Course	STRATEGIC MANAGEMENT Course: Strategic Management
Course Number	**BUAD 4500**

Dr. Eric M. Olson

University of Colorado
Colorado Springs
College of Business

http://create.mcgraw-hill.com

ISBN-10: 112122170X   ISBN-13: 9781121221703

Contents

Credits

Case 21

adidas: Will Restructuring Its Business Lineup Allow It to Catch Nike?

John E. Gamble
University of South Alabama

Adidas's 1998 acquisition of diversified sporting goods producer Salomon was expected to allow the athletic footwear company to vault over Nike to become the leader of the global sporting goods industry. Salomon had several businesses that adidas's management viewed as attractive—its Salomon ski division was the leading producer of ski equipment; TaylorMade Golf was the second-largest seller of golf equipment; and Mavic was the leading producer of high-performance bicycle wheels and rims. Other Salomon businesses included Bonfire snowboard apparel and Cliché skateboard equipment. Adidas had been the best-selling brand of sporting goods throughout the 1960s and 1970s, but Nike had overtaken adidas as leader of the athletic footwear industry in the late 1980s and had grown to three times the size of adidas by 1997.

Almost as soon as the deal was consummated, it looked doubtful that the €1.5 billion acquisition of Salomon would boost the corporation's performance. Chief concerns with the acquisition were the declining attractiveness of the winter sports industry and integration problems between the adidas footwear and apparel business and Salomon's business units. Not until 2003, five years after the acquisition, had adidas's earnings per share returned to the level that shareholders enjoyed in 1997. In addition, the company's stock price failed to return to its 1998 trading range until 2004. The Salomon winter sports business had contributed very little operating profit to the company's overall financial performance since its acquisition and the TaylorMade-adidas Golf

division had struggled at various times to deliver good earnings. However, TaylorMade seemed to have turned the corner in 2005, with sales and operating earnings improving by 12 percent and 185 percent, respectively, during the first six months of 2005. Salomon's operating loss of €54 million during the first six months of 2005 was 7 percent greater than its €50 million loss during the same period in 2004.

The company announced near the end of its second quarter 2005 that it would divest its winter sports brands and Mavic bicycle components business before the end of the year. In May 2005, Amer Sports Corporation, the maker of Atomic skis and Wilson sporting goods, agreed to acquire the winter sports and bicycle wheel businesses for €485 million. Adidas's October 2005 announcement that it would acquire Reebok International Ltd. for €3.1 billion ($3.8 billion) was the final component of a restructuring initiative that would focus the company's business lineup primarily on athletic footwear and apparel and golf equipment by 2006. Reebok also designed, marketed, and sold Rockport footwear, Ralph Lauren footwear, Greg Norman apparel, and CCM, Koho, and Jofa hockey equipment. In 2004, Rockport and Reebok's hockey brands contributed $377.6 million and $146.0 million, respectively, to the company's total sales of $3.8 billion. Reebok did not disclose the sales contributions of its Ralph Lauren or Greg Norman product lines. The acquisition would increase adidas's annual revenues to nearly €9 billion ($11 billion) and give the company a much stronger presence in North America, which accounted for 50 percent of the global

Exhibit 1   **Net Sales by Product Type and Geographic Region for Reebok International, 2002–2004**

	2004	2003	2002
Reebok International's net sales by product type			
Footwear	$2,430,311	$2,226,712	$2,060,725
Apparel	1,354,973	1,258,604	1,067,147
	$3,785,284	$3,485,316	$3,127,872
Reebok International's net sales by geographic region			
United States	$2,069,055	$2,021,396	$1,807,657
United Kingdom	474,704	444,693	416,775
Europe	810,418	692,400	607,381
Other countries	431,107	326,827	296,059
	$3,785,284	$3,485,316	$3,127,872

Source: Reebok International Ltd. 2004 10-K report.

sporting goods market. In addition, the new mix of businesses would draw adidas closer to overtaking Nike, which had 2004 revenues of $13.7 billion. Reebok's sales by product line and geographic region for 2002 through 2004 are presented in Exhibit 1.

COMPANY HISTORY

In 1920, a 20-year-old German baker-by-trade named Adolph Dassler began making simple canvas shoes in the rear of his family's small bakery in the North Bavarian town of Herzogenaurach. Dassler, a sports enthusiast, had little interest in working as a baker and wanted to make shoes for athletes competing in soccer, tennis, and track-and-field events. Adolph (nicknamed Adi) Dassler thought that proper footwear might improve an athlete's performance and began to study ways to improve athletic shoe design to give athletes wearing his shoes an edge in competitive events.

In 1924, Adi Dassler's brother, Rudolph, joined him in shoemaking to establish Gebrüder Dassler Schuhfabrik (Dassler Brothers Shoe Factory)—a new company specializing in innovative sports shoes. The two brothers realized that athletes should have shoes designed specifically for their respective sport and developed a variety of styles. In 1925, the Dasslers made their first major innovation in athletic shoe design when they integrated studs and spikes

into the soles of track-and-field shoes. The Dassler brothers also developed other key innovations in footwear such as the arch support. Many of the standard features of today's athletic footwear were developed by Dassler brothers, with Adi Dassler alone accumulating 700 patents and property rights worldwide by the time of his death in 1978.

The Dasslers were also innovators in the field of marketing—giving away their shoes to German athletes competing in the 1928 Olympic Games in Amsterdam. By the 1936 Olympic Games in Berlin, most athletes would compete only in Gebrüder Dassler shoes, including Jesse Owens, who won four gold medals in the Berlin games. By 1937, Dassler was making 30 different styles of shoes for athletes in 11 sports. All of the company's styles were distinguished from other brands by two stripes applied to each side of the shoe.

The Dasslers' sports shoe production ceased during World War II when Gebrüder Dassler Schuhfabrik was directed to produce boots for the armed forces of Nazi Germany. Adi Dassler was allowed to remain in Herzogenaurach to run the factory, but Rudolph (or Rudi) Dassler was drafted into the army and spent a year in an Allied prisoner-of-war camp after being captured. Upon the conclusion of the war, Rudi Dassler was released by the Allies and returned to Herzogenaurach to rejoin his family. The Dasslers returned to production of athletic shoes in 1947, but the company was dissolved in 1948 after the two brothers entered into a bitter feud. Rudi Dassler moved to the other side of the small village to establish his own shoe company, Puma Schuhfabrik Rudolph Dassler. With the departure of Rudi Dassler, Adi renamed the company adidas—a combination of the first three letters of his nickname and the first three letters of his last name. Adi Dassler also applied an additional stripe to the sides of adidas shoes and registered the three-stripe trademark in 1949.

The nature of the disagreement between the Dassler brothers was not known for certain, but the two never spoke again after their split and the feud became the foundation of both organizations' cultures while the two brothers were alive. The two rival companies were highly competitive, and both discouraged employees from fraternizing with cross-town rivals. An adidas spokesperson described the seriousness of the feud by stating, "Puma employees wouldn't be caught dead with adidas employees," and continuing, "It wouldn't be allowed that an adidas employee would fall in love with a Puma employee."[1]

Adi Dassler kept up his string of innovations with molded rubber cleats in 1949 and track shoes with screw-in spikes in 1952. He expanded the concept to soccer shoes in 1954 with screw-in studs, an innovation that has been partially credited for Germany's World Cup Championship that year. By 1960, adidas was the clear favorite among athletic footwear brands, with 75 percent of all track-and-field athletes competing in the Olympic Games in Rome wearing adidas shoes. The company began producing soccer balls in 1963 and athletic apparel in 1967. The company's dominance in the athletic footwear industry continued through the early 1970s with 1,164 of the 1,490 athletes competing in the 1972 Olympic Games in Munich wearing adidas shoes. In addition, as jogging became popular in the United States during in the early 1970s, adidas was the leading brand of consumer jogging shoe in the United States. Also, T-shirts and other apparel bearing adidas's three-lobed trefoil logo were popular wardrobe items for U.S. teenagers during the 1970s.

At the time of Adi Dassler's death in 1978, adidas remained the worldwide leader in athletic footwear, but the company was rapidly losing market share in the United States to industry newcomer Nike. The first Nike shoes appeared in the 1972 U.S. Olympic Trials in Eugene, Oregon, and had become the best-selling training shoe in the United States by 1974. Both Adi

Dassler and his son, Horst, who took over as adidas's chief manager after Adi Dassler's death, severely underestimated the threat of Nike. With adidas perhaps more concerned with cross-town adversary Puma, Nike pulled ahead of its European rivals in the U.S. athletic footwear market by launching new styles in a variety of colors and by signing recognizable sports figures to endorsement contracts. Even though Nike was becoming the market leader in U.S. athletic footwear market, adidas was able to retain its number one ranking among competitive athletes, with 259 gold medal winners in the 1984 Olympic Summer Games in Los Angeles wearing adidas products. Only 65 Olympic athletes wore Nike shoes during the 1984 Summer Games, but the company signed up-and-coming NBA star Michael Jordan to a $2.5 million endorsement contract after adidas passed on the opportunity earlier in the year. At the time of Horst Dassler's unexpected death in 1987, Nike was the undisputed leader in the U.S. athletic footwear market, with more than $1 billion in annual sales.

Adidas's performance spiraled downward after the death of Horst Dassler, with no clear direction from the top and quality and innovation rapidly deteriorating. By 1990, adidas had fallen to a number eight ranking in the U.S. athletic footwear market and held only a 2 percent share of the market. A number of management and ownership changes occurred between Horst Dassler's death in 1987 and 1993, when a controlling interest in the company was acquired by a group of investors led by French advertising executive Robert Louis-Dreyfus. Louis-Dreyfus launched a dramatic turnaround of the company—cutting costs, improving styling, launching new models such as the Predator soccer shoe, and creating new promotional events like the adidas Predator Cup tournament for young soccer players in Germany. The turnaround was also aided by a trend among teenagers that repopularized 1970s styles and teens' preference for niche brands that weren't likely to be purchased by adults. At year-end 1994, adidas had increased its annual sales in the United States by 75 percent from the prior year and improved its market share enough to become the third largest seller of athletic footwear in the United States, trailing only Nike and Reebok.

The company's turnaround continued in 1995 with it going public and recording annual sales of nearly €1.8 billion. In 1996, adidas outfitted more than 6,000 athletes in the Olympic Games held in

4   STRATEGIC MANAGEMENT Course: Strategic Management

Case 21   adidas: Will Restructuring Its Business Lineup Allow It to Catch Nike?   C-379

Atlanta and supplied the Official Match Ball for the European Soccer Championship. Louis-Dreyfus's turnaround also included a push in 1997 to sign athletes such as Kobe Bryant, Anna Kournikova, and David Beckham to offset the appeal of Nike's Michael Jordan with athletic footwear and apparel consumers in the United States. The company's mid-1990s image revival was also aided when celebrities such as Madonna and Elle MacPherson appeared in magazines or on television wearing adidas shoes without any prompting from the company.

Even though the company's turnaround had produced outstanding results, with sales and earnings growing at annual rates of 38.3 percent and 37.5 percent, respectively, between 1995 and 1997, the company was a distant number three in the worldwide athletic footwear and apparel industry. Nike's 1997 revenues of $9.2 billion were nearly three times greater than those of adidas, and Nike continued to grow at a fast pace as it expanded into more international markets. In addition, Nike had begun to diversify outside of athletic footwear and apparel with the 1988 acquisition of Cole-Haan and the 1995 acquisition of Bauer hockey equipment. In 1997, it was rumored that Nike was eyeing French ski maker Skis Rossignol SA. (Nike did not acquire Rossignol, but it did acquire Converse basketball shoes and Hurley skateboard equipment in 2003 and Starter athletic apparel in 2004.) In late 1997, Louis-Dreyfus and the family owners of Salomon SA, a French sports equipment manufacturer, agreed to a €1.5 billion buyout that would diversify adidas beyond footwear and apparel and into ski equipment, golf clubs, bicycle components, and winter sports apparel. The acquisition would also give adidas a stronger sales platform in North America and Asia—two markets where adidas was still struggling.

THE SALOMON SA ACQUISITION

Adidas's €1.5 billion acquisition of Salomon allowed it to surpass Reebok to become the world's second-largest sporting goods company, with projected 1998 sales of nearly €5.1 billion. Nike remained the leader of the $90 billion global sporting goods industry, but the acquisition added the number one winter sports equipment producer, the second-largest golf equipment company, and the leading producer of performance bicycle wheels and rims to adidas's lineup of businesses. The acquisition was a move toward achieving CEO Robert Louis-Dreyfus's vision of building "the best portfolio of sports brands in the world."[2]

The price of adidas's shares fell upon the announcement of the acquisition over concerns about the price adidas agreed to pay for Salomon and how the company might finance the acquisition. There was also some concern among investors that adidas did not have expertise in manufacturing sports equipment since its apparel and footwear were produced by contract manufacturers. A Merrill Lynch analyst suggested that the Salomon acquisition might prove troublesome for adidas since other athletic shoe companies had "dabbled in the hard goods segment, but they have been unsuccessful to date in making inroads."[3]

Louis-Dreyfus used 100 percent debt financing to create adidas-Salomon but was not concerned with the merged company's ability to service the debt since adidas's annual free cash flow in 1997 was projected to be more than €200 million. Adidas's 1997 results (prior to the integration of Salomon) reached record levels, with the company's annual revenues increasing 42 percent from the prior year as a result of footwear sales growing by 32 percent and apparel sales increasing by 55 percent. Gains were recorded for all geographic regions, with North American sales increasing by 66 percent during 1997, sales in Europe increasing by 31 percent, and Asia-Pacific revenues growing by 38 percent between 1996 and 1997.

Louis-Dreyfus expected the new business units to boost adidas's pretax profits by 20–25 percent in 1998 and by an additional 20 percent in 1999. He believed 2000 would be the first year shareholders would see the full potential of the acquisition. However, Louis-Dreyfus's projections never materialized, with adidas taking control of Salomon just as the winter sports equipment and golf equipment industries were becoming less attractive. The poor performance of Salomon and TaylorMade in 1998 led to a net loss of $164 million for adidas-Salomon during the first nine months of its fiscal year. To make matters worse, the integration of Mavic, Salomon, Bonfire, Cliché, and TaylorMade were not going as smoothly as Louis-Dreyfus and adidas's shareholders had expected.

adidas: Will Restructuring Its Business Lineup Allow It to Catch Nike?

5

Part 2 Cases in Crafting and Executing Strategy

Adidas's core footwear and apparel business performed commendably during 1998 to contribute to a net profit of €205 million for the fiscal year. In early 1999, adidas-Salomon's management announced that synergies from the merger would amount to less than one-half of what was initially projected. By the summer of 1999, adidas-Salomon's share price had declined by more than a third from its early 1998 high, and most large investors believed that adidas had bitten off more than it could chew with the acquisition.[4] Robert Louis-Dreyfus announced in early 2000 that he would step down from adidas-Salomon and rejoin his family's business France in early 2001. Herbert Hainer, the company's head of marketing in Europe and Asia, was tapped as his replacement to run the diversified sporting goods company.

Under Hainer's leadership, the company cut costs, introduced new apparel and footwear products, increased the company's advertising, signed additional athletes to endorsement contracts, and supplied apparel, equipment, and footwear to more than 3,000 athletes competing in 26 sports during the 2000 Olympic Games in Sydney. Also, the company expanded into company-owned retail stores in 2001 with its first adidas Originals store opening in Berlin in September, followed by stores in Tokyo, Amsterdam, and Paris by year-end. In December 2001, Hainer added to the company's lineup of sports businesses with the acquisition of Arc'Teryx, the producer of technical winter sports apparel. Adidas-Salomon recorded sales of €6.1 billion in 2001 and ended the year as the top performer in the DAX 30. The performance of adidas-Salomon's common shares is presented in Exhibit 2.

ADIDAS-SALOMON'S CORPORATE STRATEGY IN EARLY 2005

In early 2005, adidas-Salomon's businesses were organized under three units based around the company's core brands—adidas, Salomon, and TaylorMade-adidas Golf. Innovation and excellence in strategy execution were common themes in all of adidas-Salomon's three business segments. The company expected its product design teams to develop at least one major product innovation per year in each product category. In 2004, TaylorMade Golf introduced its r7 Quad driver, which was a first-of-its-kind product that incorporated four movable weights. The movable weights allowed golfers to make adjustments to the club that could produce six different ball flight trajectories. TaylorMade extended the movable weight concept to irons and hybrid clubs in 2005. The adidas Sport Performance group introduced its Roteiro soccer ball, which was the industry's first thermal-bonded soccer ball. Also, the adidas Sport Performance group and the Salomon group collaborated to develop footwear featuring a Ground Control System that adjusted for uneven ground. Adidas T-MAC HUG laceless shoes and the adidas 1 were shoe innovations developed in 2004 and 2005. The $250-per-pair adidas 1 was the first running shoe with an embedded microprocessor. The microprocessor evaluated the runner's weight, the terrain, and speed to vary the compression in the heel of the shoe with the use of mechanical shock-absorbing components.

Adidas-Salomon also relied heavily on ongoing brand-building activities to further differentiate adidas, TaylorMade, and Salomon from competing brands of sporting goods. Partnerships with major sporting events around the world and with notable athletes competing in winter sports, track and field, soccer, basketball, tennis, and golf were critical to creating a distinctive image with consumers. The company also attempted to provide its retailers with superior customer service, including on-time deliveries, since the retailer was a crucial element of the sporting goods industry value chain. Efficient supply chain management and manufacturing efficiencies were also vital to the success of the company since poor product quality might discourage repeat sales to consumers. Even though the majority of adidas-Salomon products were produced by contract manufacturers, the company employed more than 100 quality control officers to monitor supplier standards.

Adidas-Salomon management expected visible improvements in operating margins each year and anticipated that the company would achieve an overall 10 percent operating profit margin in 2006. Increased profitability in Europe, strong top-line and bottom-line growth in Asia, and steady growth in North America were expected to deliver sought-after gains in operating profit margins. The company's chief managers believed that operational efficiency coupled with product innovation would allow it to

Case 21   adidas: Will Restructuring Its Business Lineup Allow It to Catch Nike?

Exhibit 2   **Performance of adidas-Salomon's Stock Price, 1999–2005**

(a) Trend in adidas-Salomon's Common Stock Price

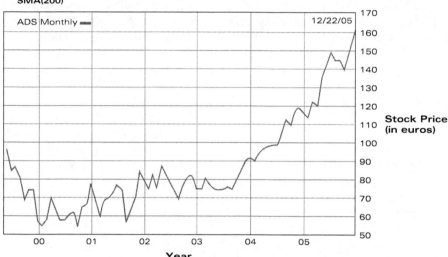

(b) Performance of adidas-Salomon's Stock Price versus the DAX 30 Index

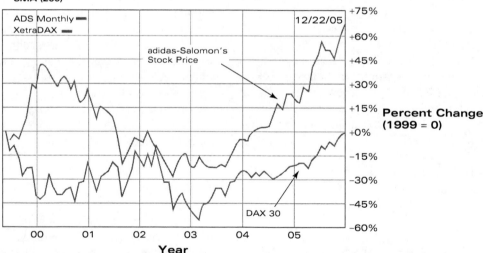

attain number one or number two positions in each sporting goods segment in which it competed.

Adidas Footwear and Apparel

Adidas footwear and apparel was organized under three categories based on the clothing needs of the consumer. The adidas Sport Performance group developed sports shoes and attire suitable for use by athletes in running, football and soccer, basketball, tennis, and general training. Adidas held number one or number two positions globally in these athletic categories and maintained its advantage primarily through innovations like its ClimaCool 360-degree footwear ventilation system, its a^3 energy management system, and endorsements by individual athletes or league sponsorships. Tim Duncan, Kevin Garnett, and Tracy McGrady were among the latest NBA athletes to endorse adidas footwear and apparel. In soccer, players such as David Beckham and Zinedine Zidane, and even entire clubs, endorsed adidas soccer shoes and clothing. Adidas was the official sponsor for the German national women's team and the UEFA European soccer league teams in Munich,

Part 2 Cases in Crafting and Executing Strategy

Amsterdam, Milan, and Madrid. Also, the adidas Roteiro was the Official Match Ball for all UEFA games. Adidas was also the official supplier to 18 National Olympic Committees competing in the 2004 Olympic Games in Athens and fully equipped athletes from 45 nations competing in 26 of the 28 disciplines included in the Olympics.

The company's Sport Heritage group was established in 2000 and designed new styles of shoes and apparel that were similar to the performance-oriented styles of the 1970s. Although athletes in the early 2000s would not compete in products based on 1970s technology, many teenagers and urban trend-followers liked the look of adidas's older products. Adidas limited distribution of its Sport Heritage products to avoid dilution of the brand.

As with Sport Heritage products, few purchasers of adidas Sport Style products were likely to wear such products while engaged in athletic endeavors. The Y-3 collection of sportswear, which was designed by Yohji Yamamoto, was based on athletic styles but would be only marginally suitable for sports. Most of the Y-3 line was best suited for consumers looking for trendy and comfortable casual wear with a mild sports influence. The line was launched in 2003, and adidas-Salomon management believed the division could eventually account for €100 million in sales. The company also believed that its Stella McCartney performance apparel line, David Beckham Sport Style line, and Mohammad Ali and Missy Elliott Heritage lines would prove successful.

North America The North American market for sporting goods showed virtually no growth between 2000 and 2004 and was characterized by fierce competition among manufacturers and deep promotional discounting by retailers. All of adidas's brand-building efforts and product innovations were directed toward building on its number four ranking in North America, which was the company's weakest region in the $33 billion global athletic footwear market. In 2004, adidas held an 8.9 percent market share—behind Nike, with 36 percent market share; Reebok, with a 12.2 percent market share; and New Balance, with an approximate 11 percent market share.

In late 2004, adidas held a 55 percent market share in soccer shoes in the United States compared to Nike's 33 percent market share. However, in the overall U.S. cleated shoe segment, Nike led adidas by a 48 to 23 percent margin. Adidas was not a contender in the $3 billion basketball category, where Nike held a 70 percent market share. Adidas, Nike, and New Balance were all tied, with about 20 percent market share each in the tennis category. Nike, asics, New Balance, and Reebok all recorded gains in the running category during the first nine months of 2004, but analysts suggested that adidas missed out on growth in the category because its new technologies had not been a hit with consumers. Sales of casual sports shoes similar to those included in the adidas Heritage and adidas Sport Style lines were up 30 percent during the first nine months of 2004, but adidas did not make the list of top four brands in the category. The category was expected to grow by 40 percent in 2005 to displace running as the second-largest category of athletic shoes in the United States.

To achieve its revenue growth objectives of 10 percent annually in 2005 and 2006, adidas developed new styles and models offered in all three adidas segments, placed a strong emphasis on basketball, established marketing partnerships with college sports teams, major league soccer, and major league baseball teams, and improved retailer relations. Also, adidas expanded distribution to additional sporting goods stores, mall-based stores, department stores, urban distribution locations, and company-owned stores. Adidas also hoped to encourage retailers to create shop-within-a-shop merchandising sections and provide permanent wall space for adidas shoes. In 2004, Foot Locker agreed to give adidas's Kevin Garnett shoes permanent wall space in its best locations and feature the sub-brand in its television and print ads. Adidas also planned to expand distribution into additional urban retail stores that might not be a part of a large chain but were close to urban consumers. Adidas estimated the U.S. urban retail market for athletic footwear and apparel to be over $6 billion. Adidas also opened company-owned retail stores in Las Vegas, New York, Chicago, and San Francisco in 2005. Store openings in Portland, Boston, Washington, Philadelphia, Los Angeles, and Atlanta were planned for 2006.

Europe Growth plans in Europe were focused on building on adidas's number one ranking in the region through its sponsorship of youth and professional soccer and continued support for running. The European athletic footwear and apparel market was growing at a modest rate, but retailers in Europe had relied even more on promotional pricing than retailers in North America. Prices for children's apparel had declined by 10 percent during 2004, and prices of adult apparel had decreased by 8.5 percent between 2003 and 2004. Adidas believed that its emphasis on product innovation and its strong brand loyalty would help protect the company from margin erosion due to price competition. Adidas also planned to increase its number of retailers in Europe by 25 percent between 2004 and 2006, with most new locations coming in emerging country markets. Adidas also intended to open additional company-owned stores in Europe during 2005 and 2006.

Asia   In 1999, adidas held a 6 percent market share in Japan, but its market share had grown to 18 percent in 2004 and its management expected a 20–24 percent market share in Japan by 2006. Adidas's increase in market share had come mainly at the expense of local brands such as asics and Mizuno. In 2004, Japan accounted for 50 percent of athletic apparel sales in Asia, but adidas and other consumer goods companies were directing considerable efforts to building brand awareness in China and other emerging Asian markets. The region's growth in gross domestic product was projected to be the highest in the world between 2005 and 2010, with much of the growth resulting from domestic-driven demand rather than exports. The size of the middle class in the region was also expected to grow dramatically in the region by 2010, with China's middle class growing from 60 million in 2002 to 160 million by 2010. Adidas's management estimated that every 1 percent increase in consumption by China's population translated into a $70 billion increase in sales of consumer goods. Adidas expected the 2008 Olympic Games in Beijing to generate interest in athletic footwear and apparel in China.

The company was rapidly adding retail stores to ensure that its products were available for purchase by China's growing consumer base. The company was adding more than 40 stores per month in urban locations in China since 55 percent of the country's population was expected to migrate from the countryside to cities by 2012. In 2004, adidas had more than 150 retail locations in only 1 province of China but expected to have more than 150 retail locations in 10 provinces by the 2008 Olympics. In 2004, adidas's revenues of more than €100 million made it the number two brand of athletic footwear and apparel in China. Nike was the leading seller of athletic goods in China. Adidas's management expected the company to double its sales in China by 2008.

Salomon

Like athletic footwear and apparel, the winter sports industry was mature, with the market declining by 3.1 percent during the 2003–2004 ski season. The 2003–2004 decline followed a 3.6 percent decline during the 2002–2003 season and a 1.8 percent decline in the 2001–2002 season. Some categories within the winter sports industry were declining at a more rapid pace, with the snowboard industry falling from €428.9 million in 2000–2001 to €344.5 million in 2003–2004. Nordic (cross-country) skiing was the only bright spot in the industry, with a 3.1 percent growth rate during the 2003–2004 ski season. The total value of worldwide winter sports equipment market in 2004 was €1.5 billion.

Revenue increases for most winter sporting goods producers had come from adding summer outdoor-inspired apparel and footwear to their product lines. Salomon was the number one producer of winter sports equipment, with a number one position in alpine (downhill) ski boots and high-end skis, a number two position in alpine skis overall and snowboard boots, and a number three position in snowboards. The company held an 80 percent market share in nordic (cross-country) ski systems. The Salomon business group also included Mavic, which was the number one brand of performance bicycle wheels and rims. The performance bicycle category was also mature, but growing a modest rate because of the popularity of road racing in the United States and Europe. Other businesses in the portfolio included Bonfire, a producer of snowboard apparel; Arc'Teryx, which produced technical winter sports apparel; and Cliché, a maker of skateboard equipment and apparel.

The businesses included in the Salomon division utilized competitive approaches similar to those of adidas-branded products. The division was committed to innovation in products in its snow, outdoor, and asphalt categories and attempted to benefit from synergies with the core adidas business when feasible. An example of such cross-division strategic fit was Salomon and adidas's collaboration on the development of the Ground Control System running shoe. Shoes using the design were marketed under both the adidas and Salomon brand names and were sold in different retail channels. The division also exploited adidas's apparel design expertise in its development of winter sports, cycling, and skateboard apparel. The collaboration between adidas and Salomon brands in apparel design had contributed to a 400 percent increase in soft goods sales for the division since 1995.

In 2004, sales for the Salomon group were nearly evenly split between winter sports hard goods and other products. The Salomon group was undertaking efforts to increase soft goods sales to 50 percent of the group's sales by expanding apparel lines, developing dedicated soft goods sales forces for each brand, and developing advertising targeting women since studies had shown that a large percentage of winter sports apparel purchases were made by women.

Improvement in operating margins was also a strategic priority at Salomon since top-line growth was limited. Since 2001, the division had shifted hardware production from France to Eastern Europe and Asia, developed a new production process in skis that lowered materials costs, reduced production time, and lowered labor costs per unit. In addition, Salomon had reduced total employment between 2002 and 2004 through early retirements and an increased number of temporary employees.

Even with Salomon management's efforts to improve operating margins for the division, there were some characteristics of the winter sports industry that precluded options that might be pursued in other industries. When asked by an investment banker why Salomon didn't shift all production to Asia, the head of Salomon, Christian Finell, responded, "The reason for this is that the main part of our business in winter sports is done in Europe. We believe it makes much more sense to have our production close to our customers. Also most of the relevant raw materials are found in Europe and not in Asia. And lead times are relatively long in this business. So by adding both the lead time and additional transportation costs it doesn't make sense to shift the production to Asia."[5]

TaylorMade-adidas Golf

TaylorMade Golf was the second largest producer of golf equipment in the $5.5 billion industry. The golf equipment industry had experience little growth since 1999 when golf's chief governing body in the United States began to ban golf clubs that it deemed performed too well. Golf equipment sales had grown dramatically during the mid- to late-1990s as golf equipment manufacturers like Callaway Golf Company, Titleist, Ping, and TaylorMade Golf introduced better-performing clubs that were more forgiving of recreational golfers' poor swing characteristics. Professional golfers using the technologically advanced equipment saw improvements in their games as well—particularly in driving distance. The United States Golf Association (USGA) began to believe that these new high-tech clubs provided a springlike effect and developed a coefficient of restitution (COR) limitation that would prevent any such effect

for golf equipment sold in the United States. Golf equipment manufacturers scoffed at the idea that clubs could produce a timed springlike or trampoline effect that could help propel the ball forward but were nevertheless obliged to discontinue research and development projects that would produce clubs exceeding a COR of 0.83.

By 2000, most golf club manufacturers had reached the 0.83 COR limitation and were compelled to find new approaches to innovation. In 2004, there was little differentiation among golf clubs until TaylorMade developed its r7 Quad driver. The driver was unique in that it allowed golfers to reposition movable weights screwed into the clubhead. The golfer could move the weights to provide a higher or lower launch angle and cause the flight path to pull to the left or fade to the right. The new innovation created 8 percent growth in driver sales for the year and made TaylorMade the number one producer of drivers and metalwoods. Prior to TaylorMade's introduction of the r7 Quad driver, Callaway Golf had held the number one position in the industry since 1991. The r7 lost its number one ranking in 2005 to Ping's G5 driver.

In 2005, the golf equipment industry had seemingly reached maturity as a sport, with the number of new participants each year barely exceeding the number who were giving up the sport. Asia's 2–3 percent annual growth in the number of new golfers made it the only geographic region to experience growth between 1999 and 2003. Poor economic conditions in the United States during 2000 caused many frequent golfers to scale back their participation levels that year, but the number of core golfers had rebounded in 2001 through 2004. However, the overall number of rounds played by golfers had declined until 2004, when the number of rounds played increased by nearly 7 percent. Exhibit 3 provides the retail value, number of units sold, and average selling price for various golf equipment categories for 1997 through 2004.

TaylorMade-adidas Golf management expected to increase sales primarily through market share gains since they had concluded that it would be unwise to count on growth of the game. TaylorMade believed it could increase market share through endorsement contracts with touring professionals on the Professional Golf Association (PGA) Tour and other professional tours and through new product innovations like the movable weight system used in its r7 driver. TaylorMade management also wished to

Case 21   adidas: Will Restructuring Its Business Lineup Allow It to Catch Nike?   **C-385**

Exhibit 3   **Retail Value, Units Sold, and Average Selling Price of Golf Equipment in the United States, 1997–2004**

	Year	Retail Value	Units Sold	Average Selling Price
Metalwoods	1997	$676.8 million	2.93 million	$231.00
	1998	601.1	2.81	214.00
	1999	583.8	2.91	201.00
	2000	599.1	2.94	204.00
	2001	626.6	2.99	210.00
	2002	608.7	3.09	197.00
	2003	660.4	3.28	201.00
	2004	654.1	3.56	184.00
Irons	1997	$533.4 million	7.12 million	$ 74.90*
	1998	485.4	6.87	70.71
	1999	447.9	6.97	64.28
	2000	475.3	7.14	66.57
	2001	459.3	7.17	64.06
	2002	456.4	7.42	61.50
	2003	461.4	7.66	60.23
	2004	482.6	8.06	59.88
Golf balls	1997	$458.7 million	19.97 million	$ 22.97†
	1998	487.4	20.06	24.30
	1999	518.1	20.46	25.32
	2000	530.8	20.80	25.52
	2001	555.6	21.32	26.06
	2002	529.9	20.81	25.46
	2003	496.4	19.85	25.01
	2004	506.3	19.98	25.34
Footwear (pairs)	1997	$214.3 million	2.48 million	$ 86.49
	1998	204.3	2.43	84.13
	1999	206.9	2.47	83.77
	2000	220.8	2.52	87.68
	2001	217.8	2.57	84.62
	2002	211.7	2.68	78.95
	2003	217.1	2.82	76.97
	2004	234.4	3.00	78.22

*Per club.
†Per dozen.
Source: Golf Datatech.

achieve revenue growth by increasing sales in Asia. The company had successfully increased its sales in Asia from 13 percent of sales in 1999 to 31 percent of sales in 2004, and the United States accounted for only 52 percent of sales in 2004 versus 69 percent of sales in 1999. TaylorMade CEO Mark King

designated Asia as a high-priority market: "Asia is very, very profitable as a region. The main reason is because the selling prices in Asia for golf equipment are higher than in any other place in the world. So the margins there are very, very strong. Profitability in North America is also very strong. The only area adidas: Will Restructuring Its Business Lineup Allow It to Catch Nike?

11

C-386   Part 2   Cases in Crafting and Executing Strategy

that we are struggling in right now a little bit is in Europe."[6] In addition, USGA rules did not apply to play in Asia and most golf club manufacturers produced models with high COR ratings for sale in Asia.

Even though TaylorMade had achieved the number one ranking in metalwoods during 2004, its market share in irons was about one-half that of industry leader, Callaway Golf Company, and its market share in putters was negligible. The division's sales of Maxfli golf balls, which was acquired by adidas-Salomon in 2002, had yet to earn profits and accounted for less than 5 percent of industry sales in 2005. Segment leader Titleist had held a 70 percent or greater market share in golf balls for decades. TaylorMade-adidas Golf's share of the metalwoods, irons, and golf footwear for January 2002–July 2004 is presented in Exhibit 4.

Like Salomon, TaylorMade-adidas Golf division attempted to benefit from adidas's core competencies in footwear and apparel design. The company offered a full line of golf apparel and footwear that was sold in golf shops in North America, Europe, and Asia. The division expected double-digit annual growth rates in apparel and footwear revenues. Exhibit 5 presents key financial data for each of adidas-Salomon's operating divisions between 1998 and 2004. The company's financial information by geographic region for 1998–2004 is presented in Exhibit 6. Income statements for and balance sheets for 2003–2004 are provided in Exhibits 7 and 8, respectively.

ADIDAS'S DIVESTITURE OF SALOMON BUSINESS UNITS AND ITS PLANNED ACQUISITION OF REEBOK

With the Amer's acquisition of Salomon's business units completed in October 2005, adidas was able to report that its revenues and earnings for the first nine months of 2005 were quite improved when compared

Exhibit 4   **Market Shares of Leading Sellers of Golf Equipment for Metalwoods, Irons, and Footwear, January 2002–July 2004**

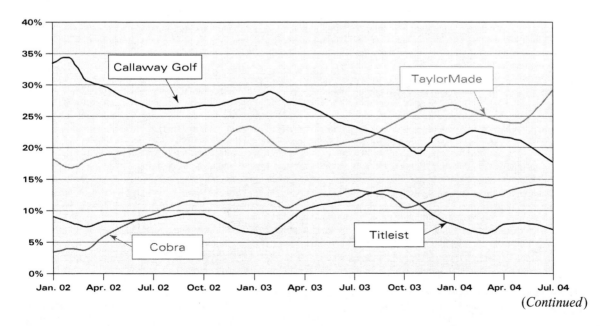

Metalwoods

(*Continued*)

Case 21   adidas: Will Restructuring Its Business Lineup Allow It to Catch Nike?   **C-387**

Exhibit 4 **Continued**

Irons

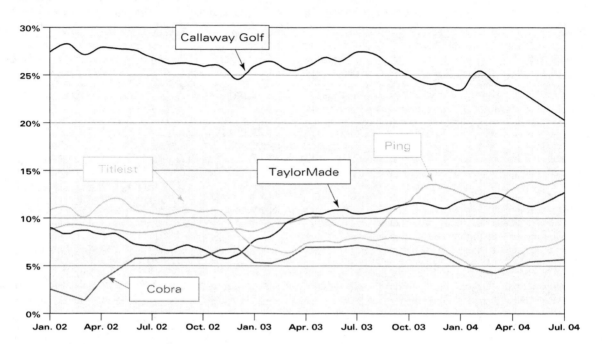

Footwear

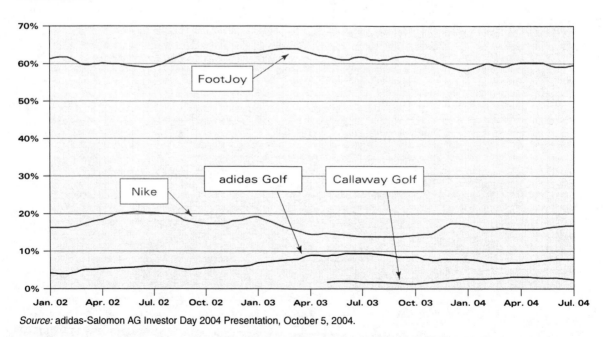

Source: adidas-Salomon AG Investor Day 2004 Presentation, October 5, 2004.

to the first nine months of 2004. The company's revenues had increased by 10 percent on a currency-neutral basis, its operating profits had increased by 12 percent, and its net income from continuing operations during the third quarter of 2005 was 28 percent better than the same period in 2004. Much of the company's sales growth was attributable to new models such as the T-Mac, which was expected to sell more than 1 million pairs in 2005 and 2006, and adidas 1, which was expected to become a €20 million product line addition by 2006. Also, adidas's Sport Heritage line was expected to account for €1 billion in sales during 2005 and the company's 680 company-owned retail stores were expected to record sales of €750 million by year-end 2005. Sales grew at double digits in all geographic regions except Europe, were sales were stable on a currency-neutral basis. Adidas-Salomon was scheduled to change its name to adidas AG during its 2006 annual stockholders' meeting.

Exhibit 5   **adidas-Salomon Financial Data by Operating Segment, 1998–2004**

	2004	2003	2002	2001	2000	1999	1998
Adidas							
Net sales	€5,174	€4,950	€5,105	€4,825	€4,672	€4,427	€4,316
Gross profit	2,284	2,008	2,004	1,845	1,907	1,827	1,818
Operating profit	523	365	343	352	391	431	412
Operating assets	1,393	2,172	2,294	1,954	2,286	1,987	1,730
Capital expenditures	85	63	84	113	93	105	102
Amortization and depreciation, excluding goodwill amortization	56	63	57	52	45	48	38
Salomon							
Net sales	€653	€658	€684	€714	€703	€587	€487
Gross profit	259	264	279	313	296	233	188
Operating profit	9	35	39	63	61	32	6
Operating assets	505	521	581	679	566	533	598
Capital expenditures	19	18	18	38	24	17	20
Amortization and depreciation, excluding goodwill amortization	7	7	7	7	7	5	7
TaylorMade-adidas Golf							
Net sales	€633	€637	€707	€545	€441	€327	€263
Gross profit	298	290	345	281	221	160	118
Operating profit	60	67	74	63	44	30	20
Operating assets	335	391	433	316	219	156	99
Capital expenditures	9	12	49	16	12	10	16
Amortization and depreciation, excluding goodwill amortization	11	9	7	6	4	4	2
Headquarters/consolidation							
Net sales	€ 18	€ 22	€ 27	€ 28	€ 19	€ 10	—
Gross profit	218	252	191	162	104	—	—
Operating profit	(12)	23	21	(3)	(59)	(14)	(22)
Operating assets	1,648	1,104	953	1,234	947	903	782
Capital expenditures	27	29	22	20	16	—	—
Amortization and depreciation, excluding goodwill amortization	28	17	26	25	23	6	6

Source: adidas-Salomon annual reports.

Case 21   adidas: Will Restructuring Its Business Lineup Allow It to Catch Nike?   C-389

Exhibit 6   **adidas-Salomon Financial Data by Geographic Region, 1998–2004**

	2004	2003	2002	2001	2000	1999	1998
Europe							
Net sales	€3,470	€3,365	€3,200	€3,066	€2,860	€2,723	€2,774
Gross profit	1,573	1,383	1,268	1,153	1,171	1,133	1,127
Operating profit	644	534	471	444	454	382	357
Operating assets	1,461	1,428	1,396	1,419	1,107	1,167	1,114
Capital expenditures	46	44	56	74	55	40	35
Amortization and depreciation, excluding goodwill amortization	30	30	27	24	22	20	19
North America							
Net sales	€1,486	€1,562	€1,960	€1,818	€1,907	€1,826	€1,784
Gross profit	534	552	742	697	729	731	713
Operating profit	79	92	162	161	177	234	276
Operating assets	768	778	969	945	862	848	666
Capital expenditures	27	22	82	68	54	26	29
Amortization and depreciation, excluding goodwill amortization	21	21	20	17	16	12	11
Asia							
Net sales	€1,251	€1,116	€1,166	€1,010	€875	€663	€383
Gross profit	615	525	562	481	416	301	156
Operating profit	244	191	189	170	129	96	26
Operating assets	480	447	505	743	455	390	201
Capital expenditures	23	12	16	15	17	18	9
Amortization and depreciation, excluding goodwill amortization	16	14	15	12	10	5	3
Latin America							
Net sales	€224	€179	€163	€178	€171	€126	€112
Gross profit	87	70	65	73	72	50	43
Operating profit	38	25	24	16	23	15	11
Operating assets	56	93	79	98	109	75	66
Capital expenditures	1	1	1	2	3	3	2
Amortization and depreciation, excluding goodwill amortization	1	1	1	2	2	1	1
Headquarters/ consolidation							
Net sales	€ 47	€ 45	€ 34	€ 40	€ 23	€ 34	€ 12
Gross profit	248	284	182	197	140	—	—
Operating profit	(426)	(352)	(369)	(316)	(346)	(239)	(254)
Operating assets	1,601	1,442	1,312	978	1,485	1,108	1,162
Capital expenditures	43	43	15	28	16	45	63
Amortization and depreciation, excluding goodwill amortization	34	30	34	35	29	25	19

Source: adidas-Salomon annual reports.

Exhibit 7   **adidas-Salomon Income Statements, 2003–2004 (in thousands except per share data)**

	2004	2003
Net sales	€6,478,072	€6,266,800
Cost of sales	3,419,864	3,453,132
Gross profit	3,058,208	2,813,668
Selling, general and administrative expenses	2,376,266	2,228,135
Depreciation and amortization (excluding goodwill)	101,764	95,519
Operating profit	580,178	490,014
Goodwill amortization	46,352	44,809
Royalty and commission income	43,166	42,153
Financial expenses, net	56,832	49,170
Income before taxes	520,160	438,188
Income taxes	196,691	166,712
Net income before minority interests	323,469	271,476
Minority interests	(9,221)	(11,391)
Net income	€ 314,248	€ 260,085
Basic earnings per share (in euros)	€6.88	€5.72
Diluted earnings per share (in euros)	€6.54	€5.72
Dividends per share (in euros)	€1.30	€1.00
Number of shares outstanding (Basic)	46,649,560	45,452,361
Number of shares outstanding (Diluted)	49,669,346	45,469,366

Source: 2004 adidas-Salomon annual report.

The Reebok acquisition, which was announced in August 2005 and was expected to be finalized sometime during the first half of 2006, would give the company pro forma aggregate 2004 revenues of €8.9 billion ($11.1 billion) and allow it to more than double its sales in North America to €3.1 billion ($3.9 billion). In addition, adidas expected to capture annual cost-sharing benefits of approximately €125 million ($150 million) within three years of the closing date. The company placed 4,531,250 shares with institutional investors in November 2005 to raise approximately €648 million to contribute to the financing of the Reebok acquisition.

Perhaps the greatest opportunity presented by the planned Reebok acquisition was the company's ability to position adidas as a technologically superior shoe designed for serious athletes, while Reebok could be positioned as leisure shoe that would sell at middle price points. In addition, the company could maintain its strategy of signing respected athletes to adidas endorsement contracts, while gaining endorsements from more edgy Reebok celebrities such as Allen Iverson, Jay-Z,

and Fifty Cent. In addition, Reebok would retain its founder and CEO Paul Fireman to lead Reebok after the acquisition.

Even though the restructured lineup of businesses offered adidas an improved chance of catching Nike in its race to be the world's largest sporting goods company, some observers were not convinced the move would prove to be any more successful than the company's 1998 acquisition of Salomon. The president of a sports marketing firm and former New Balance executive said he doubted that adidas's "German mentality of control, engineering, and production" would prove to be compatible with Reebok's "U.S. marketing-driven culture" and added, "In reality, I don't think [the merged company] is going to dent the market, because Nike is already too far ahead."[7] New Balance's CEO, Jim Davis, concurred with his former colleague's assessment by commenting, "You can try to take on Nike, but . . . Nike is Nike and will continue to be Nike."[8] A Goldman Sachs analyst added, "We fail to see how this combo will erode Nike's franchise as the global brand leader."[9]

Exhibit 8   **adidas-Salomon Balance Sheets, 2003–2004 (in thousands)**

	December 31	
Assets	**2004**	**2003**
Cash and cash equivalents	€ 195,997	€ 189,503
Short-term financial assets	258,950	89,411
Accounts receivable	1,046,322	1,075,092
Inventories	1,155,374	1,163,518
Other current assets	378,303	259,427
Total current assets	€3,034,946	€2,776,951
Property, plant and equipment, net	367,928	344,554
Goodwill, net	572,426	591,045
Other intangible assets, net	96,312	103,797
Long-term financial assets	93,134	88,408
Deferred tax assets	160,135	178,484
Other noncurrent assets	102,599	104,569
Total noncurrent assets	€1,392,534	€1,410,857
Total assets	€4,427,480	€4,187,808
Liabilities, minority interests and shareholders' equity		
Short-term borrowings	€ 185,837	€ —
Accounts payable	591,689	592,273
Income taxes	167,334	157,764
Accrued liabilities and provisions	558,121	454,573
Other current liabilities	184,332	139,095
Total current liabilities	€1,687,313	€1,343,705
Long-term borrowings	862,845	1,225,385
Pensions and similar obligations	111,321	105,264
Deferred tax liabilities	77,951	65,807
Other noncurrent liabilities	30,784	35,278
Total noncurrent liabilities	€1,082,865	€1,431,734
Minority interests	28,850	56,579
Shareholders' equity	€1,628,452	€1,355,790
Total liabilities, minority interests and shareholders' equity	€4,427,480	€4,187,808

Source: 2004 adidas-Salomon annual report.

Endnotes

[1] As quoted in "The Brothers Dassler Fight On," *Deutsche Welle,* dw-world.de.

[2] As quoted in "Adidas Foots $1.5B to Buy Sporting Firm," *USA Today,* September 17, 1997.

[3] As quoted in "Sporting Goods Consolidation Off to the Races," *Mergers & Acquisitions Report,* November 10, 1997.

[4] As quoted in "Sports Goods/Shareholders Criticize Salomon Takeover," *Handelsblatt,* May 21, 1999.

[5] Ibid.

[6] Ibid.

[7] As quoted in "Reebok and adidas: A Good Fit," *BusinessWeek Online,* August 4, 2005.

[8] Ibid.

[9] Ibid.

CASE 12

Google's Strategy in 2010

John E. Gamble
University of South Alabama

G oogle was the leading Internet search firm in 2010, with 60+ percent market shares in both searches performed on computers and searches performed on mobile devices. Google's business model allowed advertisers to bid on search terms that would describe their product or service on a cost-per-impression (CPI) or cost-per-click (CPC) basis. Google's search-based ads were displayed near Google's search results and generated advertising revenues of nearly $22.9 billion in 2009. The company also generated revenues of $761 in 2009 from licensing fees charged to businesses that wished to install Google's search appliance on company intranets and from a variety of new ventures. New ventures were becoming a growing priority with Google management since the company dominated the market for search based ads and sought additional opportunities to sustain its extraordinary growth in revenues, earnings, and net cash provided by operations.

In 2008, Google had launched its Android operating system for mobile phones, which allowed wireless phone manufacturers such as LG, HTC, and Nokia to produce Internet-enabled phones boasting features similar to those available on Apple's iPhone. Widespread use of the Internet-enabled Android phones would not only help Google solidify its lead in mobile search but also allow the company to increase its share of banner ads and video ads displayed on mobile phones. Google had also entered into alliances with Intel, Sony, DISH Network, Logitech, and other firms to develop the technology and products required to launch Google TV. Google TV was scheduled for a fall 2010 launch and would allow users to search live network and cable programming; streaming videos from providers such as Netflix, Amazon Video On Demand, and YouTube; and recorded programs on a DVR. Perhaps the company's most ambitious strategic initiative in 2010 was its desire to change the market for commonly used business productivity applications such as word processing, spreadsheets, and presentation software from the desktop to the Internet. Information technology analysts believed that the market for such applications—collectively called cloud computing—could grow to $95 billion by 2013.

While Google's growth initiatives seemed to take the company into new industries and thrust it into competition with companies ranging from AT&T to Microsoft to Apple, its CEO, Eric Schmidt, saw the new ventures as natural extensions of the company's mission to "organize the world's information and make it universally accessible and useful."[1] In a July 2010 interview with the *Telegraph,* Schmidt commented that Google's new ventures into mobile devices, television search, and cloud computing would allow the company to "organize the world's information on any device and in any way that we can figure out to do it."[2] In July 2010, it was yet to be determined to what extent Google's new initiatives would contribute to the company's growth. Some industry analysts preferred that Google focus on improving its search technology to protect its competitive advantage in search and thereby its key revenue source. There was also a concern among some that, as the company pushed harder to sustain its impressive historical growth rates, it had backed away from its commitment to "make money without doing evil."[3] While free-speech advocates had criticized Google for aiding China in its Internet censorship practices since its 2006 entry into China, authorities in the United States, Canada, Australia, Germany, Italy, the United Kingdom, and Spain were conducting investigations into Google's Street View data collection practices. It had been discovered that while Google's camera cars photographed homes and businesses along city streets, the company also captured personal data from Wi-Fi networks in the photographed homes and businesses. In addition, the U.S. House Oversight Committee was in the first phase of an investigation into Google's lobbying efforts to encourage the Obama administration to institute new policies and regulations that would be favorable to the company and the development of its new ventures.

COMPANY HISTORY

The development of Google's search technology began in January 1996 when Stanford University computer science graduate students Larry Page and Sergey Brin collaborated to develop a new search engine. They named the new search engine BackRub because of its ability to rate websites for relevancy by examining the number of back links pointing to the website. The approach for assessing the relevancy of websites to a particular search query used by other websites at the time was based on examining and counting metatags and keywords included on various websites. By 1997, the search accuracy of BackRub had allowed it to gain a loyal following among Silicon Valley Internet users. Yahoo cofounder David Filo was among the converted, and in 1998 he convinced Brin and Page to leave Stanford to focus on making their search technology the backbone of a new Internet company.

BackRub would be renamed Google, which was a play on the word *googol*—a mathematical term for a number represented by the numeral 1 followed by 100 zeros. Brin and Page's adoption of the new name reflected their mission to organize a seemingly infinite amount of information on the Internet. In August 1998, a Stanford professor arranged for Brin and Page to meet at his home with a potential angel investor to demonstrate the Google search engine. The investor, who had been a founder of Sun Microsystems, was immediately impressed with Google's search capabilities but was too pressed for time to hear much of their informal presentation. The investor stopped the two during the presentation and suggested, "Instead of us discussing all the details, why don't I just write you a check?"[4] The two partners held the investor's $100,000 check, made payable to Google Inc., for two weeks while they scrambled to set up a corporation named Google Inc. and open a corporate bank account. The two officers of the freshly incorporated company went on to raise a total of $1 million in venture capital from family, friends, and other angel investors by the end of September 1998.

Even with a cash reserve of $1 million, the two partners ran Google on a shoestring budget, with its main servers built by Brin and Page from discounted computer components and its four employees operating out of a garage owned by a friend of the founders. By year-end 1998, Google's beta version was handling 10,000 search queries per day and *PC Magazine* had named the company to its list of "Top 100 Web Sites and Search Engines for 1998."

The new company recorded successes at a lightning-fast pace, with the search kernel answering more than 500,000 queries per day and Red Hat agreeing to become the company's first search customer in early 1999. Google attracted an additional $25 million in funding from two leading Silicon Valley venture capital firms by mid-year 1999 to support further growth and enhancements to Google's search technology. The company's innovations in 2000 included wireless search technology, search capabilities in 10 languages, and a Google Toolbar browser plug-in that allowed computer users to search the Internet without first visiting a Google-affiliated Web portal or Google's home page. Features added through 2004 included Google News, Google Product Search, Google Scholar, and Google Local. The company also expanded its index of Web pages to more than 8 billion and increased its country domains to more than 150 by 2004. Google also further expanded its products for mobile phones with a short message service (SMS) feature that allowed mobile phone users to send a search request to Google as a text message. After submitting the search request to 466453 (google), a mobile phone user would receive a text message from Google providing results to his or her query.

The Initial Public Offering

Google's April 29, 2004, initial public offering (IPO) registration became the most talked-about planned offering involving an Internet company since the dot-com bust of 2000. The registration announced Google's intention to raise as much as $3.6 billion from the issue of 25.7 million shares through an unusual Dutch auction. Among the 10 key tenets of Google's philosophy (presented in Exhibit 1) was "You can make money without doing evil."[5] The choice of a Dutch auction stemmed from this philosophy, since Dutch auctions allowed potential investors to place bids for shares regardless of size. The choice of a Dutch auction was also favorable to Google since it involved considerably lower investment banking and underwriting fees and few or no commissions for brokers.

At the conclusion of the first day of trading, Google's shares had appreciated by 18 percent to make Brin and Page each worth approximately $3.8 billion. Also, an estimated 900 to 1,000 Google employees were worth at least $1 million, with 600 to 700 holding at least $2 million in Google stock. On average, each of Google's 2,292 staff members held approximately $1.7 million in company stock, excluding the holdings of the top five executives. Stanford University also enjoyed a $179.5 million windfall from its stock holdings granted for its early investment in Brin and Page's search engine. Some of Google's early contractors and consultants also profited handsomely from forgoing fees in return for stock options in the company. One such contractor was Abbe Patterson, who took options for 4,000 shares rather than a $5,000 fee for preparing a PowerPoint presentation and speaking notes for one of Brin and Page's first presentations to venture capitalists. After two splits and four days of trading, her 16,000 shares were worth $1.7 million.[6] The company executed a second public offering of 14,159,265 shares of common stock in September 2005. The number of shares issued represented the first eight digits to the right of the decimal point for the value of π (pi). The issue added more than $4 billion to Google's liquid assets.

Exhibit 2 tracks the performance of Google's common shares between August 19, 2004, and July 2010.

Google Feature Additions between 2005 and 2010

Google used its vast cash reserves to make strategic acquisitions that might lead to the development of new Internet applications offering advertising opportunities. Google Earth was launched in 2005 after the company acquired Keyhole, a digital mapping company, in 2004. Google Earth and its companion software Google Maps allowed Internet users to search and view satellite images of any location in the world. The feature was enhanced in 2007 with the addition of street-view images taken by traveling Google camera cars. Digital images, webcam feeds, and videos captured by Internet users could be linked to locations displayed by Google Maps. Real estate listings and short personal messages could also be linked to Google Maps locations. In 2010, Google further enhanced Google Maps with the inclusion of an Earth View mode that allowed users to view 3D images of various locations from the ground level. Other search features added to Google between 2005 and 2010 that users found particularly useful included Book Search, Music Search, Video Search, and the expansion of Google News to include archived news articles dating to 1900.

Google also expanded its website features beyond search functionality to include its Gmail software, a Web-based calendar, Web-based document and spreadsheet applications, its Picasa Web photo albums, and a translation feature that accommodated 51 languages. The company also released services for mobile phone uses such as Mobile Web Search, Blogger Mobile, Gmail, Google News, and Maps for Mobile. A complete list of Google services and tools for computers and mobile phones in 2010 is presented in Exhibit 3.

GOOGLE'S BUSINESS MODEL

Google's business model had evolved since the company's inception to include revenue beyond the licensing fees charged to corporations needing search capabilities on company intranets or

Exhibit 1 The 10 Principles of Google's Corporate Philosophy

1. Focus on the user and all else will follow.

From its inception, Google has focused on providing the best user experience possible. While many companies claim to put their customers first, few are able to resist the temptation to make small sacrifices to increase shareholder value. Google has steadfastly refused to make any change that does not offer a benefit to the users who come to the site:

- The interface is clear and simple.
- Pages load instantly.
- Placement in search results is never sold to anyone.
- Advertising on the site must offer relevant content and not be a distraction.

By always placing the interests of the user first, Google has built the most loyal audience on the web. And that growth has come not through TV ad campaigns, but through word of mouth from one satisfied user to another.

2. It's best to do one thing really, really well.

Google does search. With one of the world's largest research groups focused exclusively on solving search problems, we know what we do well, and how we could do it better. Through continued iteration on difficult problems, we've been able to solve complex issues and provide continuous improvements to a service already considered the best on the web at making finding information a fast and seamless experience for millions of users. Our dedication to improving search has also allowed us to apply what we've learned to new products, including Gmail, Google Desktop, and Google Maps.

3. Fast is better than slow.

Google believes in instant gratification. You want answers and you want them right now. Who are we to argue? Google may be the only company in the world whose stated goal is to have users leave its website as quickly as possible. By fanatically obsessing on shaving every excess bit and byte from our pages and increasing the efficiency of our serving environment, Google has broken its own speed records time and again.

4. Democracy on the web works.

Google works because it relies on the millions of individuals posting websites to determine which other sites offer content of value. Instead of relying on a group of editors or solely on the frequency with which certain terms appear, Google ranks every web page using a breakthrough technique called PageRank™. PageRank evaluates all of the sites linking to a web page and assigns them a value, based in part on the sites linking to them. By analyzing the full structure of the web, Google is able to determine which sites have been "voted" the best sources of information by those most interested in the information they offer.

5. You don't need to be at your desk to need an answer.

The world is increasingly mobile and unwilling to be constrained to a fixed location. Whether it's through their PDAs, their wireless phones or even their automobiles, people want information to come to them.

6. You can make money without doing evil.

Google is a business. The revenue the company generates is derived from offering its search technology to companies and from the sale of advertising displayed on Google and on other sites across the web. However, you may have never seen an ad on Google. That's because Google does not allow ads to be displayed on our results pages unless they're relevant to the results page on which they're shown. So, only certain searches produce sponsored links above or to the right of the results. Google firmly believes that ads can provide useful information if, and only if, they are relevant to what you wish to find.

Advertising on Google is always clearly identified as a "Sponsored Link." It is a core value for Google that there be no compromising of the integrity of our results. We never manipulate rankings to put our partners higher in our search results. No one can buy better PageRank. Our users trust Google's objectivity and no short-term gain could ever justify breaching that trust.

7. There's always more information out there.

Once Google had indexed more of the HTML pages on the Internet than any other search service, our engineers turned their attention to information that was not as readily accessible. Sometimes it was just a matter of integrating new databases, such as adding a phone number and address lookup and a business directory. Other efforts required a bit more creativity, like adding the ability to search billions of images and a way to view pages that were originally created as PDF files. The popularity of PDF results led us to expand the list of file types searched to include documents produced in a dozen formats such as Microsoft Word, Excel and PowerPoint. For wireless users, Google developed a unique way to translate HTML formatted files into a format that could be read by mobile devices. The list is not likely to end there as Google's researchers continue looking into ways to bring all the world's information to users seeking answers.

(Continued)

Exhibit 1   *(Concluded)*

---

8. The need for information crosses all borders.

Though Google is headquartered in California, our mission is to facilitate access to information for the entire world, so we have offices around the globe. To that end we maintain dozens of Internet domains and serve more than half of our results to users living outside the United States. Google search results can be restricted to pages written in more than 35 languages according to a user's preference. We also offer a translation feature to make content available to users regardless of their native tongue and for those who prefer not to search in English, Google's interface can be customized into more than 100 languages.

9. You can be serious without a suit.

Google's founders have often stated that the company is not serious about anything but search. They built a company around the idea that work should be challenging and the challenge should be fun. To that end, Google's culture is unlike any in corporate America, and it's not because of the ubiquitous lava lamps and large rubber balls, or the fact that the company's chef used to cook for the Grateful Dead. In the same way Google puts users first when it comes to our online service, Google Inc. puts employees first when it comes to daily life in our Googleplex headquarters. There is an emphasis on team achievements and pride in individual accomplishments that contribute to the company's overall success. Ideas are traded, tested and put into practice with an alacrity that can be dizzying. Meetings that would take hours elsewhere are frequently little more than a conversation in line for lunch and few walls separate those who write the code from those who write the checks. This highly communicative environment fosters a productivity and camaraderie fueled by the realization that millions of people rely on Google results. Give the proper tools to a group of people who like to make a difference, and they will.

10. Great just isn't good enough.

Always deliver more than expected. Google does not accept being the best as an endpoint, but a starting point. Through innovation and iteration, Google takes something that works well and improves upon it in unexpected ways. Google's point of distinction however, is anticipating needs not yet articulated by our global audience, then meeting them with products and services that set new standards. This constant dissatisfaction with the way things are is ultimately the driving force behind the world's best search engine.

Source: Google.com.

Exhibit 2   **Performance of Google's Stock Price, August 19, 2004, to July 2010**

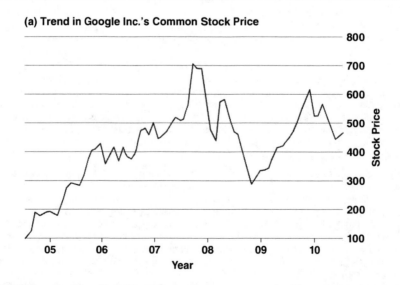

(a) Trend in Google Inc.'s Common Stock Price

(b) Performance of Google Inc.'s Stock Price Versus the S&P 500 Index

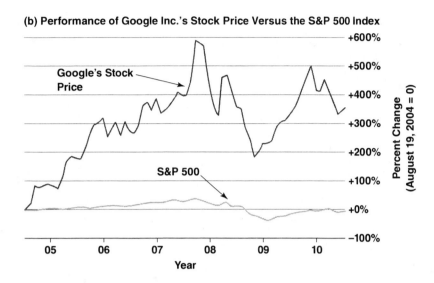

Exhibit 3   **Google' Services and Tools in 2010**

Search Features	
	Alerts
	Get email updates on the topics of your choice
	Blog Search
	Find blogs on your favorite topics
	Books
	Search the full text of books
	Checkout
	Complete online purchases more quickly and securely
	Google Chrome
	A browser built for speed, stability and security
	Custom Search
	Create a customized search experience for your community
	Desktop
	Search and personalize your computer
	Directory
	Search the web, organized by topic or category
	Earth
	Explore the world from your computer
	Finance
	Business info, news, and interactive charts

(Continued)

C-180   **Part 2**   Cases in Crafting and Executing Strategy

Exhibit 3   *(Continued)*

Search Features	
	GOOG-411 Find and connect with businesses from your phone
	Google Health Organize your medical records online
	iGoogle Add news, games and more to your Google homepage
	Images Search for images on the Web
	Maps View maps and directions
	News Search thousands of news stories
	Patent Search Search the full text of US Patents
	Product Search Search for stuff to buy
	Scholar Search scholarly papers
	Toolbar Add a search box to your browser
	Trends Explore past and present search trends
	Videos Search for videos on the Web
	Web Search Search billions of Web pages

Google Tools and Web Applications	
	Code Developer tools, APIs and resources
	Labs Explore Google's technology playground
	Blogger Share your life online with a blog—it's fast, easy, and free

(Continued)

Exhibit 3   *(Concluded)*

Google Tools and Web Applications	
	Calendar Organize your schedule and share events with friends
	Docs Create and share your online documents, presentations, and spreadsheets
	Google Mail Fast, searchable email with less spam
	Groups Create mailing lists and discussion groups
	Knol Share what you know
orkut	**Orkut** Meet new people and stay in touch with friends
	Picasa Find, edit and share your photos
	Reader Get all your blogs and news feeds fast
	Sites Create Web sites and secure group wikis
	SketchUp Build 3D models quickly and easily
	Talk IM and call your friends through your computer
	Translate View Web pages in other languages
	YouTube Watch, upload and share videos

Google Mobile Applications	
	Maps for mobile View maps, your location and get directions on your phone
	Search for mobile Search Google wherever you are

Source: Google.com.

websites. The 2000 development of keyword-targeted advertising expanded its business model to include revenues from the placement of highly targeted text-only sponsor ads adjacent to its search results. Google was able to target its ads to specific users based on the user's browsing history. The addition of advertising-based revenue allowed Google to increase annual revenues from $220,000 in 1999 to more than $86 million in 2001. A summary of Google's financial performance between 2001 and 2009 is presented in Exhibit 4. The company's balance sheets for 2008 and 2009 are presented in Exhibit 5.

Google Search Appliance

Google's search technology could be integrated into a third party's website or intranet if search functionality was important to the customer. Google's Site Search allowed enterprises ranging from small businesses to public companies to license Google's search appliance for use on their websites for as little as $100 per year. The Google Search Appliance was designed for use on corporate intranets to allow employees to search company documents. The Search Appliance included a variety of security features to ensure that only employees with proper authority were able to view restricted documents. The Google Mini Search Appliance was designed for small businesses with 50,000 to 300,000 documents stored on local PCs and servers. The Google Mini hardware and software package could be licensed online (at www.google.com/enterprise/mini) at prices ranging from $2,990 to $9,900, depending on document count capability. Google's more robust search appliance had a document count capability of up to 30 million documents and was designed for midsized to global businesses. Licensing fees for the Google Search appliance ranged from $30,000 to $600,000, depending on document count capability.

AdWords

Google AdWords allowed advertisers, either independently through Google's automated tools or with the assistance of Google's marketing teams, to create text-based ads that would appear alongside Google search results. AdWords users could evaluate the effectiveness of their advertising expenditures with Google through the use of performance reports that tracked the effectiveness of each ad. Google also offered a keyword targeting program that suggested synonyms for keywords entered by advertisers, a traffic estimator that helped potential advertisers anticipate charges, and multiple payment options that included charges to credit cards, debit cards, and monthly invoicing.

Larger advertisers were offered additional services to help run large, dynamic advertising campaigns. Such assistance included the availability of specialists with expertise in various industries to offer suggestions for targeting potential customers and identifying relevant keywords. Google's advertising specialists helped develop ads for customers that would increase click-through rates and purchase rates. Google also offered its large advertising customers bulk posting services that helped launch and manage campaigns including ads using hundreds or thousands of keywords.

Google's search-based ads were priced using an auction system that allowed advertisers to bid on keywords that would describe their product or service. Bids could be made on a cost-per-impression (CPI) or cost-per-click (CPC) basis. Most Google advertisers placed bids based on CPC frequency rather than how many times an ad was displayed by Google. Google's auction pricing model assigned each bidder a Quality Score, which was determined by the advertiser's past keyword click-through rate and the relevance of the ad text. Advertisers with high Quality Scores were offered lower minimum bids than advertisers with poor quality scores.

Google allowed users to pay a CPC rate lower than their bid price if their bid was considerably more than the next highest bid. For example, an advertiser who bid $0.75 per click for a particular keyword would be charged only $0.51 per click if the next highest bid was only $0.50. The AdWords discounter ensured that advertisers paid only 1 cent more than the next highest bid, regardless of the actual amount of their bid.

AdSense

Google's AdSense program allowed Web publishers to share in the advertising revenues generated by Google's text ads. The AdSense program served content-relevant Google text ads to pages

Exhibit 4 Financial Summary for Google, 2001–2009 ($ thousands, except per share amounts)

	2009	2008	2007	2006	2005	2004	2003	2002	2001
Revenues	$23,650,563	$21,795,550	$16,593,986	$10,604,917	$ 6,138,560	$3,189,223	$1,465,934	$439,508	$86,426
Costs and expenses:									
Cost of revenues	8,844,115	8,621,506	6,649,085	4,225,027	2,577,088	1,457,653	625,854	131,510	14,228
Research and development	2,843,027	2,793,192	2,119,985	1,228,589	599,510	225,632	91,228	31,748	16,500
Sales and marketing	1,983,941	1,946,244	1,461,266	849,518	468,152	246,300	120,328	43,849	20,076
General and administrative	1,667,294	1,802,639	1,279,250	751,787	386,532	188,151	286,060	45,935	24,658
Contribution to Google Foundation	—	—	—	—	90,000	201,000	—	—	—
Non-recurring portion of settlement of disputes with Yahoo	—	—	—	—	—	—	—	—	—
Total costs and expenses	15,338,377	15,163,581	11,509,586	7,054,921	4,121,282	2,549,031	1,123,470	253,042	75,462
Income (loss) from operations	8,312,186	6,631,969	5,084,400	3,549,996	2,017,278	640,192	342,464	186,466	10,964
Impairment of equity investments		(1,094,757)							
Interest income (expense) and other, net	69,003	316,384	589,580	461,044	124,399	10,042	4,190	-1,551	-896
Income (loss) before income taxes	8,381,189	5,853,596	5,673,980	4,011,040	2,141,677	650,234	346,654	184,915	10,068
Provision for income taxes	1,860,741	1,626,738	1,470,260	933,594	676,280	251,115	241,006	85,259	3,083
Net income (loss)	$ 6,520,448	$ 4,226,858	$ 4,203,720	$ 3,077,446	$ 1,465,397	$ 399,119	$ 105,648	$ 99,656	$ 6,985
Net income (loss) per share:									
Basic	$20.62	$13.46	$13.53	$10.21	$5.31	$2.07	$0.77	$0.86	$0.07
Diluted	$20.41	$13.31	$13.29	$9.94	$5.02	$1.46	$0.41	$0.45	$0.04
Number of shares used in per share calculations: (in thousands)									
Basic	316,220	314,031	310,806	301,403	275,844	193,176	137,697	115,242	94,523
Diluted	319,473	317,570	316,210	309,548	291,874	272,781	256,638	220,633	186,776
Net cash provided by operating activities	$ 9,316,198	$ 7,852,857	$ 5,775,410	$ 3,580,508	$ 2,459,422	$ 977,044	$ 395,445	$155,265	n/a
Net proceeds from public offerings	—	—	—	2,063,549	4,287,229	1,161,466	—	—	—
Cash, cash equivalents, and marketable securities	24,484,775	15,845,771	14,218,613	11,243,914	8,034,247	2,132,297	334,718	146,331	n/a
Total assets	40,496,778	31,767,575	25,335,806	18,473,351	10,271,813	3,313,351	871,458	286,892	n/a
Total long-term liabilities	1,745,087	1,226,623	610,525	128,924	107,472	43,927	33,365	n/a	n/a
Total stockholders' equity	36,004,224	28,238,862	22,689,679	17,039,840	9,418,957	2,929,056	588,770	173,953	n/a

Source: Google, Form S-1, filed April 29, 2004; Google, 2009 10-K report.

Exhibit 5   **Google's Balance Sheets, 2008–2009 ($ thousands, except per share amounts)**

	As of December 31	
	2009	2008
Assets		
Current assets:		
Cash and cash equivalents	$10,197,588	$ 8,656,672
Marketable securities	14,287,187	7,189,099
Accounts receivable, net of allowance of $16,914 and $32,887	3,178,471	2,642,192
Deferred income taxes, net	644,406	286,105
Income taxes receivable	23,244	—
Prepaid revenue share, expenses and other assets	836,062	1,404,114
Total current assets	29,166,958	20,178,182
Prepaid revenue share, expenses and other assets, non-current	416,119	433,846
Deferred income taxes, net, non-current	262,611	—
Non-marketable equity securities	128,977	85,160
Property and equipment, net	4,844,610	5,233,843
Intangible assets, net	4,774,938	996,690
Goodwill	4,902,565	4,839,854
Total assets	$40,496,778	$31,767,575
Liabilities and Stockholders' Equity		
Current liabilities:		
Accounts payable	$ 215,867	$ 178,004
Accrued compensation and benefits	982,482	811,643
Accrued expenses and other current liabilities	570,080	480,263
Accrued revenue share	693,958	532,547
Deferred revenue	285,080	218,084
Income taxes payable, net	—	81,549
Total current liabilities	2,747,467	2,302,090
Deferred revenue, long-term	41,618	29,818
Income taxes payable, long-term	1,392,468	890,115
Deferred income taxes, net, non-current	—	12,515
Other long-term liabilities	311,001	294,175
Commitments and contingencies		
Stockholders' equity:		
Convertible preferred stock, $0.001 par value, 100,000 shares authorized; no shares issued and outstanding	—	—
Class A and Class B common stock, $0.001 par value per share: 9,000,000 shares authorized; 315,114 (Class A 240,073, Class B 75,041) and par value of $315 (Class A $240, Class B $75) and 317,772 (Class A 243,611, Class B 74,161) and par value of $318 (Class A $244, Class B $74) shares issued and outstanding, excluding 26 and zero Class A shares subject to repurchase at December 31, 2008 and 2009	318	315
Additional paid-in capital	15,816,738	14,450,338
Accumulated other comprehensive income	105,090	226,579
Retained earnings	20,082,078	13,561,630
Total stockholders' equity	36,004,224	28,238,862
Total liabilities and stockholders' equity	$40,496,778	$31,767,575

Source: Google, 2009 10-K report.

on Google Network websites. For example, an Internet user reading an article about the state of the economy at Reuters.com would see Google text ads by investment magazines and companies specializing in home business opportunities. Google Network members shared in the advertising revenue whenever a site visitor clicked on a Google ad displayed on their sites. The more than 1 million Google Network members did not pay a fee to participate in the program and received about 60 percent of advertising dollars generated from the ads. Google's AdSense program also allowed mobile phone operators to share in Google revenues if text and image ads were displayed on mobile handsets. Also, owners of dormant domain names, Web-based game sites, video sites, and news feed services could also participate in the AdSense program. The breakdown of Google's revenues by source for 2003 through 2009 is presented in Exhibit 6.

Other Revenue Sources

The company's 2006 acquisition of YouTube allowed it to receive advertising revenues for ads displayed during Internet videos, while its 2008 acquisition of DoubleClick allowed the company to generate advertising revenues through banner ads. The company's 2008 launch of Google Checkout generated fees of as much as 2 percent of the transaction amount for purchases made at participating e-retailer sites. Google's business model was further expanded in 2008 to include licensing fees paid by users of its Web-based Google Apps document and spreadsheet software.

GOOGLE'S STRATEGY AND COMPETITIVE POSITION IN 2010

Google's Strategies to Dominate Internet Advertising

Google's multiple acquisitions since its 2004 IPO, and its research and development activities, were directed at increasing the company's dominance in Internet advertising. The addition of Google Maps, local search, airline travel information, weather, Book Search, Gmail, Blogger, and other features increased traffic to Google sites and gave the company more opportunities to serve ads to Internet users. Also, the acquisition of Double-Click in 2008 allowed Google to diversify its Internet advertising beyond search ads to include banner ads. However, not all of Google's acquisitions and innovations had resulted in meaningful contributions to the company's revenues. Even though more than 12 billion videos were watched on YouTube each month, the online video site's advertising revenues in 2009 were estimated at less than $300 million. Also, the company's internally developed social networking site, Orkut, had failed to match the success of competing social networking sites Facebook.com and MySpace.com.

Google's strategy to dominate Internet advertising also entailed becoming the number one search engine used not only in the United States but also across the world. In 2010, Google's search-based ads could be delivered to Internet users

Exhibit 6 Google's Revenues by Source, 2003–2009 ($ thousands)

	2009	2008	2007	2006	2005	2004	2003
Advertising revenues:							
Google websites	$15,722,486	$14,413,826	$10,624,705	$ 6,332,797	$3,377,060	$1,589,032	$ 792,063
Google Network websites	7,166,318	6,714,688	5,787,938	4,159,831	2,687,942	1,554,256	628,600
Total	22,888,804	21,128,514	16,412,643	10,492,628	6,065,002	3,143,288	1,420,663
Licensing and other revenues	761,759	667,036	181,343	112,289	73,558	45,935	45,271
Total revenues	$23,650,563	$21,795,550	$16,593,986	$10,604,917	$6,138,560	$3,189,223	$1,465,934

Source: Google, 2007 and 2009 10-K reports.

in 41 different languages. More than 50 percent of the company's 2009 revenues and traffic were generated from outside the United States, and the percentage of sales from outside the United States was expected to grow as Google entered emerging markets like Russia and China. China was a particularly attractive market for Google since it had more Internet users (300+ million) than any other country in the world. However, Google's 2006 entry into China was accompanied by challenges, including strong competition from local search provider Baidu and requirements by the Chinese government to censor search results that were critical of the government. Google complied with government censorship requirements until early 2010, when cyberattacks originating in China stole proprietary computer code from Google and information from the Gmail accounts of several Chinese human rights activists. Google first responded to the hacking incidents by stating that it would withdraw from the Chinese search market and then shifted to a strategy of redirecting users of its censored Google.cn site in China to its uncensored Hong Kong search site, Google.com.hk. The Chinese government was able to block search results from Google's Hong Kong site, but the new policy ended Google's involvement in China's censorship practices. To avoid breaking Chinese law prohibiting the distribution of information not authorized by the government,

Google agreed in June 2010 to stop the automatic redirects to its Hong Kong site. Instead, it presented Google.cn users with a link to Google.com.hk. In 2009, 64 percent of Internet searches in China were performed by Baidu, while Google held a 31 percent share of searches in that country. A breakdown of Google's revenues and long-lived assets by geographic region for 2006 through 2009 is presented in Exhibit 7.

Mobile Search and Google's Entry into the Market for Smartphones

In 2010, 234 million Americans ages 13 and older owned and used mobile phones. More than 30 percent of mobile phone users accessed the Internet from mobile devices, and a rapidly growing number of mobile phone users were exchanging basic mobile phones for smartphones. Smartphones like Research in Motion's Blackberry and Apple's iPhone could connect to the networks of wireless carriers to make phone calls, access the Internet, or run various Internet applications. Between February 2010 and May 2010, the number of smartphone users had grown by 8.1 percent to reach 49.1 million.

The company's introduction of its Android operating system for smartphones in 2008 was expected to allow it to increase its 60-plus percent

Exhibit 7   Google's Revenues and Long-Lived Assets by Geographic Region, 2006–2009 (in thousands)

Revenues	Year Ended December 31			
	2009	2008	2007	2006
United States	$11,193,557	$10,635,553	$ 8,698,021	$ 6,030,140
United Kingdom	2,986,040	3,038,488	2,530,916	1,603,842
Rest of the world	9,470,966	8,121,509	5,365,049	2,970,935
Total revenues	$23,650,563	$21,795,550	$16,593,986	$10,604,917

Long-Lived Assets	As of December 31			
	2009	2008	2007	2006
United States	$ 9,432,113	$ 9,782,825	$ 7,334,877	$ 5,070,694
Rest of the world	1,897,707	1,806,568	711,791	362,810
Total long-lived assets	$11,329,820	$11,589,393	$ 8,046,668	$ 5,433,504

Source: Google, 2007 and 2009 10-K reports.

Exhibit 8 **U.S. Smartphone Platform Market Share Rankings, Selected Periods, September 2009–May 2010**

Smartphone Platform	Share of Smartphone Subscribers			
	September 2009	December 2009	February 2010	May 2010
RIM (Blackberry)	42.6%	41.6%	42.1%	41.7%
Apple iPhone	24.1	25.3	25.4	24.4
Microsoft Windows Mobile	19.0	18.0	15.1	13.2
Google Android	2.5	5.2	9.0	13.0
Palm	8.3	6.1	5.4	4.8
Others	3.5	3.8	3.0	2.9
Total	100.0%	100.0%	100.0%	100.0%

Source: ComScore.com.

share of mobile searches and expand the market for other types of Internet ads delivered on mobile devices. Android was not a phone, but an operating system that Google made available free of charge to any phone manufacturer wishing to market mobile devices with Internet capability. Android's core applications included Wi-Fi capability, e-mail, a Web-based calendar, Google Earth maps, a browser, and GPS. T-Mobile was the first wireless provider to market an Android phone. Its $179 G1 was launched in September 2008 and included essentially the same features found on the more expensive Apple iPhone. By 2010, all major mobile phone providers had added smartphone models running Android software to its lineup of handsets. In addition, Google marketed its own Nexus One smartphone, which was produced by HTC and was compatible with all major wireless carrier 3G and 4G networks. Google was also collaborating with Verizon to develop a tablet computer similar to Apple's iPad that would run on Verizon's wireless networks.

Google's Android software had achieved remarkable success, despite its late entry into the market, with its market share increasing from zero in 2008 to 13.0 percent in May 2010—see Exhibit 8. Google also allowed mobile apps developers to use the Android operating system free of licensing fees. The worldwide market for mobile apps was expected to increase from $4.1 billion in 2009 to $17.5 billion by 2012. In 2010, more than 10,000 free and paid apps were available at Google's Android Market and more than 60 percent of mobile developers were actively working on new

apps for Android. About 50 percent of mobile developers were developing new apps for the iPhone and phones running Microsoft's Windows Mobile platform. Also in 2010, Google acquired AdMob, which had developed technology to deliver banner ads to smartphones and other mobile phones able to connect to the Internet. The transaction provided AdMob stockholders with Google shares worth $750 million.

Google's Strategic Offensive to Control the Desktop

Google's senior management believed that, in the very near future, most computer software programs used by businesses would move from local hard drives or intranets to the Internet. Many information technology analysts agreed that cloud computing would become a common software platform and could grow to a $95 billion market by 2013. Moving software applications to the cloud offered many possible benefits to corporate users, including lower software acquisition costs, lower computing support costs, and easier collaboration among employees in different locations. The beta version of Google Apps was launched in 2006 as a free word processing and spreadsheet package for individuals, but was relaunched in 2008 as a competing product to Microsoft Office. Google Apps was hosted on computers in Google's data centers and included Gmail, a calendar, instant messaging, word processing, spreadsheets, presentation software, and file storage space. Google Apps could be licensed by corporate customers at $50 per user per year. The licensing fee for the Microsoft Office and Outlook package was typically $350 per user per year. Industry analysts estimated Google Apps users at about 25 million and paid subscribers at about 1.5 million in 2010. Microsoft estimated Microsoft Office users at about 500 million in 2010.

Google's Chrome browser, which was launched in September 2008, and Chrome operating system (OS) launched in July 2009 were developed specifically to accommodate cloud computing applications. The bare-bones Chrome browser was built on a multiprocessor design that would allow users to operate spreadsheets, word processing, video editing, and other applications on separate tabs that could be run simultaneously. Each tab operated independently so that if one tab crashed, other applications running from Google's data centers were not affected. The Chrome browser also provided Google with a defense against moves by Microsoft to make it more difficult for Google to deliver relevant search-based ads to Internet users. Microsoft's Internet Explorer 8 allowed users to hide their Internet address and viewing history, which prevented Google from collecting user-specific information needed for ad targeting. Mozilla's Firefox browser employed a similar feature that prevented third parties from tracking a user's viewing habits. The clean-running Chrome OS was an open source operating system specifically designed as a platform for cloud computing applications.

Late in 2009, Google entered into agreements with Acer, Hewlett-Packard, and Lenovo to begin producing netbooks that would use the Chrome OS and Chrome browser to access the cloud-based Google Apps productivity software. Chrome OS netbooks were expected to be available for purchase by consumers and businesses in late 2010. Worldwide market share statistics for the leading browsers in September 2008 and June 2010 are presented in Exhibit 9.

Google's Initiatives to Expand Search to Television

In mid-2010, Google entered into an alliance with Intel, Sony, Logitech, Best Buy, DISH Network, and Adobe to develop Google TV. Google TV would be built on the Android platform and would run the Chrome browser software to search live network and cable programming; streaming

Exhibit 9   **Worldwide Browser Market Share Rankings, September 2008 and June 2010**

Browser	September 2008	June 2010
Internet Explorer	74%	60%
Firefox	19	24
Chrome	1	7
Safari	3	5
Opera	2	3
Others	1	1
Total	100%	100%

Source: "Google Rekindles Browser War," *Wall Street Journal Online,* July 7, 2010.

videos from providers such as Netflix, Amazon Video On Demand, and YouTube; and recorded programs on a DVR. Google TV users would also be able to use their televisions to browse the Web and run cloud-based applications such as Google Apps. Google TV was expected to be integrated into DISH Network's satellite service by fall 2010, while Sony was on schedule for fall 2010 shipments of Google TV–compatible high-definition televisions (HDTVs). Logitech was also on track for fall 2010 shipments of Google TV set-top boxes that would be compatible with all brands of HDTVs and Google TV accessories such as HD cameras that could be used for video chats.

Google acquired On2 Technologies, which was the leading developer of video compression technology, in February 2010 in a $124 million stock and cash transaction. The acquisition of On2 was expected to improve the video streaming capabilities of Google TV. Google also lobbied heavily during 2009 and 2010 to encourage the Obama administration to adopt a "Net neutrality" policy that would require Internet providers to manage traffic in a manner that would not restrict high-bandwidth services such as Internet television. The company was also testing an ultrafast broadband network in several cities across the United States that was as much as 100 times faster than what was offered by competing Internet providers. Google management had stated that the company did not intend to launch a nationwide Internet service, but did want to expose consumers to Internet applications and content that would be possible with greater bandwidth and faster transmission speeds.

GOOGLE'S INTERNET RIVALS

Google's ability to sustain its competitive advantage among search companies was a function of its ability to maintain strong relationships with Internet users, advertisers, and websites. In 2010, Google was the world's most-visited Internet site, with nearly 147 million unique Internet users going to Google sites each month to search for information. Google management believed its primary competitors to be Microsoft and Yahoo. A comparison of the percentage of Internet searches among websites offering search capabilities in July 2006, June 2009, and May 2010 is shown in Exhibit 10.

Exhibit 10 **U.S. Search Engine Market Share Rankings, July 2006, June 2009, and May 2010**

Search Entity	Percent of Searches		
	July 2006	June 2009	May 2010
Google Sites	43.7%	65.0%	63.7%
Yahoo Sites	28.8	19.6	18.3
Microsoft Sites	12.8	8.4	12.1
Ask.com	5.4	3.9	3.6
AOL	5.9	3.1	2.3
Others	3.4	n.m.	n.m.
Total	100.0%	100.0%	100.0%

n.m. = not material.

Source: ComScore.com.

Yahoo

Yahoo was founded in 1994 and was the third-most-visited Internet destination worldwide in 2010, with 130.5 million unique visitors each month. Facebook was the second-most-visited website, with 132 million unique visitors each month in 2010. Almost any information available on the Internet could be accessed through Yahoo's Web portal. Visitors could access content categorized by Yahoo or set up an account with Yahoo to maintain a personal calendar and e-mail account, check the latest news, check local weather, obtain maps, check TV listings, watch a movie trailer, track a stock portfolio, maintain a golf handicap, keep an online photo album, or search personal ads or job listings.

Yahoo also hosted websites for small businesses and Internet retailers and had entered into strategic partnerships with 20 mobile phone operators in the United States and Europe to provide mobile search and display ads to their customers. Yahoo accounted for about 35 percent of searches performed on mobile phones in 2010. Yahoo's broad range of services allowed it to generate revenues from numerous sources—it received fees for banner ads displayed at Yahoo.com, Yahoo! Messenger, Yahoo! Mail, Flickr, or mobile phone customers; it received listing fees at Yahoo! Autos, Cars.com, and Yahoo! Real Estate; it received revenues from paid search results at Yahoo! Search; it shared in travel agency booking fees made at Yahoo! Travel; and it received subscription fees from its registered users at Rivals.com, Yahoo! Games, Yahoo! Music, and Yahoo! Personals.

Yahoo's relationship with Google dated to 2000 and, since that time, had oscillated between cooperative and adversarial. Yahoo was among Google's earliest customers for its search appliance, but Yahoo began to distance itself from Google in 2002 when it began acquiring companies with developed search technologies. Yahoo replaced Google with its own search capabilities in February 2004. Yahoo later levied a patent infringement charge against Google that resulted in a settlement that gave Google ownership of the technology rights in return for 2.7 million shares of Google stock. Yahoo attempted to renew its relationship with Google in 2008 in hopes of reversing a decline in profitability and liquidity that began in 2006. After averting a hostile takeover by Microsoft in June 2008, Yahoo reached an agreement with Google that would allow Yahoo to host Google search ads. The partnership would provide Yahoo with an estimated $800 million in additional revenues annually, most of which would go directly to its bottom line. However, Google withdrew from the agreement in November 2008 after receiving notification from the U.S. Justice Department that the alliance would possibly violate antitrust statutes. Shortly after being notified that Google was withdrawing from the deal, Yahoo's chief managers told business reporters that the company was "disappointed that Google has elected to withdraw from the agreement rather than defend it in court."[7] In July 2009, Microsoft and Yahoo finally came to an agreement that would make Microsoft Bing Yahoo's imbedded search engine for a period of 10 years. A summary of Yahoo's financial performance between 2003 and 2009 is presented in Exhibit 11.

Microsoft Online Services

Microsoft Corporation recorded fiscal 2009 revenues and net income of approximately $58.4 billion and $14.6 billion, respectively, through the sales of computer software, consulting services, video game hardware, and online services. Windows 7 and Microsoft Office accounted for more than one-half of the company's 2009 revenues and nearly all of its operating profit. The company's online services business recorded sales of nearly $3.1 billion and an operating loss of almost $2.3 billion during fiscal 2009. Microsoft's online services business generated revenues from banner ads displayed at the company's MSN Web portal and its affiliated websites, search-based ads displayed with Bing results, and subscription fees from its MSN

dial-up service. A financial summary for Microsoft Corporation and its Online Services Division is provided in Exhibit 12.

Microsoft's search business was launched in November 2004 as Live Search to compete directly with Google and slow whatever intentions Google might have to threaten Microsoft in its core operating system and productivity software businesses. Microsoft's concern with threats posed by Google arose shortly after Google's IPO, when Bill Gates noticed that many of the Google job postings on its site were nearly identical to Microsoft job specifications. Recognizing that the position announcements had more to do with operating-system design than search, Gates e-mailed key Microsoft executives, warning, "We have to watch these guys. It looks like they are building something to compete with us."[8] Gates later commented that Google was "more like us than anyone else we have ever competed with."[9]

Gates speculated that Google's long-term strategy involved the development of Web-based software applications comparable to Word, Excel, PowerPoint, and other Microsoft products. Microsoft's strategy to compete with Google was keyed to making Live Search more effective than Google at providing highly relevant search results. Microsoft believed that any conversion of Google users to Live Search would reduce the number of PC users who might ultimately adopt Google's Web-based

Exhibit 11   Selected Financial Data for Yahoo, 2003–2009 ($ thousands)

	2009	2008	2007	2006	2005	2004	2003
Revenues	$ 6,460,315	$ 7,208,502	$ 6,969,274	$ 6,425,679	$ 5,257,668	$3,574,517	$1,625,097
Income from operations	386,692	12,963	695,413	940,966	1,107,725	688,581	295,666
Net income	597,992	418,921	639,155	731,568	1,877,407	839,553	237,879
Cash and cash equivalents	1,275,430	2,292,296	1,513,930	1,569,871	1,429,693	823,723	415,892
Marketable securities	3,242,574	1,229,677	849,542	1,967,414	2,570,155	2,918,539	2,150,323
Working capital	2,877,044	3,040,483	937,274	2,276,148	2,245,481	2,909,768	1,013,913
Total assets	14,936,030	13,689,848	12,229,741	11,513,608	10,831,834	9,178,201	5,931,654
Long-term liabilities	699,666	715,872	384,208	870,948	1,061,367	851,782	822,890
Total stockholders' equity	12,493,320	11,250,942	9,532,831	9,160,610	8,566,415	7,101,446	4,363,490

Source: Yahoo, 2007 and 2009 10-K reports.

Exhibit 12   **Selected Financial Data for Microsoft Corporation and Microsoft's Online Services Business Unit, 2006–2009 ($ millions)**

Microsoft Corporation	Fiscal Year Ended June 30			
	2009	2008	2007	2006
Revenue	$58,437	$60,420	$51,122	$44,282
Operating income	20,363	22,492	18,524	16,472
Net income	14,569	17,681	14,065	12,599
Cash, cash equivalents, and short-term investments	$31,447	$23,662	$23,411	$34,161
Total assets	77,888	72,793	63,171	69,597
Long-term obligations	11,296	6,621	8,320	7,051
Stockholders' equity	39,558	36,286	31,097	40,104
Microsoft's Online Services Business Unit	**2009**	**2008**	**2007**	**2006**
Revenue	$ 3,088	$ 3,214	$ 2,441	$ 2,296
Operating income (loss)	(2,253)	(1,233)	(617)	5

Source: Microsoft, 2007 and 2009 annual reports.

word processing, spreadsheet, and presentation software packages. In 2008, Microsoft paid more than $100 million to acquire Powerset, which was the developer of a semantic search engine. Semantic search technology offered the opportunity to surpass the relevancy of Google's search results since semantic search evaluated the meaning of a word or phrase and considered its context when returning search results. Even though semantic search had the capability to answer questions stated in common language, semantic search processing time took several seconds to return results. The amount of time necessary to conduct a search had caused Microsoft to limit Powerset's search index to only articles listed in Wikipedia. Microsoft's developers were focused on increasing the speed of its semantic search capabilities so that its search index could be expanded to a greater number of Internet pages. The company's developers also incorporated some of Powerset's capabilities into its latest-generation search engine, Bing, which was launched in June 2009.

Microsoft's search agreement with Yahoo was engineered to allow the company to increase its Internet search market share and achieve advertising scale necessary to make its online services business profitable. The addition of Yahoo's 130.5 million unique monthly users was expected to double exposure for Microsoft's banner ads to more than 200 million unique monthly users. Banner ads comprised the bulk of Microsoft's online advertising revenues, since its Bing search engine accounted for only 12 percent of online searches in 2010. Even though the market for display ads was only about one-half the size of the search ad market in 2009, the advertising spending on banner ads was expected to double by 2012 to reach $15 billion.

Microsoft was also moving forward with its own approach to cloud computing. The company's 2008 launch of Windows Live allowed Internet users to store files online at its password-protected SkyDrive site. SkyDrive's online file storage allowed users to access and edit files from multiple locations, share files with coworkers who might need editing privileges, or make files available in a public folder for wide distribution. Azure was Microsoft's most ambitious cloud computing initiative in 2010 and was intended to allow businesses to reduce computing costs by allowing Microsoft to host its operating programs and data files. In addition to reducing capital expenditures for software upgrades and added server capacity, Azure's offsite hosting provided data security in the event of natural disasters such as fires or hurricanes.

ISSUES CONCERNING GOOGLE'S PERFORMANCE AND BUSINESS ETHICS IN 2010

During its first quarter of fiscal 2010, Google had been able to achieve year-over-year revenue growth of 23 percent, while most companies in almost every industry struggled as the U.S. economy continued to falter. So far, it appeared that Google's business model and strategy had insulated it from the effects of the recession and it was in position to pursue its growth strategies. The company's strategic priorities in 2010 focused on expanding its share of mobile search and smartphone platforms, pushing forward with its plans to become the dominant provider of cloud computing solutions, increasing search advertising revenues from markets outside the United States, and extending search to television. Some analysts believed the company's priorities should also include the development of semantic search capabilities, while others were concerned that the company had strayed from its 10 Principles—specifically, Principle 6, "You can make money without doing evil."

Free-speech advocates had criticized Google for its complicity in China's censorship of Internet content since it launched its Chinese site in 2006, while privacy advocates complained that Google Map's street view mode violated privacy rights. The New Zealand government addressed privacy rights by requiring Google to blur the faces of all individuals photographed by its camera cars. The most serious issue involving Google's Street View involved Google management's decision to allow the company's camera cars to capture Wi-Fi data emitted from homes and businesses while photographing the route. In May 2010, authorities in the United States, Canada, Australia, Germany, Italy, the United Kingdom, and Spain were conducting investigations into Google's data collection activities to determine if prosecution of company managers was

warranted. Google cofounder Sergey Brin said the company "screwed up" by collecting personal data through wireless networks in an attempt to improve its mapping system.[10]

Also, the company's lobbying efforts to encourage the Obama administration to institute policies to promote Net neutrality had drawn the scrutiny of the U.S. House Oversight Committee. The primary concern of the House Oversight Committee involved communications between the company and its former head of public policy and government affairs, Andrew McLaughlin, who had been appointed to the position of White House deputy chief technology officer. Ethics rules created by an executive order signed by President Obama barred all White House officials from communicating with lobbyists or a company potentially affected by pending policy matters. A Freedom of Information Act (FOIA) request by a consumer group found that McLaughlin regularly communicated with Google executives to discuss the administration's push to have the Internet regulated by the Federal Communications Commission to promote Net neutrality. McLaughlin's e-mails could be obtained under the FOIA since all White House e-mail accounts were required to be archived under federal law. The House Oversight Committee was particularly disturbed by McLaughlin's alleged use of a personal Gmail account to avoid having his communications with Google executives archived and subject to FOIA requests.

Some analysts believed that pressure to achieve the revenue and earnings growth necessary to maintain Google's lofty stock price may have caused Google management to make decisions that pushed the bounds of its corporate philosophy. The company's revenues and earnings growth had begun to slow in recent years, and the sluggish U.S. economy seemed unlikely to give Google a dramatic boost in revenues in 2010. It remained to be determined if Google's strategies could sustain its growth and stock performance in a manner that would adhere to the company founders' early beliefs.

ENDNOTES

1 Google, www.google.com/corporate/, accessed July 13, 2010.

2 Quoted in "Google's Eric Schmidt: You Can Trust Us with Your Data," *UK Telegraph,* July 1, 2010.

3 Google, www.google.com/corporate/tenthings.html, accessed July 13, 2010.

4 Quoted in Google's Corporate Information, www.google.com/corporate/history.html.

5 Google, "Our Philosophy," www.google.com/corporate/tenthings.html.

6 "For Some Who Passed on Google Long Ago, Wistful Thinking," *Wall Street Journal Online,* August 23, 2004.

7 Quoted in "With Google Gone, Will Microsoft Come Back to Yahoo?" *Fortune,* November 5, 2008.

8 Quoted in "Gates vs. Google," *Fortune,* April 18, 2005.

9 Ibid.

10 Quoted in "Google Faces European Probes on Wi-Fi Data," *Wall Street Journal Online,* May 20, 2010.

case 32

Kmart: Striving for a Comeback

John E. Gamble
University of South Alabama

In March 2003 Kmart Corporation was entering what its management hoped would be the last two months of bankruptcy protection that had allowed it to continue its operations even though it had been delinquent on obligations of more than $4.7 billion owed to creditors, vendors, and leaseholders. The bankruptcy, which was filed in January 2002, was the largest bankruptcy in U.S. retailing history and was the culmination of decades of poor strategy execution that resulted in an overall deterioration of Kmart's competitive position in the discount retail industry and a roller-coaster earnings history.

Specific problems that contributed to Kmart's bankruptcy were poor supply chain management, poor customer service, frequent stockouts of popular items, excessive inventory of slow-selling items, poor store housekeeping, unsound pricing strategies, and too many deteriorating stores built in the 1960s and 1970s. To make matters worse, as Kmart committed blunder after blunder in strategy execution during the 1980s and 1990s, Wal-Mart's distribution efficiency was becoming the global benchmark across all industries and the department store operator Dayton Hudson was perfecting its strategy for its Target stores that made designer-inspired apparel and housewares available at discount prices. Kmart's problems and competitive liabilities had long been obvious not only to industry insiders but also to the company's board of directors, employees, and customers, but the problems had been unresolved throughout a series of five executive regime changes dating to the late 1980s—three of which had occurred between June 2000 and January 2003.

Kmart's most recent CEO, Julian Day, who was installed in January 2003, began his tenure with the company in March 2002, when as chief operating officer he aided outgoing CEO James Adamson in the implementation of Kmart's restructuring plan. The reorganization plan, which focused on improving the company's weak competitive position and restoring financial solvency, included the closure of 600 stores and elimination of 52,000 employees, the restructuring of Kmart's supply chain, the elimination of slow-moving inventory, and the development of new private-label soft goods licensed from Disney and Joe Boxer that might compete with more expensive branded apparel. Upon his acceptance of the new position, Day stated the company would emerge from bankruptcy by April 30, 2003, and was poised to be a contender in the U.S. discount retail industry as it had achieved "a discernible shift in the company's internal culture, . . . repositioned itself as a high/low retailer of exclusive proprietary brands, . . . and restructured the store base and distribution network to protect and strengthen Kmart's competitive position in key markets."[1]

When the company closed out its fiscal 2002 books on January 31, 2003, the plan had yet to achieve any great successes with Kmart Corporation recording a net loss of $3.2 billion for the year and experiencing a sales decline of 18.5 percent during the fourth quarter of 2002 while rivals Wal-Mart and Target achieved sales growth of 12.3 percent and 9.0 percent, respectively, during the quarter. In addition, Kmart's sales per square foot (a key performance measure in retailing) of $212 during 2002 trailed Wal-Mart's sales per square foot of $404 and Target's sales per square foot of $263 by an unacceptable margin. Exhibit 1 presents a summary of Kmart's financial performance between 1992 and 2002. The company's common shares were delisted by the New York Stock Exchange in December 2002.

---

[1]Quoted in Kmart Corporation press release, January 19, 2003.

exhibit 1 **Selected Financial and Operating Statistics, Kmart Corporation, 1992–2002 (dollars in millions, except per share data)**

	2002	2001	2000	1999	1998	1997	1996	1995	1994	1993	1992
Summary of operations											
Total sales	$30,762	$36,151	$37,028	$35,925	$33,674	$32,183	$31,437	$31,713	$29,563	$28,039	$26,470
Cost of sales, buying and occupancy	26,258	29,853	29,732	28,161	26,357	25,167	24,390	24,675	22,331	20,732	19,087
Selling, general and administrative expenses	6,544	7,588	7,366	6,569	6,288	6,174	6,274	6,876	6,651	6,241	5,830
Restructuring, impairment and other charges	705	1,091	—	—	19	114	—	—	—	—	—
Interest expense, net	155	344	287	280	293	363	453	434	479	467	411
Continuing income (loss) before income taxes, preferred dividend, and reorganization items	(2,900)	(2,725)	(370)	959	755	407	330	(313)	102	(306)	1,142
Chapter 11 reorganization items, net	(362)	183	—	—	—	—	—	—	—	—	—
Net income (loss) from continuing operations	(3,262)	(2,612)	(268)	594	491	242	231	(230)	96	(179)	745
Discontinued operations, net	43	166	—	(230)	—	—	(451)	(341)	200	(795)	196
Net income (loss)	($ 3,219)	($ 2,446)	($ 268)	$ 364	$ 491	$ 242	($ 220)	($ 571)	$ 296	($ 974)	$ 941
Per share of common stock											
Basic:											
Continuing income (loss)	($6.44)	($5.29)	($0.53)	$ 1.21	$ 1.00	$ 0.50	$ 0.48	($0.51)	$ 0.19	($0.41)	$ 1.63
Discontinued operations	$0.08	$0.34	$ —	($0.47)	$ —	$ —	($0.93)	($0.74)	$ 0.44	($1.74)	$ 0.43
Net income (loss)	($6.36)	($4.95)	($0.53)	$0.74	$ 1.00	$ 0.50	($0.45)	($1.24)	$ 0.65	($2.13)	$ 2.06
Book value	($0.59)	$6.42	$12.09	$12.73	$11.84	$10.89	$10.51	$10.99	$13.15	$13.39	$16.64
Financial data											
Total assets	$11,238	$14,183	$14,815	$15,192	$14,238	$13,614	$14,286	$15,033	$16,085	$15,875	$16,769
Liabilities subject to compromise	7,969	8,093	—	—	—	—	—	—	—	—	—
Long-term debt	—	330	2,084	1,759	1,538	1,725	2,121	3,922	1,989	2,209	2,995
Long-term capital lease obligations	623	857	943	1,014	1,091	1,179	1,478	1,586	1,666	1,609	1,612
Capital expenditures	252	1,385	1,089	1,277	981	678	343	540	1,021	793	1,187
Depreciation and amortization	737	824	777	770	671	660	654	685	639	650	566
Basic weighted average shares outstanding (millions)	506	494	483	492	492	487	486	460	457	457	456
Number of stores	1,829	2,114	2,105	2,171	2,161	2,136	2,261	2,310	2,481	2,486	2,435
U.S. Kmart store sales per comparable selling square footage	$ 212	$ 235	$ 236	$ 233	$ 222	$ 211	$ 201	$ 195	$ 181	$ 160	$ 152
U.S. Kmart total selling square footage (millions)	139	154	153	155	154	151	156	160	166	182	181

Source: Kmart Corporation annual reports.

COMPANY HISTORY AND BACKGROUND

Kmart's roots in the discount retail industry can be traced to 1899 when Sebastian S. Kresge opened a five-and-dime store in downtown Detroit, Michigan. Kresge's 5- and 10-cent pricing strategy appealed to turn-of-the-century working families and allowed him to expand the S. S. Kresge Company chain to 85 stores with $10 million in sales by 1912. Kresge was known for his bold and innovative strategies, which included expansion into Canada in 1929, the development of a mall-based store concept in the first suburban shopping center in 1937, the use of newspaper advertising circulars in the 1940s, and the introduction of checkout lines in the 1950s. When Sebastian Kresge retired as CEO of the company in 1959, his successor, Harry Cunningham, began to investigate new store concepts that included a wider variety of household items and apparel than what was found in five-and-dimes. Cunningham opened the first Kmart full-line discount store in Garden City, Michigan, in 1962. The new store concept was an instant hit with consumers, and Cunningham responded by opening an average of about three new Kmart stores each month over the next four years. At the time of Sebastian Kresge's death in 1966, the S. S. Kresge Company operated 753 Kresge variety stores and 162 Kmart full-line discount stores with combined annual sales of over $1 billion.

Throughout the remainder of the 1960s and 1970s, Kresge management continued to increase the number of Kmart stores and replaced existing Kresge stores with Kmart stores. In 1976, the S. S. Kresge Company opened 271 stores and thus became the only retailer to ever open 17 million square feet of retailing space in one year. By year-end 1976, Kresge operated 1,206 Kmart stores and 441 Kresge five-and-dime stores. The company changed its name to Kmart Corporation in early 1977 since its Kmart stores had generated nearly 95 percent of the company's 1976 domestic revenues. In 1981 the company opened its 2,000th Kmart location.

During the 1980s and early 1990s Kmart management diversified the company into additional retailing businesses rather than rely only on new Kmart store openings to generate revenue growth. In 1984 Kmart acquired Builders Square (a chain of warehouse-style home centers) and Walden Book Company, which operated Waldenbooks stores in all 50 states. PayLess Drug Stores, Inc., and Bargain Harold's Discount Outlets (a Canadian retailer) were acquired in 1985. In 1988 three start-up businesses—American Fare hypermarts (giant stores carrying a huge variety of household, apparel, and supermarket merchandise), Pace Membership warehouse clubs, and Office Square warehouse-style office supply stores—were added to the corporation's portfolio of retail businesses.

The Sports Authority (a 10-store chain of sporting goods superstores) was acquired in 1990 to complement and strengthen Kmart's own Sports Giant stores started in 1989; the Sports Giant stores were subsequently renamed and integrated into the Sports Authority chain. Kmart also acquired a 22 percent interest in OfficeMax office supply superstores in 1990 and increased its interest in the business to over 90 percent in 1991. In 1992, Kmart management acquired Borders, Inc. (a chain of 22 book superstores in the midwestern and northeastern United States); purchased a chain of 13 discount stores in the Czech Republic and Slovakia; acquired Bizmart (a 105-store chain of office supply stores); and announced that it would open up to 100 Kmart stores in Mexico in a 50–50 joint venture with Mexican retailer El Puerto de Liverpool. The company also entered into a joint venture with Metro Limited to open discount stores in Singapore in 1994.

The following year, Kmart's board brought in new executive management after concluding that the company's diversification moves had done little to improve revenues and had actually damaged earnings by distracting management's attention from the company's core discount store business. With its sales growing at an annual rate of only 7.7 percent between 1980 and 1990, Kmart Corporation lost its position as the world's largest discount chain in 1990 to Wal-Mart. Kmart's position had weakened further by 1995, following annual sales rate growth of only 1.2 percent between 1990 and 1995. Wal-Mart's sales, by comparison, had grown at annual rates of 34.8 percent and 23.5 percent over the same respective periods. Exhibit 2 presents a financial comparison of Kmart Corporation, Target, and Wal-Mart Stores for selected years between 1980 and 2002.

exhibit 2 **Comparative Financial Performance of Target, Kmart, and Wal-Mart, 1980, 1990, 1995–2002**

Year	Sales* (in millions of dollars)			Operating Profit* (in millions of dollars)			Operating Profit as a Percent of Sales			Net Income* (in millions of dollars)			Net Income as a Percentage of Sales		
	Target	Kmart	Wal-Mart	Target	Kmart	Wal-Mart	Target	Kmart	Wal-Mart	Target†	Kmart	Wal-Mart	Target†	Kmart	Wal-Mart
1980	$ 1,531	$14,118	$ 1,643	$ 91	n.a	n.a	5.9%	n.a	n.a.	n.a.	$ 429	$ 56	n.a.	3.0%	3.4%
1990	8,175	29,775	32,602	466	1,151	2,212	5.7	3.9%	6.8%	n.a.	756	1,291	n.a.	2.5	4.0
1995	15,807	31,713	93,627	721	162	5,247	4.6	0.5	5.6	n.a.	(571)	2,740	n.a.	−1.8	2.9
1996	17,853	31,437	104,859	1,048	773	5,722	5.9	2.5	5.5	n.a.	(220)	3,056	n.a.	−0.7	2.9
1997	20,368	32,183	117,558	1,287	728	6,503	6.3	2.3	5.5	n.a.	242	3,526	n.a.	0.8	3.0
1998	23,014	33,674	137,634	1,578	1,010	8,120	6.9	3.0	5.9	n.a.	491	4,430	n.a.	1.5	3.2
1999	26,080	35,925	165,013	2,022	1,239	10,105	7.8	3.4	6.1	n.a.	364	5,377	n.a.	1.0	3.3
2000	29,278	37,028	191,329	2,223	(83)	11,490	7.6	−0.2	6.0	n.a.	(268)	6,295	n.a.	−0.7	3.3
2001	32,588	36,151	217,799	2,546	(2,381)	12,077	7.8	−6.6	5.5	n.a.	(2,446)	6,671	n.a.	−6.8	3.1
2002	36,917	30,762	246,525	3,088	(2,745)	13,644	8.4	−8.9	5.5	n.a.	(3,219)	8,039	n.a.	−10.5	3.3

n.a. = not available.

*The fiscal year end for all three retailers occurs on or near January 31 of each year. In Wal-Mart's case, data for the period January 31, 1979, through January 31, 1980, are reported in Wal-Mart's annual report as 1980 results. Because the company's fiscal year results really cover 11 months of the previous calendar year, this exhibit shows Wal-Mart's 1996 fiscal results in the 1995 row, its 1997 fiscal results in the 1996 row, and so on. This adjustment makes Wal-Mart's figures correspond more to the same time frame as the calendar year data for Kmart and Target, which both report results as if the 11-month period dictated the year rather than the closing month.

†Net income is not reported for Target Corporation's Target stores. The company's retail chains include Mervyn's, Marshall Field's, and Target. The company does not make net income figures available for its different chains.

Source: Company annual reports.

KMART UNDER JOSEPH ANTONINI, 1987–1995

Kmart's strategy of growth via diversification into a variety of retail businesses was initiated by Bernard Fauber, the company's chief executive officer from 1980 to 1987. However, most of Kmart's acquisitions were orchestrated by Joseph Antonini, who succeeded Fauber as Kmart's chairman, CEO, and president in 1987. Both Fauber and Antonini believed that entry into specialty retail stores would provide the company with greater growth opportunities than would be possible with only the Kmart chain of discount stores. The move to expand Kmart's scope of retail operations was intended to position the company in such fast-growing product categories as drugstore merchandise, office supplies, books, building materials, and sporting goods. Antonini also believed it made good strategic sense for Kmart to be involved in warehouse clubs and hypermarts because such stores were simply a larger-scale and slightly modified retailing format of the traditional discount stores that Kmart was already operating. Antonini saw the purchase of the discount stores in the Czech Republic and Slovakia and the joint ventures in Mexico and Singapore as valuable ways to begin positioning Kmart more aggressively in international retail markets.

Antonini's second strategic initiative to stimulate revenue growth focused on a $3.5 billion "renewal" program in 1991 to modernize, expand, or relocate Kmart's 2,435 discount stores. Most of these stores were built during the company's dramatic growth period in the 1960s and 1970s and had undergone little or no remodeling or renovation since they were constructed. Antonini wanted to increase the size of Kmart stores from a typical 80,000 square feet to about 100,000 square feet so that a wider variety of merchandise could be offered to consumers. The modernized Kmart stores provided brighter lighting, wider aisles, more modern and colorful interior signs, and more attractive merchandise displays. In 1992 he announced that the company would launch as many as 500 Super Kmart Centers that, like American Fare, would include both a discount store and a grocery store in a 160,000–180,000-square-foot building. By 1994 the sales of the renovated and new Super Kmart Centers were 23 percent above the sales of the chain's older, unrefurbished stores.

Antonini also initiated efforts to increase the volume of apparel sold in Kmart stores. He believed that increased sales of high-margin apparel would provide the stores with better operating margins and allow the company to offer lower everyday pricing on nonapparel items, like household items and health and beauty products. The company improved the styling and quality of its private-label apparel and began to include more natural fibers and less polyester in its garments. Kmart used endorsements from Jaclyn Smith and Kathy Ireland to create private-label branded lines of apparel to appeal to fashion-conscious and designer-conscious shoppers. Antonini also added national brands of apparel and footwear like Wrangler, Hanes, L.A. Gear, and Brittania to the company's merchandise mix.

Attempts to Cure Kmart's Longstanding Inventory Management Problems

Joseph Antonini also believed that the company needed to correct its long-running inability to maintain proper inventory levels in its stores. Kmart had been confronted with this problem for years, but the company had never really been able to resolve it. Most Kmart stores either frequently stocked out of popular items and/or were burdened with excess stocks of slow-moving items that eventually had to be marked down significantly. Antonini believed that Kmart's decentralized buying and merchandising process was at the root of the company's poor inventory management practices. Typically, Kmart buyers negotiated purchases with manufacturers, distribution people shipped products to stores, advertising specialists coordinated the company's advertising, and a separate marketing staff was responsible for promotions. Additionally, the company's store managers were authorized to purchase merchandise specific to their geographic locale and to place special ads in local area newspapers.

Antonini and Kmart's chief information officer, David Carlson, implemented a number of state-of-the-art information systems to correct the inventory management problems in the company's 2,000+ stores. In 1990 Kmart launched a GTE Spacenet satellite-based network that linked individual Kmart stores with the Kmart corporate office in Troy, Michigan, and some suppliers. The system allowed

Cases in Crafting and Executing Strategy

Kmart management to eliminate its traditional decentralized inventory management process and adopt a centralized process that was intended to reduce escalating inventory costs while meeting local preferences and price sensitivities. The GTE Spacenet communication system allowed management to implement its Central Merchandising Automated Replenishment (CMAR) system that was jointly developed by Kmart's information systems staff and Electronic Data Systems, a leading supplier of data processing services. The CMAR system allowed Kmart's corporate office to keep track of every sale in each store. All scanner data were transmitted via a local area network to a Unix server in the back room of each individual store. At the end of every day, the server transmitted sales data to the corporate headquarters via the GTE Spacenet satellite.

The next morning Kmart product category managers studied the sales data from each store; later in the day they placed orders with vendors to replenish each store's inventory. Vendors that were members of Kmart's Partners in Merchandise Flow program were allowed to monitor the scanner data themselves and ship to Kmart distribution centers when they determined it was necessary to maintain Kmart's desired inventory levels. The distribution centers used a cross-docking system that helped keep inventory levels at the distribution center to a minimum. A senior executive at Kmart explained how centralized category management allowed the company to reduce expenses and keep products that consumers wanted on the shelves:

> Category management has been very successful for us. It's shifted our entire focus to the front door. Years ago we were busy with shipments—looking at what was coming in the back door from our suppliers. Today we have a front-door focus in that we are focusing on the consumer and what the register tape tells us she's taking out the front door. We've seen dramatic improvements in turnover. In fact, we used to call our distribution centers "warehouses" because products would come in and sometimes just sit there. Now they are truly distribution centers with goods flowing in and right out, often within a day or two.[2]

Kmart identified about 1,500 hard-line categories and several hundred soft-line categories and selected managers to make all buying and merchandising decisions—including pricing, assortments, and promotions—for their assigned category of products. Each category manager used the scanner data available from CMAR and demographic profiles and consumer purchasing behavior data provided by third parties such as Nielsen Marketing Research to make their purchasing decisions. Each category manager was required to develop a sales plan, a gross margin plan, and a turnover plan that was presented to the senior marketing executives at the beginning of the financial year.

Kmart spent about $160 million annually to create and implement information systems like CMAR technology and other state-of-the art computer systems during Antonini's tenure as Kmart's top executive. The company implemented electronic data interchange (EDI) systems with some suppliers that attempted to reduce the company's dependence on paper-based transaction processing. The company also developed the ShopperTrack system, which used backroom computers and ceiling-mounted sensors to monitor how many customers were in each department throughout the day. The system used the tracking data to project store and department customer counts at 15-minute intervals. Store managers were instructed to use this information to schedule employee staffing at the store's checkout stations and merchandise departments.

Difficulties in Implementing and Executing Antonini's Strategy

At the outset, both Wall Street and Kmart investors reacted favorably to Antonini's moves to diversify the corporation into a number of attractive discount retail segments, to renovate and enlarge Kmart stores, to improve merchandise selection, quality and availability, and to improve information systems. The consensus was that these moves would allow the company to grow faster and to compete more effectively against its major rivals. However, as efforts to implement the strategy continued to unfold, events made it increasingly clear that Kmart was being outmaneuvered by its rivals; Wal-Mart, in particular, was leaving Kmart far behind (see Exhibit 2). Kmart's sales per store continued to run near $180 per square foot in 1994, despite the merchandising efforts initiated by Antonini and other Kmart execu-

[2]Quoted in "Kmart's Category Approach," *Discount Merchandiser*, May 1994, p. 118.

tives. Also, Kmart's pricing continued to average 10 to 15 percent above its chief competitors, as Kmart sought to boost its subpar store margins and make up for the higher selling, general, and administrative expenses brought on by relatively low sales volumes per square foot of selling space.

Moreover, while Fauber and Antonini built Kmart's retailing portfolio far beyond its core discount store base, Kmart management never was able to transform any of its acquisitions into enterprises able to compete successfully against key segment rivals in terms of sales, net income, or efficient inventory management. In almost every retailing business that Kmart diversified into, it trailed the industry leader by a considerable distance. Sales volumes at Builders Square stores were only one-third of those at industry leader Home Depot. The company's Pace warehouse clubs never were able to match the selection and pricing of Sam's Clubs and, in the end, many of Pace's store locations were eventually sold to Wal-Mart.

Knowledgeable retail analysts attributed the failure of Kmart's American Fare stores in part to poor store design and poor store management. PayLess Drugs, Waldenbooks, and OfficeMax were all weak-performing businesses under Kmart's management, posting either operating losses or minimal operating profits.

Joseph Antonini attributed some of Kmart's difficulties in the apparel segment of its core retail discount business to rapidly shifting market conditions rather than weak strategy on Kmart's part. For example, although the Kathy Ireland and Jaclyn Smith apparel lines were successfully positioned as national brands in the minds of shoppers, as the company had planned, the initial success proved short-lived. By 1994, sales of the two apparel lines were sagging because of changing buyer preferences. Antonini, whose background and experience had been largely in apparel and soft lines, explained the reasons for the downturn: "Substantial shifts are taking place. For example, clothes just don't mean as much as they did five years ago, focus groups tell us. Designer names are not driving shoppers to stores, but in many ways have the opposite effect. Today, Mom is usually the last family member to get a new outfit. She is sacrificing for her family."[3] Antonini, in a 1994 *Forbes* in-

terview, said that the U.S. economy played a role in undermining some of Kmart's merchandising efforts: "The economy is hurting, disposable income is down, and people are spending money only on essential products. The fringe items—and I consider apparel to be a fringe item—aren't selling anywhere across the country like they used to."[4]

Antonini's expectation that sales of higher-margin apparel items would allow the company to offer lower prices on thousands of other items sold in Kmart stores didn't pan out either. As it turned out, Kmart was at a cost disadvantage relative to Wal-Mart and was not able to meet Wal-Mart's pricing on many items. In addition, Wal-Mart management was intent on being the low-price leader and chose not to allow competitors to price popular items below what Wal-Mart charged. A Wal-Mart executive gave the following explanation of the importance of the company's five-point operating cost advantage in setting its pricing strategy: "It's very simple. We're not going to be undersold. What that means is, that in an all-out price war, [our competitors] will go broke 5% before we will."[5]

When asked about Wal-Mart's meteoric climb to the top of the full-line discount industry, Antonini stated that Wal-Mart managers, whom he at times referred to as "snake oil salesmen,"[6] came across as successful largely because Wal-Mart was new to the industry and consumers were inclined to try out a new store. In 1994 he commented, "They have enjoyed the advantage of being the new show in town in many of our markets."[7] Antonini suggested that Wal-Mart's newcomer advantage was very similar to the new retail shopping excitement that Kmart was able to create during its period of rapid growth in the 1960s and 1970s.

Kmart's Image with Consumers   Surveys of U.S. discount store shoppers commissioned by *Chain Store Age Executive* found three consistent negative images that customers attributed to Kmart: out-of-stock merchandise, poor housekeeping, and indifferent service. Additionally, the consumers sur-

---

[3]Quoted in "Antonini: On Changes in the Marketplace," *Discount Merchandiser,* December 1994, p. 12.

[4]Quoted in "The Best-Laid Plans . . . ," *Forbes,* January 3, 1994, p. 44.

[5]Quoted in "The High Cost of Second Best," *Fortune,* July 26, 1993, p. 99.

[6]Quoted in ibid.

[7]Quoted in "Kmart's Agenda for Recovery." *Discount Merchandiser,* July 1994, p. 14.

veyed found Wal-Mart's locations more convenient and believed that Wal-Mart offered better pricing and product selection than Kmart. Antonini's store renovation and remodeling strategy was directed at eliminating Wal-Mart's pricing and selection advantage. However, in 1995—the company's fourth year into its renovation, relocation, and remodeling strategy—sales per square foot at Kmart remained flat at around $195, resulting in selling, general, and administrative expense ratios that were far above Wal-Mart's because the typical Wal-Mart store had sales per square foot of over $370. The higher expense ratios kept Kmart's bottom-line performance from materially improving.

Kmart's Store Renovation and Renewal Program

Wall Street analysts were very critical of Kmart's efforts to upgrade its stores. Many investors were displeased with Kmart management's use of the proceeds of a $1 billion equity issue in 1991. At the time the new shares of stock were sold, management had indicated that the capital was to be used to renovate and refurbish older Kmart stores and build new Super Kmart Centers. As it turned out, a big portion of the money spent in its "renewal" program went into acquiring new specialty retail stores rather than renovating older Kmart stores. Wall Street analysts made the following comments about Kmart's store renewal efforts.

> They aren't doing full renovations, just repainting or putting in new linoleum instead of gutting the stores entirely and redesigning them. And that has hurt them. It's back to the old Kmart culture where it's better to spend money on new stores and expand the chain.
>
> Even Betty Crocker got a new hairdo. I just drove by a Kmart store sign and it looked like a Howard Johnson should be next to it, circa 1957. They have a long way to go before getting rid of the popcorn smell when you walk in the door.[8]

Some shareholders and industry analysts suggested that the lack of management commitment to the store renewal program was a result of the company's past strategies. Kmart had achieved great success during the 1960s and 1970s as a result of its rapid addition of stores. The company's stock jumped from $0.50 per share when the first Kmart store was opened in 1962 to $32 in 1972. Some investors believed that the era of store growth at Kmart helped mold a managerial mind-set that favored putting more emphasis on store expansion than on proper management of existing stores and on merchandising efforts to boost annual sales at each existing store.

Continuing Inventory Problems

Even though Kmart had invested far more than its industry rivals on developing systems and procedures to correct its inventory-related problems, the problems still existed. Kmart stores still were faced with frequent stockouts of merchandise, and some of Kmart's vendors had criticized Kmart's buying procedures, stating that the corporate office frequently placed orders for merchandise and then later canceled the orders. A Kmart executive explained the difficulties of implementing its centralized merchandising strategy:

> Bringing this decision-making power to the desktop is a hurdle. Category management evolved with computer systems, but it's still a challenge to get these high-powered PCs on everyone's desktops and to have them linked together via local area networks. Furthermore, some buyers may not be computer literate or used to dealing with scanner and syndicated data. So it can be an educational process as well as a hardware installation process. Most of our buyers started out as store managers, so to them it's attractive to think, "Oh, I'll call my old store to see how this product is doing." We have to get them additionally looking at and relying on this internal computer data, syndicated third party data, and quantitative information. It also takes a certain kind of person, someone who knows merchandising, who knows computer processing, who knows about financing, who knows a little about advertising—someone who knows enough about everything, as opposed to being a specialist in just one area. The information and the software available are just tools. You still need an experienced person who can tie it all together.[9]

In a January 28, 2002, interview published in *Crain's Detroit Business,* David Carlson, Kmart's chief information officer between 1984 and 1995, provided further understanding of why Antonini's efforts to cure Kmart's inventory management problems failed:

> One of the core problems was that there was just way too much merchandise, and the stores didn't have adequate volume to justify the assortment. I produced reports that showed our inventory turns in the fishing

[8]Quoted in "Attention Bottom Fishers," *Financial World,* March 28, 1995, p. 31.

[9]Ibid., pp. 119–20.

rod category were abysmal. But the merchants were never able to move in the right direction of editing what was carried in the stores to ensure higher-moving items were in stock. The number of items just kept growing. Too often customers would go to Kmart and stores would be out of stock, or shelves would be full of the wrong products. If headquarters said you had to carry 13 toasters, you carried 13 toasters. Never mind the fact that the bottom-five were each selling one or less a year.

Customer Service Problems Some Kmart stores were plagued with unresponsive customer service. A 1994 *Forbes* article cited customer complaints of indifferent Kmart employees who, when asked for a specific item in the store, would wave their hand in a general direction. One disgruntled shopper complained, "At the superstores in Farmington Hills or Southfield, the help is surly and uncooperative and you can never find the products that you need and have to have."[10]

FLOYD HALL'S TURNAROUND EFFORTS, 1995–2000

Kmart's board of directors appointed Floyd Hall as the company's new chairman, chief executive officer, and president in June 1995. Hall, who was recruited from Grand Union Supermarkets, had engineered Target's growth during the 1980s and had more recently gotten Grand Union back on track. Floyd Hall accepted the position with the intention of turning around Kmart within three years and then moving on to other ventures. He said, "I'm just trying to build a team . . . get a good succession plan and new policies and practices in place."[11] Hall and the board quickly assembled a new top-level management team—with 12 new vice presidents in marketing, product development, strategic planning, finance, administration, merchandising, information systems, and other key areas. The 12 new vice presidents had an average of 27 years of retail experience. When Hall asked his new management team to review and evaluate

Kmart's competitive position, he found that Kmart trailed Wal-Mart by a considerable distance on every key performance indicator. Wal-Mart's customers averaged 32 store visits per year, while Kmart's customers averaged 15 visits per year. Kmart's sales per square foot in 1994 were $185, compared to Wal-Mart's $379 and Target's $282. Only 19 percent of Kmart shoppers considered themselves loyal to the chain, while 46 percent of Wal-Mart shoppers considered themselves loyal Wal-Mart shoppers. Hall stated, "The most devastating news I saw in all the research was that 49% of Wal-Mart's shoppers drive past a Kmart to get to Wal-Mart."[12]

Hall believed that Kmart must be fixed "department by department" and that management must not try to "put a Band-Aid on our problems. This requires surgery."[13] Hall's first priority was to close nearly 400 Kmart stores and divest all noncore businesses from the company's portfolio between 1995 and 1997. Hall also initiated over $900 million in cost reductions during 1995 and 1996 by consolidating the company's Canadian operations with its U.S. operations, clearing out $700 million in old inventory, and using the company's volume buying power to reduce the cost of benefits for its 300,000 employees.

Some of the portfolio restructuring actually had taken place in the months just before Antonini's departure. Kmart sold PayLess Drug Stores in 1993 and spun off OfficeMax and Sports Authority as independent, stand-alone companies in late 1994. The initial public offerings of stock in OfficeMax and in Sports Authority were completed in December 1994, with Kmart retaining a 25 percent equity ownership in OfficeMax and a 30 percent equity ownership in Sports Authority. In addition, the company's 21.5 percent interest in Cole Myer, an Australian retailer, was sold in 1994.

In 1995 and 1996, Hall and Kmart's new management team sold the company's Czech and Slovak stores for $115 million; completed public offerings of stock to divest the company's remaining interests in OfficeMax and Sports Authority (netting the company an after-tax gain of $155 million); sold the assets of the Kmart auto centers to Penske for $84 million; completed a public stock offering of Borders Bookstores group (which resulted in an after-tax loss

---

[10]Quoted in "The Antonini Transcript," *Discount Store News,* April 17, 1995, p. 12.

[11]Quoted in "Kmart Is Down for the Count," *Fortune,* January 15, 1996, p. 103.

[12]Ibid., p. 102.

[13]Quoted in "Kmart: Who's in Charge Here?" *Business Week,* December 4, 1995, p. 107.

Cases in Crafting and Executing Strategy

of $185 million); and sold the Rite Aid drugstore chain for $257 million. The company also discontinued its joint ventures in Singapore and Mexico in 1996 and divested its 162-store Builders Square home improvement chain for a mere $10 million in 1997.

A Near Bankruptcy as Floyd Hall Begins a Turnaround

Floyd Hall and the other members of Kmart's top management team were confronted with a potentially devastating financial crisis during the last half of 1995 that was a result of Kmart's poor cash flow and the financial decisions made by previous Kmart management. As was common with most retailers, Kmart management had a long-standing preference of financing new store construction off the company's balance sheet. Groups of newly constructed stores were sold to pension funds, insurance companies, and other such organizations, who then leased the stores back to Kmart on long-term lease agreements. This was a hidden financial obligation, since long-term lease payment obligations were not required, under accounting rules then prevailing, to be shown as a long-term liability on Kmart's balance sheet; the company had only to report current-year lease payments as an operating expense on its annual income statement.

In the early 1990s, Kmart's financial officers had agreed to special "put provisions" in a number of Kmart's store leasing agreements in exchange for better lease terms from the financing organizations. The put provisions stipulated that if Kmart's bond rating was downgraded to junk-bond status, then Kmart would immediately be obligated to buy back the leased stores from the lease owner. Kmart's contingent liability under the put provisions amounted to about $600 million. In July 1995—just one month after Hall became Kmart's CEO—Kmart was placed on credit watch by various credit rating agencies as an indication that they were considering downgrading Kmart's bond rating. The credit watch placement prevented Kmart from borrowing on 30–60-day commercial paper over the October–November period to pay suppliers for shipping the volume of goods needed to build its Christmas inventory. In order to have ample inventories for the Christmas season, Kmart was forced to activate a $2 billion backup revolving line of credit, adding interest costs and fur-

ther straining Kmart's already precariously thin profit margins and cash flows. To make matters worse, the covenants of Kmart's $2 billion revolving line of credit stated that if the leaseholders exercised their put options, any borrowings under the line of credit would immediately become due and payable. Kmart's accounts payable to its vendors already exceeded $3.5 billion for its purchases for Christmas inventory. The potential for Kmart to be faced with obligations to its vendors and creditors totaling $6 billion, compounded by swirling rumors, drove the company's stock price down to $5¾ per share—50 percent of its book value.

As Wall Street rumors predicted, Kmart's long-term debt was downgraded to junk bond status in January 1996. Hall and Kmart financial officers had already visited with the leaseholders in late December of 1995 and negotiated an agreement for them not to immediately exercise the put options and demand payment. With temporary agreements in place, Hall and Kmart financial executives used the company's available cash to pay vendors in a manner sufficiently timely to ensure continued shipments of merchandise. As Kmart paid its suppliers, management continued talks with the 70 banks that funded Kmart's line of credit. Kmart's creditors agreed to allow the company to suspend principal payments on its debt for 18 months while Hall and Kmart's financial officers negotiated a new financing proposal with a consortium of banks led by Chemical Bank. Chemical Bank agreed to put a consortium of lenders together to provide Kmart with $3.7 billion to refinance its obligations under the revolving line of credit and the leased-store debt associated with put options—contingent on the company's ability to raise $750 million through an equity issue. The close call with bankruptcy came to an end in June 1996, when Kmart issued $1 billion in convertible preferred shares and signed a new $3.7 billion financing agreement with Chemical Bank.

Attracting Customers to Kmart

Floyd Hall and his new management team developed a combination of new strategies and improved implementation techniques to better compete with low-cost leader Wal-Mart and rapidly growing Target.

A New Merchandising and Distribution Strategy Kmart had been confronted with serious inventory management problems as far back as the early 1980s, and the new management team saw inventory management as the single biggest problem that had to be corrected. A big part of the solution, they believed, lay in eliminating many slow-selling items and unpopular brands and reducing the number of vendors. Under Antonini's centralized merchandising strategy, Kmart carried one or two national brands, an assortment of second- and third-tier brands, and some private-label brands. The new top management team found that many of the second- and third-tier brands cluttered store shelves and frequently did not sell without deep markdowns. Kmart's new merchandising executives eliminated some second-tier brands and most third-tier brands and began to develop its private-label brands to fill the gaps in its merchandise mix left by the removal of the lesser-known brands.

Kmart also completely redesigned the Martha Stewart Everyday bed and bath collection and relaunched the brand in 1997. The Martha Stewart private-label line of linens, towels, and other bed and bath products had been created during the Antonini era; however, under Antonini, the brand had not done particularly well because of inadequate promotion and a limited product line. The reintroduced Martha Stewart bed and bath collection included a wider variety of products—linens, bath towels, beach towels, draperies, pillows, blankets, lawn and garden products, baby products, and paint.

Company management took a series of steps to improve its working relationships with suppliers, to correct stockouts, and to reduce its distribution costs. Kmart began a Collaborative Forecasting and Replenishment program with vendors that shared Kmart's customer and product information with its suppliers over the Internet. The company also upgraded its IBM Inventory Forecasting and Replenishment Modules system to shorten its replenishment cycle by a full day. Kmart's chief information officer, Donald Norman, said that the company had reduced the amount of time to replenish some merchandise from 40 hours to 18 hours.

Improving Kmart's Store Productivity and Relative Cost Position

Despite the efforts of Kmart executives, at year-end 1996 Kmart's store productivity still trailed Wal-Mart's by a wide margin. Kmart had sales of $201 per square foot of retail space, compared to sales of $379 per square foot for Wal-Mart. While Kmart's new superstores achieved higher sales volumes than the company's older stores, they did not attract customers in sufficient volume to come close to matching sales per square foot at Wal-Mart. Kmart executives saw increased store traffic as the key to improving store productivity and lowering prices.

Hall developed and rolled out a redesign of existing stores that was intended to attract more customers to Kmart stores. The company tested its high-frequency Pantry concept during 1995 in selected stores and announced in 1997 that it would expand the Pantry concept to as many as 1,800 stores during the next three years. The Pantry concept was a redesign of existing stores that took items typically found in a convenience store and placed them in the front of Kmart stores. Merchandise that was already sold in Kmart stores—diapers, paper towels, bread, milk, dog food, beverages, snack foods, and so on—was gathered and placed in one department, then supplemented by additional dry grocery items. Kmart rearranged remaining store merchandise so that frequently purchased items like small appliances and soft lines (underwear, T-shirts, socks, and fleece products) were placed near the Pantry area. The cost to convert an existing Kmart store to the new Pantry concept was $600,000 versus $10 million for a new 100,000-square-foot Kmart store or $20 million for a new 180,000-square-foot Super Kmart Center.

Changes in Structure, Communications, Culture, and Rewards

Concerned that the attitudes and performance of Kmart store managers and associates were adversely impacting shopper visits and loyalty, Hall brought all Kmart store managers together in 1996 for the company's first-ever store managers' meeting. At the meeting, the executive team explained the company's mission and strategy and what individual store managers' roles were in implementing the strategy. The executive team also made it clear that they intended to end Kmart's historically insular, turf-wary organizational culture and adopt a more team-oriented atmosphere at both corporate headquarters and in the stores. The company also announced its new management development program to help the company develop future store-level and corporate-level managers from within its ranks.

Kmart corporate management also unveiled a new organizational structure during the conference that reduced the number of stores that each district manager was responsible for from 28 to 14. This reduction was intended to allow district managers to have the time necessary to visit every store in their districts more frequently and to provide better coaching to store managers. Within the stores, associates no longer had at-large responsibility but instead were assigned to departments. Kmart executives believed that giving associates defined areas of responsibility would create a feeling of ownership within their department and encourage employees to offer better service.

A new incentive compensation plan for store managers was developed to replace Kmart's old managerial pay plan. Previously, Kmart managers were paid a salary plus a bonus based on store sales. Under the new compensation plan, store managers were eligible for both bonuses and stock options. The new bonus plan tied 50 percent of a store manager's bonus to meeting the store's budget objectives for the year and 50 percent to the store's customer satisfaction rating. The customer satisfaction rating was determined by the results of independent mystery shoppers who visited each store 28 times per year.

Hall's Success in Getting Kmart on Track

By 1999, Floyd Hall's turnaround efforts were showing signs of success: More than 1,600 Kmart stores had been remodeled with wider aisles, brighter lighting, and lower shelving; the Martha Stewart line accounted for $1 billion per year in sales; and operating expenses had fallen by more than $500 million. Hall was also able to put together a string of three consecutive profitable years. The company's sales per square foot of $233 at year-end 1999 approached Target's sales per square foot of $253, though it still trailed Wal-Mart's sales per square foot of $360. However, many consumers still found Kmart's customer service unacceptable; the company's distribution system still had many bottlenecks; shelves still lacked best-selling items; stores had too much inventory of items consumers rarely needed; and, most important, the company found itself unattractively positioned between Wal-Mart's low prices and Target's more upscale merchandising. Even though Floyd Hall had expected to serve as Kmart's CEO for only three years, he remained CEO until May 2000, when he was succeeded by former CVS executive Charles Conaway.

CHARLES CONAWAY AND KMART'S BANKRUPTCY, JUNE 2000–MARCH 2002

Charles Conaway was selected as Hall's replacement in June 2000 by Kmart's board of directors, based largely on the 39-year-old Conaway's performance while president and chief operating officer of the rapidly growing drugstore chain CVS Corporation. Kmart board member James Adamson commented, "Floyd got us to Point B, now Chuck has got to get us beyond."[14] Some analysts questioned the hiring of Conaway, noting that even though he was known as an operations whiz at CVS, he had not managed a chain as large as the 2,100-store Kmart and had no experience with soft goods such as apparel. Conaway moved decisively after he was installed as Kmart's new CEO. His first official action was to replace Hall's top management team with a group of 40-ish retail veterans who became known at Kmart headquarters as "the frat boys."[15] Conaway also replaced many higher-level managers outside the corporate office with 500 outsiders from companies such as Wal-Mart, Coca-Cola, and Sears. Conaway expanded the number of district managers from 150 to 275—reducing the number of stores in each territory from 14 to 8. Conaway also expanded the number of geographic regions from six to eight and added 25 regional managers—a new level of management between district managers and senior regional vice presidents. Conaway believed that the smaller districts and additional management oversight would improve Kmart's poor customer service.

Conaway's Strategy and Execution Approaches to Revitalize Kmart

Conaway and members of Conaway's new management team crafted a strategy that addressed the discount chain's poor inventory management, muddled marketing strategy, and pricing disadvantage relative

[14]Quoted in "A Kmart Special: Better Service," *Business Week,* September 4, 2000, p. 80.

[15]"Kmart's Last Chance," *Business Week,* March 11, 2002, online edition.

to Wal-Mart. Conaway's team tackled the company's poor image by closing 78 of the company's poorest-performing and most run-down stores, revising the company's advertising campaign to cut more than $200 million in annual advertising expenditures and eliminate its newspaper circulars used since the 1940s, improving the company's e-commerce capabilities, and improving its merchandise quality.

Conaway adopted the marketing slogan "Kmart: The authority for moms, home, and kids" and placed greater emphasis on private-label brands such as Kathy Ireland and Jaclyn Smith women's wear, Martha Stewart Everyday home collection, Sesame Street kids' wear, and Route 66 jeans in attempt to differentiate Kmart from Wal-Mart and Target. Conaway also entered into a new seven-year contract with Martha Stewart Living that called for the company to launch a new line of Martha Stewart products every six months. The original line and its extensions proved successful, with Martha Stewart products accounting for $1.5 billion in sales by year-end 2002. Analysts were less satisfied with the company tag line; many believed it failed to convey meaning to consumers and believed that the Kathy Ireland, Jaclyn Smith, Sesame Street, and Route 66 private-label brands did not come close to either Kmart's own Martha Stewart line or Target's exclusive brands such as Mossimo in terms of quality or style.

Conaway also wanted Kmart customers to be able to purchase standard and differentiated products sold in Kmart stores over the Internet. Under Conaway the company expanded its e-commerce capabilities beyond its Kmart.com Web site through the development of a BlueLight.com venture with Softbank. Kmart committed $55 million to the e-commerce venture, which initially began as a free Internet service for Kmart customers and evolved into a discount e-tailing site where consumers could purchase any of 100,000 items typically found in Kmart stores. Kmart eventually paid its venture partner $84 million in cash and stock to gain control of BlueLight.com.

Kmart's boldest strategies under Conaway involved a $1.7 billion investment in new information technology systems to improve Kmart's supply chain management and a Blue Light Always plan to beat Wal-Mart on price on 38,000 stock-keeping units (SKUs). Kmart's Play to Win information technology initiative was designed to resolve Kmart's supply chain problems. When Conaway became the company's CEO, Kmart's in-stock rating stood just below 90 percent, while more than 99 percent of Wal-Mart's products were always in stock. Conaway also learned that Kmart had 15,000 trailers of unsold merchandise sitting outside stores because there was no space available for the merchandise inside. In addition, Kmart's 4.39 inventory turns per year were just over one-half of Wal-Mart's 7.29 turns. The president of a retail industry consulting firm, commenting on Kmart's poor inventory management and its 15,000 trailers of overflow merchandise, said, "Trucks and trailers are supposed to move product. They are not supposed to be a warehouse on wheels."[16]

The Play to Win program was designed to improve supply chain management by keeping track of what was selling in stores, store inventory levels, warehouse inventory levels, and shipments en route to stores. Kmart contracted with i2 Technologies, a highly regarded systems designer, but had great difficulty in implementing the supply chain technology program since the software had integration problems with Kmart's existing computing systems and because of the vast amount of data to process. For example, Kmart's 2,100 stores might stock more than 70,000 items each—creating 140 million possible data points to track. Analysts claimed that Conaway's $1.7 billion plan failed, in part, because it attempted to do too much too soon, but they did commend him for eliminating $700 million in inventory, including Kmart's 15,000 trailers of overflow merchandise, during his brief stay with the company. A former Kmart executive suggested that Kmart's inventory management program also failed because, even under Conaway, point-of-sale data available through the system were ignored by Kmart's buying department, with purchasing decisions based on which vendors were willing to pay the largest slotting fees rather than what products Kmart shoppers wanted. Conaway also invested $200 million for new Internet-enabled IBM SurePOS point-of-sales systems in all 2,100 stores to speed customer checkout and built two new distribution centers to improve productivity and the flow of goods to over one-half of Kmart's stores. The company incurred a $195 restructuring charge related to the relocation of its distribution centers.

[16]Quoted in "Kmart Misses Mark Amid Tech Field," *Investor's Business Daily,* April 25, 2002, p. A10.

Kmart's Blue Light Always plan was developed by Conaway's most notable and influential hire, Mark Schwartz—his choice for chief operating officer. Schwarz was a former Wal-Mart executive who had been second in command of Wal-Mart's Supercenters operations at one time but who also had other responsibilities at Wal-Mart, including managing an unrelated real estate investment firm that filed for bankruptcy in 1996 and was dissolved under his leadership. Schwartz left Wal-Mart in 1998, not long after the failure of the real estate firm, to become head of Hechinger Company, a home improvement chain that was in need of a turnaround. Under Schwartz, Hechinger built up excessive inventory, ran out of cash, and filed for bankruptcy within weeks of Schwartz's departure for Big V Supermarkets, which was also looking for a turnaround. Big V also filed for bankruptcy just weeks after Schwartz left to become Kmart's chief operating officer.

Many industry analysts believed that Schwartz's Blue Light Always pricing strategy, which attempted to beat Wal-Mart on price every day on 38,000 SKUs (and ultimately underprice Wal-Mart on 50,000 items), was the biggest reason for Kmart's slide into bankruptcy as compared to any of the other management gaffes. Analysts noted that no matter how much Kmart was willing to cut price, Wal-Mart, which was light-years ahead of Kmart in terms of efficiency, could cut more. Some observed that Kmart declaring a price war against Wal-Mart was comparable to Luxembourg declaring war against the United States. Similarly, they were unimpressed with the idea of revising the Blue Light Special concept. A business professor with Northwestern University's Kellogg School of Management commented, "The underlying principle behind a Blue Light Special was 'you are going to be surprised in a positive way when you walk in the store.' You don't know what you'll see, but you will see something. It may have worked in 1965, but in 1995 or 2000 consumers are too busy, so they don't go to the store to be surprised."[17]

Kmart's Slide into Bankruptcy

Kmart's Blue Light Always pricing strategy and Schwartz's decision to build $8.3 billion worth of in-ventory for the Christmas shopping season led to the company's January 22, 2002, bankruptcy after Kmart had a disastrous holiday season in which sales declined by 1 percent during the month of December 2001, while Wal-Mart's sales increased by 8 percent and Target's sales increased by 0.6 percent. With sales failing to materialize, many of Kmart's suppliers went unpaid after the holiday season concluded. Kmart's food supplier, Fleming Companies, stopped its shipments of food items to Kmart stores the day before Kmart's bankruptcy after it failed to receive its weekly payment from Kmart for approximately $78 million worth of food. Although Kmart management attempted to avert bankruptcy by putting together an emergency financial package to pay its creditors and suppliers, lenders balked and a last-minute bailout in early 2002 failed to materialize.

Kmart Corporation's bankruptcy filing enabled it to restructure payments on $4.7 billion in debt and keep shipments of inventory coming from suppliers since bankruptcy courts give vendors who continue to ship goods first priority in repayment status. On the day of the bankruptcy filing, Charles Conaway commented, "After considering a wide range of alternatives, it became clear that this course of action was the only way to truly resolve the company's most challenging problems."[18] In the quarter prior to Kmart's bankruptcy filing, the company's sales per square foot reached $243—an improvement, but well below Wal-Mart's sales per square foot of $410. In addition, its selling, general, and administrative (SG&A) expenses as a percentage of sales were 22.7 percent, compared to Wal-Mart's SG&A-to-sales ratio of 17.3 percent, and its prices averaged 3.8 percent higher than Wal-Mart's pricing on comparable products despite its efforts to underprice Wal-Mart with its Blue Light Always campaign. Exhibit 3 presents Kmart's statements of operations for fiscal 1999 through fiscal 2002. Its balance sheets and cash flow statements are presented in Exhibits 4 and 5, respectively. Exhibit 6 presents a listing of Kmart's contractual obligations and other commercial commitments at fiscal year-end 2001.

---

[17]Quoted in "Kmart Struggles to Escape Oblivion," *The Business*, January 27, 2002, p. 17.

[18]Quoted in "Kmart Lays Out Plans to Trim Its Size, Boost Efficiency, in Bankruptcy Filing," *The Wall Street Journal Online*, January 22, 2002.

exhibit 3 **Consolidated Statement of Operations for Kmart Corporation, Fiscal 2000–2003 (dollars in millions, except per share data)**

	Fiscal Year Ended January			
	2003	**2002**	**2001**	**2000**
Sales	$30,762	$36,151	$37,028	$35,925
Cost of sales, buying, and occupancy	26,258	29,853	29,732	28,161
Gross margin	4,504	6,298	7,296	7,764
Selling, general and administrative expenses	6,544	7,588	7,366	6,569
Equity (loss) income in unconsolidated subsidiaries	34	—	(13)	44
Restructuring, impairment and other charges	739	1,091	—	—
Continuing (loss) income before interest, reorganization items, income taxes and dividends on convertible preferred securities of subsidiary trust	(2,745)	(2,381)	(83)	1,239
Interest expense, net (contractual interest for fiscal year 2001 was $352)	155	344	287	280
Reorganization items, net	386	(183)	—	—
(Benefit from) provision for income taxes	(24)	—	(148)	315
Dividends on convertible preferred securities of subsidiary trust, net of income taxes of $0, $25 and $27, respectively (contractual dividend for fiscal year 2001 was $72, net of tax)	—	70	46	50
Net (loss) income from continuing operations	(3,262)	(2,612)	(2)	594
Discontinued operations, net of income taxes	43	166	—	(230)
Net (loss) income	($3,219)	($2,446)	($ 268)	$ 364
Basic earnings (loss) per common share				
Net (loss) income from continuing operations	($6.44)	($5.29)	($0.53)	$1.21
Discontinued operations	$0.08	$0.34	—	($0.47)
Net (loss) income	($6.36)	($4.95)	($0.53)	$0.74
Diluted (loss) earnings per common share				
Net (loss) income from continuing operations	($6.44)	($5.29)	($0.53)	$1.15
Discontinued operations	$0.08	$0.34	—	($0.41)
Net (loss) income	($6.36)	($4.95)	($0.53)	$0.74
Basic weighted average shares (millions)	506.4	494.1	482.8	491.7
Diluted weighted average share (millions)	506.4	494.1	482.8	561.7

Source: 2001 Kmart Corporation revised 10K report and 2002 Kmart Corporation 10K report.

Cases in Crafting and Executing Strategy

exhibit 4 **Kmart's Consolidated Balance Sheets, Fiscal Years 2001–2003 (dollars in millions)**

	As of January 29, 2003, January 30, 2002, and January 31, 2001		
	2003	2002	2001
Assets			
Current assets			
Cash and cash equivalents	$ 613	$ 1,245	$ 401
Merchandise inventories	4,825	5,796	6,350
Other current assets	664	800	925
Total current assets	6,102	7,841	7,676
Property and equipment, net	4,892	6,093	6,522
Other assets and deferred charges	244	249	617
Total assets	$11,238	$14,183	$14,815
Liabilities and shareholders' equity			
Current liabilities			
Long-term debt due within one year	$ —	$ —	$ 68
Accounts payable	1,248	89	2,190
Accrued payroll and other liabilities	710	420	1,691
Taxes other than income taxes	162	143	187
Total current liabilities	2,120	652	4,136
Long-term debt and notes payable	—	330	2,084
Capital lease obligations	623	857	943
Other long-term liabilities	181	132	883
Total liabilities not subject to compromise	$ 2,924	$ 1,971	$ 8,046
Liabilities subject to compromise	$ 7,969	$ 8,093	—
Company obligated mandatorily redeemable convertible preferred securities of a subsidiary trust holding solely 7¾% convertible junior subordinated debentures of Kmart (redemption value of $898 and $898, respectively)	$ 646	$ 889	$ 887
Common stock, $1 par value, 1,500,000,000 shares authorized; 503,294,515 and 486,509,736 shares issued, respectively	519	503	487
Capital in excess of par value	1,922	1,695	1,578
Retained earnings	(2,742)	1,032	3,817
Total liabilities and shareholders' equity	$11,238	$14,183	$14,815

Source: 2001 Kmart Corporation revised 10K report and 2002 Kmart Corporation 10K report.

exhibit 5 **Kmart's Consolidated Statements of Cash Flows, Fiscal Years 2000–2003 (dollars in millions)**

	Years Ended January 29, 2003, January 30, 2002, January 31, 2001, and January 26, 2000			
	2003	2002	2001	2000
Cash flows from operating activities				
Net (loss) income	($3,219)	($2,446)	($ 268)	$ 364
Adjustments to reconcile net income (loss) to net cash provided by operating activities:				
Discontinued operations	(43)	(166)	—	230
Inventory writedown	1,291	163	—	—
Restructuring, impairment and other charges	739	1,091	728	—
Reorganization items, net	386	(183)	—	—
Depreciation and amortization	737	824	777	770
Equity loss (income) in unconsolidated subsidiaries	(34)	—	13	(44)
Dividends received from Meldisco	45	51	44	38
Decrease (increase) in inventories	(168)	560	335	(544)
Increase (decrease) in accounts payable	401	1,046	(137)	169
Deferred income taxes and taxes payable	23	(55)	(204)	258
Changes in other assets	161	295	29	(127)
Changes in other liabilities	67	(23)	14	133
Cash used for store closings	(134)	(230)	(217)	(80)
Net cash provided by operating activities	252	927	1,114	1,084
Net cash used for reorganization items	135	(6)	—	—
Cash flows from investing activities				
Capital expenditures	(252)	(1,385)	(1,089)	(1,277)
Investment in BlueLight.com	—	(45)	(55)	—
Acquisition of Caldor leases	—	—	—	(86)
Net cash used for investing activities	(252)	(1,430)	(1,144)	(1,363)
Cash flows from financing activities				
Net borrowings on DIP credit facility	(330)	330	—	—
Proceeds from issuance of debt	—	1,494	400	300
Payments on debt	(31)	(320)	(73)	(90)
Debt issuance costs	(42)	(49)	(3)	(3)
Payments on capital lease obligations	(94)	(86)	(78)	(77)
Payments of dividends on preferred securities of subsidiary trust	—	(72)	(73)	(80)
Purchase of convertible preferred securities of subsidiary trust	—	—	(84)	—
Issuance of common shares	—	56	53	63
Purchase of common shares	—	—	(55)	(200)
Net cash provided by (used for) financing activities	(497)	1,353	87	(87)
Net change in cash and cash equivalents	(632)	844	57	(366)
Cash and cash equivalents, beginning of year	1,245	401	344	710
Cash and cash equivalents, end of year	$ 613	$1,245	$ 401	$ 344

Source: 2001 Kmart Corporation revised 10K report and 2002 Kmart Corporation 10K report.

exhibit 6 **Kmart's Contractual Obligations and Other Commercial Commitments at Fiscal Year-End 2001**

Contractual Obligations	Payments Due by Period				
	Within 1 Year	Within 2–3 Years	Within 4–5 Years	After 5 Years	Total
Long-term debt	$1,151	$ 714	$ 728	$1,083	$ 3,676
Capital lease obligations	234	433	344	1,232	2,243
Operating leases	728	1,374	1,177	6,355	9,634
Other long-term obligations	143	248	165	90	646
Total contractual cash obligations	$2,256	$2,769	$2,414	$8,760	$16,199

Other Commercial Commitments	Amount of Commitment Expiration Per Period				
	Within 1 Year	Within 2–3 Years	Within 4–5 Years	After 5 Years	Total
Trade lines of credit	$162	$ —	$ —	$ —	$162
Standby letters of credit	98	—	—	—	98
Guarantees	49	102	125	365	641
Total commercial commitments	$309	$102	$125	$365	$901

Source: 2001 Kmart Corporation revised 10K report.

KMART'S RESTRUCTURING PROGRAM AND PLANNED EMERGENCE FROM BANKRUPTCY, MARCH 2002–APRIL 2003

Five days prior to Kmart's January 22, 2002, bankruptcy filing, its board of directors promoted board member James Adamson to the position of chairman of the board, a position previously held by CEO Charles Conaway. Adamson had been a member of Kmart's board of directors since 1996 and was among those enthralled by the youthful Conaway during the selection process for Floyd Hall's replacement. Adamson was the retired chairman and CEO of Advantica Restaurant Group, which operated the Denny's, Coco's, and Carrows restaurant chains. Adamson had also held executive positions with Revco, Target, and B. Dalton Booksellers prior to joining Kmart's board. Kmart's board named Adamson to the additional position of CEO when Charles Conaway resigned in March 2002.

Kmart's board believed that Adamson was a good choice to head up Kmart during its bankruptcy because of his retailing experience and his experience operating under bankruptcy protection. While Adamson was its chairman and CEO, Advantica filed for bankruptcy protection and successfully emerged from Chapter 11 a year later. Adamson's restructuring plan for Kmart included the following components, some of which had been initiated by Charles Conaway prior to his exit from the company:

- An announcement in March 2002 that the company would close 284 stores and eliminate 22,000 jobs before year-end. The terminations and store closings would result in a charge against earnings of $1.3 billion.
- Liquidation of $758 million in inventory in the closed stores, some of which was transferred from remaining stores.
- Reduction of annual overhead expenses by $130 million.
- Utilization of a $2 billion debtor-in-possession financing that would be used to supplement Kmart's cash flow during its reorganization.
- Development of a new advertising phrase, "The Stuff of Life." The company hoped to win

customer loyalty by claiming to be the "store that understands what really matters in life."[19] The campaign was supported by an advertising budget of \$20–\$30 million and artistic 30-second television spots directed by filmmaker Spike Lee.

- Sale of BlueLight.com for \$8.4 million to an Internet service provider. BlueLight.com had incurred undisclosed millions in losses and sold products to fewer than 1 percent of its visitors during the fourth quarter of 2001. Kmart continued to make products available to consumers over the Internet at Kmart.com after the sale.

- Development of a prototype store that had futuristic icons, wider aisles, lower shelves, and brighter lighting. Martha Stewart Everyday, Joe Boxer, Disney, and Sesame Street products were located in dedicated sections rather than spread about the store.

- An announcement in January 2003 that the company would close an additional 316 stores and eliminate 25,000 more jobs. The store closings were expected to result in the liquidation of an additional \$1.5 billion in inventory for closed and remaining stores.

LEGAL WORRIES FOR KMART'S BOARD AND FORMER MANAGEMENT IN EARLY 2003

Three days after Kmart filed for bankruptcy, an anonymous letter from a Kmart employee addressed to the Securities and Exchange Commission (SEC), Kmart's auditors (PricewaterhouseCoopers), and the company's board of directors initiated investigations into Kmart's accounting practices. The investigations were led by the SEC, the U.S. Attorney's Office for Eastern Michigan, and the company's board of directors. The letter was followed by more than a dozen additional letters from different Kmart employees, all of whom suggested that Kmart executives told finance department employees to deviate from standard accounting practices and that those executives

also made misleading or deceptive statements to investors. As a result of Kmart's internal investigation, its financial statements for fiscal 1999 through the first two quarters of 2002 were restated because of the improper recording of vendor allowances that provided discounts or rebates to Kmart based on certain sales volumes of merchandise supplied by vendors. In numerous instances, Kmart recorded the discounts even though the sales volumes necessary to receive the allowances were not achieved. The audit had the effect of increasing Kmart's 2001 expenses by approximately \$100 million. After Kmart had completed its audit and the letter campaign continued, James Adamson sent an e-mail to all employees asking them to end the letter campaign and report potential violations of the company's Code of Conduct through proper channels.

The letter-writing campaign also brought oversight attention to \$28.9 million in retention loans granted to Charles Conaway and other top executives just days prior to Kmart's bankruptcy. The loans, which did not require a repayment, were questioned by investigators since the individual loan amounts were unusually high (e.g., Charles Conaway received a \$5 million retention loan, Mark Schwartz received a \$3 million loan, and a manager who had been with the company only two months received a loan for \$1.75 million) and since Kmart suppliers had gone unpaid for goods shipped to and sold by Kmart. Conaway and his top management team also received generous severance packages—Conaway received severance pay of \$4 million when he left the company in March 2002.

James Adamson launched a stewardship review of Kmart's outgoing management team in May 2002—agreeing to pay Conaway's severance package but suspending the severance pay of several members of Conaway's team. Kmart also suspended \$2 million in annual special retirement benefits for 20 former executives in June 2002. Some critics of Conaway questioned the veracity of Adamson's review since his own employment contract with Kmart granted him a \$2.5 million "inducement payment" to take the job of Kmart's CEO and provided such perks as weekly private plane service between his residences in Detroit, New York, and Florida; limousine service in Michigan and New York; and temporary accommodations in a \$320-per-night hotel near Kmart's headquarters. In addition, Adamson was the chairman of Kmart's board of directors' audit committee

[19]Quoted in "Kmart Pitches Family Values in New TV Spots by Spike Lee," *The Wall Street Journal Online,* February 25, 2002.

in 2000 and 2001, which was the period under examination for accounting irregularities.

Adamson stepped down as Kmart's CEO on January 19, 2003. Julian Day was selected to lead the company through the remaining months of bankruptcy. The investigation initiated by Kmart's board disclosed the following findings on January 27, 2003:

- Former officers were grossly derelict in performing their duties.
- Former managers failed to provide the board with important information concerning Kmart's retention loan program.
- Former senior executives authorized the purchase of $850 million in additional inventory for the Christmas 2002 shopping season that Kmart didn't need.
- In September 2001, former executives created "Project Slow It Down," in which the company avoided payments to vendors and told vendors who asked about payments that the invoices had been paid.
- Former officers hired unqualified employees and provided them with extraordinary compensation packages.

On February 27, 2003, the U.S. Justice Department filed criminal indictments against two former Kmart executives—Joseph A. Hofmeister, a divisional vice president of merchandising within Kmart's drugstore operations, and Enio Montini, a senior vice president and general merchandise manager for Kmart's drugstore division. Legal experts believed that the Justice Department had indicted the two relatively low-level managers to help gain their cooperation in investigating the actions of higher-ranking Kmart managers.

Apple Inc. in 2010

Lou Marino
The University of Alabama

John E. Gamble
University of South Alabama

Despite the effects of ongoing poor economic conditions in the United States, Apple Inc. celebrated record quarterly revenues and unit sales of computers during its third quarter of 2010. In addition, the company's newly released iPad tablet computer had sold 3.3 million units between its April 3, 2010, launch and the June 26, 2010, quarter end. The company also sold 8.4 million iPhones during the quarter. Most of the smartphone units sold during the third quarter of 2010 were iPhone 3GS models since the new iPhone 4 launched only four days prior to the close of the quarter. Although there had been some criticism of the antenna design of the iPhone 4, more than 3 million iPhone 4 units had been purchased by July 16, 2010, with only 1.7 percent being returned by dissatisfied customers. By comparison, the iPhone 3GS had a 6 percent return rate.

Apple's chief operating officer, Tim Cook, commented to the *Wall Street Journal* that the company was selling iPads and iPhones "as fast as we can make them" and was "working around the clock to try to get supply and demand in balance."[1] Some analysts were projecting that Apple would sell nearly 12 million iPad tablet computers by year-end 2010. However, others were concerned that once Apple aficionados had purchased an iPad to complement their iPhone, iPod, or Mac, further sales growth might be difficult to achieve. A former Apple executive commented, "The first five million will be sold in a heartbeat. But let's see: you can't make a phone call with it, you can't take a picture with it, and you have to buy content that before now you were not willing to pay for. That seems tough to me."[2]

Analysts were also concerned with the general decline in iPod unit sales and worried that Apple might have to struggle to sustain its growth in the smartphone market. The iPod had been important in the company's resurgence in the past decade, but sustained growth in iPhone sales were critical to the company's financial performance, since iPhone sales accounted for $5.33 billion of the company's third-quarter 2010 revenues of $15.7 billion. Research in Motion (RIM) had been known for innovative smartphones since it introduced the BlackBerry in 1999, but Google's development of the Android operating system for smartphones had allowed HTC, LG, Nokia, and Samsung to introduce smartphones that matched many of the iPhone's best features. In addition, Microsoft's Windows Mobile 7 operating system, planned for a late-2010 launch, was expected to surpass some of the capabilities of the iPhone operating system. Google was also a growing threat to Apple, since many computer makers were developing new tablet computers similar to the iPad that would run the Android operating system; the two companies seemed to be headed for a future battle in mobile ads.

COMPANY HISTORY AND FINANCIAL PERFORMANCE

Steven Wozniak and Steven Jobs founded Apple Computer in 1976 when they began selling a crudely designed personal computer called the

Apple I to Silicon Valley computer enthusiasts. Two years later, the partners introduced the first mass-produced personal computer (PC), the Apple II. The Apple II boasted the first color display and eventually sold more than 10,000 units. While the Apple II was relatively successful, the next revision of the product line, the Macintosh (Mac), would dramatically change personal computing through its user-friendly graphical user interface (GUI), which allowed users to interact with screen images rather than merely type text commands.

The Macintosh that was introduced in 1984 was hailed as a breakthrough in personal computing, but it did not have the speed, power, or software availability to compete with the PC that IBM had introduced in 1981. One of the reasons the Macintosh lacked the necessary software was that Apple put very strict restrictions on the Apple Certified Developer Program, which made it difficult for software developers to obtain Macs at a discount and receive informational materials about the operating system.

With the Mac faring poorly in the market, founder Steve Jobs became highly critical of the company's president and CEO, John Sculley, who had been hired by the board in 1983. Finally, in 1985, as Sculley was preparing to visit China, Jobs devised a boardroom coup to replace him. Sculley found out about the plan and canceled his trip. After Apple's board voted unanimously to keep Sculley in his position, Jobs, who was retained as chairman of the company but stripped of all decision-making authority, soon resigned. During the remainder of 1985, Apple continued to encounter problems and laid off one-fifth of its employees while posting its first ever quarterly loss.

Despite these setbacks, Apple kept bringing innovative products to the market, while closely guarding the secrets behind its technology. In 1987, Apple released a revamped Macintosh computer that proved to be a favorite in K–12 schools and with graphic artists and other users needing excellent graphics capabilities. However, by 1990, PCs running Windows 3.0 and Word for Windows were preferred by businesses and consumers and held a commanding 97+ percent share of the market for personal computers.

In 1991, Apple released its first-generation notebook computer, the PowerBook and, in 1993, Apple's board of directors opted to remove Sculley from the position of CEO. The board chose to place the chief operating officer, Michael Spindler, in the vacated spot. Under Spindler, Apple released the PowerMac family of PCs in 1994, the first Macs to incorporate the PowerPC chip, a very fast processor co-developed with Motorola and IBM. Even though the PowerMac family received excellent reviews by technology analysts, Microsoft's Windows 95 matched many of the capabilities of the Mac OS and prevented the PowerMac from gaining significant market share. In January 1996, Apple asked Spindler to resign and chose Gil Amelio, former president of National Semiconductor, to take his place.

During his first 100 days in office, Amelio announced many sweeping changes for the company. He split Apple into seven distinct divisions, each responsible for its own profit or loss, and he tried to better inform the developers and consumers of Apple's products and projects. Amelio acquired NeXT, the company Steve Jobs had founded upon his resignation from Apple in 1985. Steve Jobs was rehired by Apple as part of the acquisition. In 1997, after recording additional quarterly losses, Apple's board terminated Amelio's employment with the company and named Steve Jobs interim CEO.

Apple introduced the limited feature iMac in 1998 and the company's iBook line of notebook computers in 1999. The company was profitable in every quarter during 1998 and 1999, and its share price reached an all-time high in the upper $70 range. Jobs was named permanent CEO of Apple in 2000 and, in 2001, oversaw the release of the iPod. The iPod recorded modest sales until the 2003 launch of iTunes—the online retail store where consumers could legally purchase individual songs. By July 2004, 100 million songs had been sold and iTunes had a 70 percent market share among all legal online music download services. The tremendous success of the iPod helped transform Apple from a struggling computer company into a powerful consumer electronics company.

By 2005, consumers' satisfaction with the iPod had helped renew interest in Apple computers, with its market share in personal computers growing from a negligible share to 4 percent. The company also exploited consumer loyalty and satisfaction with the iPod to enter the market for smartphones with the 2007 launch of the iPhone.

Much of Apple's turnaround could be credited to Steve Jobs, who had idea after idea for how to improve the company and turn its performance around. He not only consistently pushed for innovative new ideas and products but also enforced several structural changes, including ridding the company of unprofitable segments and divisions.

The success of the turnaround could also be attributed to the efforts of Tim Cook, Apple's chief operating officer. While Jobs provided the vision for the organization, Cook and the other members of the executive staff and the board of directors were responsible for ensuring that all operations of Apple ran efficiently and smoothly. Between mid-2008 and mid-2009, when Steve Jobs took a leave of absence to receive a liver transplant, Cook took on the role of acting CEO.

A summary of Apple's financial performance for fiscal years 2005 through 2009 is provided in Exhibit 1. The company's net sales by operating segment and product line and unit sales by product line for 2005 through 2009 are provided in Exhibit 2.

OVERVIEW OF THE PERSONAL COMPUTER INDUSTRY

The personal computer industry was relatively consolidated, with five sellers accounting for 78.5 percent of the U.S. shipments and 60.3 percent of worldwide shipments in 2009—see Exhibit 3. Prior to the onset of the recession that began in 2008, the PC industry was expected to grow at a rate of 5–6 percent, to reach $354 billion by 2012. However, the effects of the recession caused a dramatic decline in industry revenues in 2008 and 2009.

PC industry shipments grew by a healthy 22.4 percent during the second quarter of 2010 as businesses were forced to replace aging computers. The sharp spike in shipments was not expected to continue throughout the year, with analysts expecting a 12.6 percent increase in worldwide shipments for the full year 2010. PC shipments in emerging markets were expected to grow at 18.5 percent to allow demand in emerging markets to overtake demand for PCs in developed countries by the end of 2010. Shipments of PCs in developed countries were expected to increase by only 7.2 percent in 2010 and were not expected to reach double-digit rates until 2011. Industry revenues were projected to grow more slowly than shipments because average selling prices had declined steadily since 2008.

Both businesses and consumers were tending to replace desktop PCs with portable PCs such as laptops and netbooks. Total shipments of portable PCs grew by 18.4 percent in 2009, with consumer purchases of portable PCs growing by 38 percent during the year. Low-end laptops and netbooks accounted for the majority of consumer portable PC sales in 2009. The sale of desktop computers was expected to decline in all country markets except emerging markets in Asia, which would allow portable PCs to make up 70 percent of industry shipments by 2012.

APPLE'S COMPETITIVE POSITION IN THE PERSONAL COMPUTER INDUSTRY

Even though a larger percentage of Apple's revenues were increasingly coming from noncomputer products, the company still saw computers as its core business. Apple's proprietary operating system and strong graphics-handling capabilities differentiated Macs from PCs, but many consumers and business users who owned PCs were hesitant to purchase a Mac because of Apple's premium pricing and because of the learning curve involved with mastering its proprietary operating system. The company's market share in the United States had improved from 4 percent in 2005 to 8 percent in 2009 primarily because of the success of the iPod and iPhone. These products created a halo effect whereby some consumers (but not business users) switched to Apple computers after purchasing an iPod or iPhone.

Apple's computer product line consisted of several models in various configurations. Its desktop lines included the Mac Pro (aimed at professional and business users); the iMac (targeted toward consumer, educational, and business use); and Mac mini (made specifically for consumer use). Apple had three notebook product

Exhibit 1   Summary of Apple, Inc.'s Financial Performance, 2005–2009 ($ millions, except share amounts)

Income Statement Data	2009	2008	2007	2006	2005
Net Sales					
Domestic	$ 19,870	$ 18,469	$ 14,128	$ 11,486	$ 8,334
International	16,667	14,010	9,878	7,829	5,597
Total net sales	36,537	32,479	24,006	19,315	13,931
Costs and Expenses					
Cost of sales	23,397	21,334	15,852	13,717	9,889
Research and development (R&D)	1,333	1,109	782	712	535
Selling, general and administrative (SG&A)	4,149	3,761	2,963	2,433	1,864
Total operating expenses	5,482	4,870	3,745	3,145	2,399
Operating income	7,658	6,275	4,409	2,453	1,643
Other income and expense	326	620	599	365	165
Income before provision for income taxes	7,984	6,895	5,008	2,818	1,808
Provision for income taxes	2,280	2,061	1,512	829	480
Net income	$ 5,704	$ 4,834	$ 3,496	$ 1,989	$ 1,328
Earnings per common share—diluted	$6.29	$5.36	$3.93	$2.27	$1.55
Shares used in computing earnings per share—diluted (in thousands)	907,005	902,139	889,292	877,526	856,878

Balance Sheet Data (as of September 30)	2009	2008	2007	2006	2005
Cash, cash equivalents, and short-term investments	$ 23,464	$ 24,490	$ 15,386	$ 10,110	$ 8,261
Accounts receivable, net	3,361	2,422	1,637	1,252	895
Inventories	455	509	346	270	165
Property, plant, and equipment, net	2,954	2,455	1,832	1,281	817
Total assets	53,851	39,572	25,347	17,205	11,516
Current liabilities	19,284	14,092	9,299	6,443	3,487
Noncurrent liabilities	6,737	4,450	1,516	778	601
Shareholders' equity	$ 27,832	$ 21,030	$ 14,532	$ 9,984	$ 7,428

Source: Apple Inc., 2007 and 2009 10-K reports.

Exhibit 2   Apple, Inc.'s Net Sales by Operating Segment, Net Sales by Product, and Unit Sales by Product, 2005–2009 ($ millions)

	2009	2008	2007	2006	2005
Net Sales by Operating Segment					
Americas net sales	$16,142	$14,573	$11,596	$ 9,415	$ 6,950
Europe net sales	9,365	7,622	5,460	4,096	3,073
Japan net sales	1,831	1,509	1,082	1,211	920
Retail net sales	6,574	6,315	4,115	3,246	2,350
Other Segments net sales [a]	2,625	2,460	1,753	1,347	998
Total net sales	$36,537	$32,479	$24,006	$19,315	$13,931
Net Sales by Product					
Desktops [b]	$ 4,308	$ 5,603	$ 4,020	$ 3,319	$ 3,436
Portables [c]	9,472	8,673	6,294	4,056	2,839
Total Macintosh net sales	$13,780	$14,276	10,314	7,375	6,275
iPod	8,091	9,153	8,305	7,375	4,540
Other music related products and services [d]	4,036	3,340	2,496	1,885	899
iPhone and related products and services [e]	6,754	1,844	123	—	—
Peripherals and other hardware [f]	1,470	1,659	1,260	1,100	1,126
Software, service, and other sales [g]	2,406	2,207	1,508	1,279	1,091
Total net sales	$36,537	$32,479	$24,006	$19,315	$13,931
Unit Sales by Product:					
Desktops [b]	3,182	3,712	2,714	2,434	2,520
Portables [c]	7,214	6,003	4,337	2,869	2,014
Total Macintosh unit sales	10,396	9,715	7,051	5,303	4,534
Net sales per Macintosh unit sold [h]	$1,326	$1,469	$1,463	$1,391	$1,384
iPod unit sales	54,132	54,828	51,630	39,409	22,497
Net sales per iPod unit sold [i]	$149	$167	$161	$195	$202
iPhone unit sales	20,731	11,627	1,389	—	—

[a]Other segments include Asia Pacific and FileMaker.
[b]Includes iMac, eMac, Mac mini, Power Mac, and Xserve product lines.
[c]Includes MacBook, MacBook Pro, iBook, and PowerBook product lines.
[d]Consists of iTunes Music Store sales, iPod services, and Apple-branded and third-party iPod accessories.
[e]Derived from handset sales, carrier agreements, and Apple-branded and third-party iPhone accessories.
[f]Includes sales of Apple-branded and third-party displays, wireless connectivity and networking solutions, and other hardware accessories.
[g]Includes sales of Apple-branded operating system, application software, third-party software, AppleCare, and Internet services.
[h]Derived by dividing total Macintosh net sales by total Macintosh unit sales.
[i]Derived by dividing total iPod net sales by total iPod unit sales.
Source: Apple Inc., 2007 and 2009 10-K reports.

Exhibit 3 U.S. and Global Market Shares of Leading PC Vendors, 2000 and 2005–2009

A. U.S. Market Shares of the Leading PC Vendors, 2000 and 2005–2009

2009 Rank	Vendor	2009 Shipments (in 000s)	2009 Market Share	2008 Shipments (in 000s)	2008 Market Share	2007 Shipments (in 000s)	2007 Market Share	2006 Shipments (in 000s)	2006 Market Share	2005 Shipments (in 000s)	2005 Market Share	2000 Shipments (in 000s)	2000 Market Share
1	Hewlett Packard[1]	18,781	26.9%	16,218	24.7%	16,759	23.9%	11,600	21.5%	12,456	19.5%	5,630	11.5%
2	Dell	17,099	24.5	19,276	29.4	19,645	28.0	20,472	31.2	21,466	33.6	9,645	19.7
	Compaq[1]	—	—	—	—	—	—	—	—	—	—	7,761	15.9
3	Acer[1]	7,983	11.4	6,106	9.3	3,860	5.5	1,421	2.2	n.a.	n.a.	n.a.	n.a.
4	Apple	5,579	8.0	5,158	7.9	4,081	5.8	3,109	4.7	2,555	4.0	n.a.	n.a.
5	Toshiba	5,379	7.7	3,788	5.8	3,509	5.0	2,843	4.3	2,327	3.6	n.a.	n.a.
	Others	15,008	21.5	15,026	22.9	22,235	31.7	23,350	35.7	25,070	39.2	18,959	38.8
	All vendors	69,829	100.0%	65,571	100.0%	70,088	100.0%	65,481	100.0%	63,874	100.0%	48,900	100.0%

B. Worldwide Market Shares of the Leading PC Vendors, 2000 and 2005–2009

2009 Rank	Vendor	2009 Shipments (in 000s)	2009 Market Share	2008 Shipments (in 000s)	2008 Market Share	2007 Shipments (in 000s)	2007 Market Share	2006 Shipments (in 000s)	2006 Market Share	2005 Shipments (in 000s)	2005 Market Share	2000 Shipments (in 000s)	2000 Market Share
1	Hewlett Packard[1]	59,942	20.3%	54,293	18.9%	50,526	18.8%	38,838	16.5%	32,575	15.7%	10,327	7.4%
2	Dell	38,416	13.1	42,388	14.7	39,993	14.9	39,094	16.6	37,755	18.2	14,801	10.6
	Compaq[1]	—	—	—	—	—	—	—	—	—	—	17,399	12.5
3	Acer[2]	38,377	13.0	31,377	10.9	21,206	7.9	13,594	5.8	9,845	4.7	n.a.	n.a.
4	Lenovo/IBM[3]	24,887	8.5	21,870	7.6	20,224	7.5	16,609	7.1	12,979	6.2	9,308	6.7
5	Toshiba	15,878	5.4	13,727	4.8	10,936	4.1	9,292	3.9	7,234	3.5	n.a.	n.a.
	Others	116,709	39.7	123,910	43.1	126,075	46.9	117,971	50.1	107,450	51.7	80,640	58.0
	All vendors	294,208	100.0%	287,566	100.0%	268,960	100.0%	235,397	100.0%	207,837	100.0%	139,057	100.0%

n.a. = not available; sales and market shares for these companies in the years where n.a. appears are included in the "Others" category because the company was not in the top 5 in shipments or market share.

[1]Compaq was acquired by Hewlett-Packard in May 2002.

[2]Acer acquired Gateway in 2007 and Packard Bell in 2008. Data for Acer includes shipments for Gateway starting in Q4 2007 and shipments for Packard Bell starting in Q1 2008, and only Acer data for prior periods.

[3]Lenovo, a Chinese computer company, completed the acquisition of IBM's PC business in 2005. The numbers for Lenovo/IBM for 2000 reflect sales of IBM branded PCs only; the numbers for 2005–2009 reflect their combined sales beginning in the second quarter of 2005. In 2007, Lenovo rebranded all IBM PCs as Lenovo.

Source: International Data Corp.

lines as well: MacBook Pro (for professional and advanced consumer users), the MacBook (designed for education users and consumers), and the MacBook Air (designed for professional and consumer users).

The MacBook Air was Apple's most recent notebook introduction. The MacBook Air was designed to target users who valued both portability and power. The notebook featured a 13.3-inch screen, a full-size keyboard, a built-in video camera, and cutting-edge wireless connectivity. This sleek notebook measured only 0.76 inches at its maximum height when closed and weighed only three pounds. The MacBook Air had won critical acclaim for both its design and its ease of use, and was one of the products helping Apple gain ground in the competitive computer industry. All Apple computers were priced at a steep premium compared to PCs and laptops offered by Dell, HP, and other rivals. The company lowered the prices of all its computer models by 10 percent or more in June 2009, with the price of the MacBook Pro falling to $1,199 and the MacBook Air getting a $300 price cut, to $1,499.

APPLE'S RIVALS IN THE PERSONAL COMPUTER INDUSTRY

Hewlett-Packard

Hewlett-Packard (HP) was broadly diversified across segments of the computer industry with business divisions focused on information technology consulting services, large enterprise systems, software, personal computers, printers and other imaging devices, and financial services. The company's Personal Systems Group (PSG), which manufactured and marketed HP and Compaq desktop computers and portable computers, was its largest division, accounting for revenues of $35.3 billion in 2009. HP recorded total net revenues of $114.6 billion in 2009, with information technology services contributing nearly $34.7 billion, imaging and printing devices contributing $24 billion, and enterprise systems accounting for about $15.4 billion. The company's financial services and software business units accounted for sales of about $6 billion in 2009.

HP's sales of personal computers declined by 16.5 percent between 2008 and 2009 as the recession forced consumers and businesses to reduce expenditures and capital investments. Handheld computers and workstations were affected most by the recession, with sales declining by 52.2 percent and 33.7 percent, respectively, during 2009. The company's sales of desktop computers were affected not only by the recession but also by business users' and consumers' growing preference for portable computers over desktop models. HP portable computers were harmed least by the recession, with a 10.8 percent decline in sales between 2008 and 2009. HP did sustain some growth in emerging markets despite the recession in developed countries. Exhibit 4 provides the revenue contribution by PSG product line for 2005 through 2009.

Dell Inc.

Dell Inc. was the world's second-largest seller of personal computers, with revenues of $52.9 billion for the fiscal year ending January 29, 2010.

Exhibit 4   **Hewlett-Packard Personal Systems Group, Net Revenue ($ millions)**

Product	2009	2008	2007	2006	2005
Notebooks	$20,210	$22,657	$17,650	$12,005	$ 9,763
Desktop PCs	12,864	16,626	15,889	14,641	14,406
Workstations	1,261	1,902	1,721	1,368	1,195
Handhelds	172	360	531	650	836
Other	798	750	618	502	541
Total	$35,305	$42,295	$36,409	$29,166	$26,741

Source: Hewlett-Packard, 2007 and 2008 10-K reports.

Exhibit 5   Dell's Revenues by Product Category, Fiscal 2008–Fiscal 2010 ($ millions)

Fiscal Year Ended	January 29, 2010		January 30, 2009		February 1, 2008	
	Dollars	% of Revenue	Dollars	% of Revenue	Dollars	% of Revenue
Servers and networking	$ 6,032	11%	$ 6,512	11%	$ 6,486	11%
Storage	2,192	4	2,667	4	2,429	4
Services	5,622	11	5,351	9	4,980	8
Software and peripherals	9,499	18	10,603	17	9,927	16
Mobility	16,610	31	18,604	30	17,961	29
Desktop PCs	12,947	25	17,364	29	19,350	32
Totals	$52,902	100%	$61,101	100%	$61,133	100%

Source: Dell Inc., 2010 10-K report.

Exhibit 5 presents Dell's revenues by product category for fiscal 2008 through fiscal 2010. The recession significantly affected Dell's financial performance in late 2008, when its fourth-quarter sales declined by 48 percent from the same period in the prior year. The revenue decline was a result of an overall decline in unit sales and strong price competition in both desktop PCs and portables. In addition, Dell's net earnings fell from $2.9 billion in fiscal 2008 to $2.5 billion in fiscal 2009 to $1.4 billion in fiscal 2010. The company offered a wide range of desktop computers and portables, ranging from low-end, low-priced models to state-of-the-art, high-priced models. The company also offered servers; workstations; peripherals such as printers, monitors, and projectors; and Wi-Fi products.

Acer

Taiwan-based Acer was the world's second-largest portable computer provider and third-largest desktop computer manufacturer in 2010. Acer's 2009 consolidated revenues rose by approximately 13 percent from the previous year to reach $18.3 billion, while operating income increased by 17 percent to reach $488 million. Its 40.5 percent annual growth in global PC shipments between 2005 and 2009 ranked first among the industry's leading sellers. The company's largest and one of its fastest-growing geographic segments was the Europe/Middle East/Africa segment, which accounted for 52 percent of the company's PC, desktop, and notebook sales. A summary of the company's financial performance between 2006 and 2009 is presented in Exhibit 6.

Exhibit 6   Financial Summary for Acer Incorporated, 2006–2009 ($ thousands)

	2009	2008	2007	2006
Revenue	$18,264,125	$16,186,102	$15,252,801	$10,577,113
Gross profit	1,855,993	1,697,374	1,565,278	1,150,865
Operating income	488,102	416,962	336,211	224,993
Operating margin	2.7%	2.6%	2.2%	2.1%
Income before income taxes	476,759	438,723	498,736	408,481
Net income	$361,248	$347,919	$427,774	$308,080

Source: Acer Incorporated Financial Snapshot, http://www.acer-group.com/public/Investor_Relations/financial_snapshot.htm.

Acer's multibrand strategy—which positioned Acer, Gateway, eMachines, and Packard Bell at distinct price points in the market for PCs—had helped it become one of the fastest-growing vendors in the United States. The company based its competitive strategy on its four pillars of success: a winning business model, competitive products, an innovative marketing strategy, and an efficient operation model. The company's computer offering included desktop and mobile PCs, LCD monitors, servers and storage, and high-definition TVs and projectors. In 2009, the company entered the market for smartphones with the launch of its Liquid line of stylish, high-end smartphones, which used Google's Android operating system.

APPLE'S COMPETITIVE POSITION IN THE PERSONAL MEDIA PLAYER INDUSTRY

Although Apple didn't introduce the first portable digital music player, the company held a 73 percent market share digital music players in 2010 and the name iPod had become a generic term used to describe digital media players. When Apple launched its first iPod, many critics did not give the product much of a chance for success, given its fairly hefty price tag of $399. However, the iPod's sleek styling, ease of use, and eventual price decreases allowed it to develop such high levels of customer satisfaction and loyalty that rivals found it difficult to gain traction in the marketplace.

The most popular portable players in 2010 not only played music but could be connected to Wi-Fi networks to play videos, access the Internet, view photos, or listen to FM high-definition radio. The iPod Touch was the best-selling media player in 2010, but electronics sector reviewers generally agreed that Microsoft's Zune, Archos's Vision models, and Sony's X-series media players compared quite favorably to the iPod Touch. In addition, electronics reviewers found that inexpensive MP3 music players offered by SanDisk, Creative, iRiver, and others generally performed as well as Apple's more basic iPod models. However, none of Apple's key rivals in the media player industry had been able to achieve a market share greater than 5 percent in 2010. Most consumers did not find many convincing reasons to consider any brand of media player other than Apple.

In 2010, Apple offered four basic styles in the iPod product line:

- *The iPod Shuffle*—a basic flash-based player with no screen, FM radio, or voice recorder. The 4 gigabyte (GB) model was capable of storing 1,000 songs, and its rechargeable lithium polymer battery provided up to 10 hours of playback time.

- *The iPod Nano*—a multimedia player offered in 8 GB (8 hours of video or 2,000 songs) and 16 GB (16 hours of video or 4,000 songs) sizes that used a click wheel interface to navigate the player's controls. It allowed users to view photos and videos as well as to listen to music in Apple's Advanced Audio Coding (AAC) format, and it provided up to 24 hours of music playback and 5 hours of video playback on a single charge.

- *The iPod Classic*—a hard-drive-based click-wheel-controlled multimedia player offered with a 160 GB hard drive that, similar to the smaller Nano, played music in Apple's AAC format and showed videos and photos. The 160 GB player held up to 40,000 songs or 200 hours of video and provided up to 36 hours of audio playback or 6 hours of video playback on a single charge.

- *The iPod Touch*—a multimedia flash memory player controlled though an innovative touch screen interface that was a feature of the iPhone. It was offered in 8 GB (1,750 songs, 10 hours of video), 32 GB (7,000 songs, 40 hours of video), and 64 GB (14,000 songs, 80 hours of video) sizes, and provided up to 30 hours of music playback and 6 hours of video playback on a single charge. This multimedia player featured a wide 3.5-inch screen and built-in Wi-Fi, which allowed users to connect to the Internet and access e-mail, buy music from the iTunes store, and surf the Web from wireless hotspots. Touch users also had access to maps, the weather, and stocks, and the ability to write notes to themselves. The Touch featured an accelerometer that detected when the Touch rotated and automatically changed the display from portrait to landscape.

iTunes

Aside from the iPod's stylish design and ease of use, another factor that contributed to the popularity of the iPod was Apple's iPod/iTunes combination. In 2010, more than 50 million customers visited the iTunes Store to purchase and download music, videos, movies, and television shows that could be played on iPods, iPhones, or Apple TV devices. (Apple TV was a device that allowed users to play iTunes content on televisions.) Also in 2010, Apple's iTunes Store recorded its 10-billionth download since its launch in 2003. Additionally, iTunes was the world's most popular online movie store, with customers purchasing and renting more than 50,000 movies each day. Apple did not offer an iTunes subscription service, although a July 2010 survey by research firm NPD Group found that 7 to 8 million iPod owners would have a strong interest in subscribing to a service that would allow them to stream iTunes music and videos.

The success of the iPod/iTunes combination gave iTunes a 69 percent share of the U.S. digital music market in 2010. Since downloads accounted for about 40 percent of all music sales in the United States, iTunes' commanding share of the digital music sales also gave it a 27 percent share of total U.S. music sales. Amazon.com was the second-largest seller of digital music in the United States, with an 8 percent share of the market. Amazon.com and Walmart were tied for second in total U.S. music sales, with 12 percent market shares.

APPLE'S COMPETITIVE POSITION IN THE MOBILE PHONE INDUSTRY

The first version of the iPhone was released on June 29, 2007, and had a multitouch screen with a virtual keyboard, a camera, and a portable media player (equivalent to the iPod) in addition to text messaging and visual voice mail. It also offered Internet services including e-mail, Web browsing (using access to Apple's Safari Web browser), and local Wi-Fi connectivity. More than 270,000 first-generation iPhones were sold during the first 30 hours of the product's launch. The iPhone was named *Time* magazine's Invention of the Year in 2007.

The iPhone 3G was released in 70 countries on July 11, 2008, and was available in the United States exclusively through AT&T Mobility. The iPhone 3G combined the functionality of a wireless phone and an iPod, and allowed users to access the Internet wirelessly at twice the speed of the previous version of the iPhone. Apple's new phone also featured a built-in global positioning system (GPS) and, in an effort to increase adoption by corporate users, was compatible with Microsoft Exchange.

The iPhone 3GS was introduced on June 19, 2009, and included all of the features of the iPhone 3G but could also launch applications and render Web pages twice as fast as the iPhone 3G. The iPhone 3GS also featured a 3-megapixel camera, video recording, voice control, and up to 32 GB of flash memory. The iPhone 4 was launched on June 24, 2010, with the 16 GB model priced at $199 on a two-year AT&T contract and the 32 GB model priced at $299 on a two-year AT&T contract. Upgrades over the 3GS included video-calling capabilities (only over a Wi-Fi network), a higher resolution display, a 5-megapixel camera including flash and zoom, 720p video recording, a longer-lasting battery, and a gyroscopic motion sensor to enable an improved gaming experience. The iPhone 4 sold more than 1.7 million units within three days of its launch.

Similar to the iTunes/iPod partnership, Apple launched the App Store for the iPhone. The App Store allowed developers to build applications for the iPhone and to offer them either for free or for a fee. In January 2010, more than 3 billion apps had been downloaded by iPhone and iPod Touch users. Both Apple and Google had begun to embed ads into mobile apps to both create additional revenue sources and to allow app developers to earn revenues from apps that could be downloaded free of charge.

While worldwide shipments of mobile phones declined from 1.19 billion in 2008 to 1.27 billion in 2009 because of poor economic conditions in the United States and many other major country markets, worldwide sales of mobile phones grew by 21.7 percent during the first quarter of 2010 as economies in most countries began to improve. However, industry analysts did not expect the 21.7 percent year-over-year sales increase during the first quarter of 2010 to continue throughout the year and projected annual sales growth of about 11 percent for 2010. The growth in shipments of smartphones during the first quarter of 2010 outpaced the growth in basic-feature phone shipments by a considerable margin. The shipments of smartphones grew by 56.7 percent during the first quarter of 2010, while shipments of basic-feature phones increased by 18.8 percent between the first quarter of 2009 and the first quarter of 2010. The rapid growth in demand for smartphones during early 2010 allowed Research in Motion (RIM) to become the first company producing only smartphones to become a Top 5 vendor in the industry—see Exhibit 7.

Developing countries such as China offered the greatest growth opportunities but also presented challenges to smartphone producers. For example, there were 700 million mobile phone users in China, but popular-selling models were quickly counterfeited, it was difficult to develop keyboards that included the thousands of commonly used characters in the Chinese language, and most consumers preferred inexpensive feature phones over smartphones. Nevertheless, many analysts expected China to account for 10 percent of worldwide smartphone shipments within the near term. Apple planned to begin selling the iPhone in China in 2010 through a network of 25 flagship stores located in the country's largest cities. The iPhone would be available in 80 countries by year-end 2010.

With the market for smartphones growing rapidly and supporting high average selling prices, competition was becoming more heated. Google's entry into the market with its Android operating system had allowed vendors such as HTC, Motorola, Acer, and Samsung to offer models that matched many of the features of the iPhone. In addition, Microsoft's Windows Mobile 7, which was planned for a late-2010 launch, was expected to exceed the capabilities of the iPhone operating system with live tiles of rotating pictures, e-mail messages, and social-networking feeds. In addition, smartphones operating on Windows Mobile 7 would have all of the functionality of a Zune media player just as the iPhone included all of the functionality of the iPod Touch. While iPhones and Android phones primarily targeted consumers enthralled with clever and helpful Web apps, RIM had built a number one position in the smartphone market by appealing to businesspeople who needed the

ability to check e-mail; maintain appointment calendars; receive fax transmissions; and open, edit, and save Microsoft Office and Adobe PDF files. Hewlett-Packard entered the market for smartphones in May 2010 with its $1.2 billion acquisition of Palm. However, Palm had lost its edge in innovation years before and was primarily popular with users who had purchased Palm Pilots in the company's heyday. Exhibit 8 presents market shares for the leading smartphone brands between 2006 and the first quarter of 2010.

APPLE'S ENTRY INTO THE MARKET FOR TABLET COMPUTERS

Apple entered the market for tablet computers with its April 3, 2010, launch of the iPad. Tablet computers such as the iPad allowed users to access the Internet, read and send e-mail, view photos, watch videos, listen to music, read e-books, and play video games. In addition, Apple's iPad could run 11,000 apps developed specifically for the iPad and most of the 225,000-plus apps developed for the iPhone and iPod Touch. Apple sold more than 3 million iPads within the first 90 days the product was on the market. Industry analysts expected that 13 million tablet computers would be sold in 2010, with Apple accounting for almost all shipments of tablet computers. The market for tablet computers was expected to increase to 46 million units by 2014. By comparison, the market for portable PCs was expected to grow to 398 million units by 2014.

Tablet computers had been on the market since the late 1990s, but only Apple's version had gained any significant interest from consumers and business users. Previous-generation tablet computers required the use of a stylus to launch applications and enter information. Most users found the stylus interface to be an annoyance and preferred to use a smartphone or laptop when portability was required. Dell, Acer, Hewlett-Packard, and Nokia were all racing to get touch-screen tablet computers to market but would be unable to do so until very late 2010 or early 2011 because of the technological differences between tablet computers and PCs. Tablet computers were technologically similar to smartphones and

C-152   **Part 2**   Cases in Crafting and Executing Strategy

Exhibit 7   **Worldwide Market Shares of Leading Mobile Phone Vendors, 2000 and 2005–2009**

Q1 2010 Rank	Vendor	Q1 2010		2009		2008		2007	
		Shipments (in millions)	Market Share	Shipments (in millions)	Market Share	Shipments (in millions)	Market Share	Shipments (in millions)	Market Share
1	Nokia	107.8	36.6%	431.8	38.3%	468.4	39.4%	437.1	38.3%
2	Samsung	64.3	21.8	227.2	20.1	196.8	16.5	161.1	14.1
3	LG	27.1	9.2	117.9	10.5	100.8	8.5	80.5	7.1
4	RIM	10.6	3.6	n.a.	n.a.	n.a.	n.a.	n.a.	n.a.
5	Sony Ericsson	10.5	3.6	57.0	5.1	96.6	8.1	103.4	9.1
	Others	74.6	25.3	293.8	26.0	327.7	27.5	358.8	31.4
	All vendors	294.9	100.0%	1,127.8	100.0%	1,190.1	100.0%	1,140.9	100.0%

n.a. = not available; sales and market shares for these companies in the years where n.a. appears are included in the "Others" category because the company was not in the top 5 in shipments or market share.

Source: International Data Corp.

Exhibit 8   U.S. Smartphone Platform Market Share Rankings, Selected Periods, September 2009–May 2010

Smartphone Platform	Share of Smartphone Subscribers			
	September 2009	December 2009	February 2010	May 2010
RIM (BlackBerry)	42.6%	41.6%	42.1%	41.7%
Apple iPhone	24.1	25.3	25.4	24.4
Microsoft Windows Mobile	19.0	18.0	15.1	13.2
Google Android	2.5	5.2	9.0	13.0
Palm	8.3	6.1	5.4	4.8
Others	3.5	3.8	3.0	2.9
Total	100.0%	100.0%	100.0%	100.0%

Source: ComScore.com.

shared almost no components with PCs. The primary reason tablet computers could not use PC components was that the small size of tablet computers limited battery size. The small battery size prevented the use of energy-hungry PC components and required that tablet computers run the limited-capability microprocessors and operating systems found in smartphones. This minimal processing capability made tablet computers suitable only for viewing information and prevented the devices from running applications such as Microsoft Word, Excel, or PowerPoint.

Intel's new Atom microprocessor and Microsoft's Windows Mobile 7 would both be suitable for use in tablet computers and were expected to arrive to market in late 2010. PC manufacturers unwilling to wait for the development of the Atom and Windows Mobile 7 were designing tablet computers that used smartphone microprocessors and Google's Android operating system. Analysts believed that HP's 2010 acquisition of Palm was motivated more by the desire to use the Palm operating system in HP tablet computers than the company's interest in entering the smartphone market. Smartphone manufacturer Archos was the only vendor offering a viable competing product to the iPad in mid-2010. E-readers such as Amazon's Kindle were not considered direct competitors to the iPad since dedicated reading devices could not browse the Internet, view videos, play music, or perform other media tasks. In addition, e-readers carried prices in the $99–$189 range, which was considerably lower than the $499–$829 range charged by Apple for various iPad models.

APPLE'S PERFORMANCE GOING INTO THE FOURTH QUARTER OF 2010

Apple set a number of records with its third-quarter 2010 performance. The company's quarterly revenue of 15.7 billion was its highest-ever quarterly sales figure, and the company set a new record for quarterly shipments of computers, with 3.47 million Macs shipped during the quarter. The company also sold 3.3 million iPads by the June 26, 2010, close of the quarter. By comparison, it took the first iPod 20 months to reach 1 million units in sales—the iPad hit the 1-million-unit mark within 30 days of its April 3, 2010, launch. In addition, Apple sold 8.4 million iPhones during the third quarter of 2010, which was 61 percent more than what was sold during the same period in 2009. The increase in iPhone sales came primarily from sales of iPhone 3GS models since the iPhone 4 launched only four days before the quarter end. Unit sales for the iPod declined by 8.6 percent between the third quarter of 2009 and the third quarter of 2010, although iPod revenues increased by 4 percent to reach $1.5 billion as consumers purchased a higher percentage of iPod Touch models rather than lower-priced iPod Shuffle, iPod Nano, and iPod Classic models.

However, the company did face some concerns going into the fourth quarter of 2010. The U.S. Justice Department had launched a preliminary inquiry into the company's tactics in the digital music industry. Specifically, the government was investigating reports that Apple had discouraged music labels from participating in an Amazon promotion by threatening to withdraw marketing support for songs included in Amazon's promotion that were also sold by the iTunes Store. Also, Steve Jobs was called upon to personally intervene in a flap involving the antenna design of the iPhone 4. Shortly after the iPhone 4 launch, the media widely reported that the iPhone 4's antenna design caused calls to be dropped if users touched the lower edges of the phone. The company reported that the company had received fewer returns of iPhone 4s than iPhone 3GS models at its launch. To calm the media frenzy that he dubbed "Antennagate," Steve Jobs called a press conference to announce that the company would provide free bumper cases to iPhone 4 buyers concerned with reception problems caused by touching the metal edge of the phone.

ENDNOTES

[1] Quoted in "New Gadgets Power Apple Sales," *Wall Street Journal Online,* July 21, 2010.

[2] Quoted in "Doing the iPad Math: Utility + Price + Desire," *New York Times,* April 2, 2010, p. B1.

Starbucks' Strategy and Internal Initiatives to Return to Profitable Growth

Arthur A. Thompson
The University of Alabama

Amit J. Shah
Frostburg State University

Since its founding in 1987 as a modest nine-store operation in Seattle, Washington, Starbucks had become the world's premier roaster and retailer of specialty coffees, with 8,812 company-owned stores and 7,852 licensed stores in more than 50 countries as of April 2010 and annual sales of about $10 billion. But the company's 2008–2009 fiscal years were challenging. Sales at company-owned Starbucks stores open 13 months or longer declined an average of 3 percent in 2008 and another 5 percent in 2009. Company-wide revenues declined from $10.4 billion in fiscal year 2008 to $9.8 billion in fiscal year 2009. During fiscal 2009, Starbucks closed 800 underperforming company-operated stores in the United States and an additional 100 stores in other countries, restructured its entire operations in Australia (including the closure of 61 stores), and reduced the number of planned new store openings by more than 200. Starbucks' global workforce was trimmed by about 6,700 employees. The company's cost-reduction and labor-efficiency initiatives resulted in savings of about $580 million. Exhibit 1 shows the performance of Starbucks' company-operated retail stores for the most recent five fiscal years.

In his November 2009 letter to company shareholders, Howard Schultz, Starbucks' founder, chairman of the board, and chief executive officer, said:

> Two years ago, I expressed concern over challenges confronting our business of a breadth and magnitude unlike anything I had ever seen before. For the first time, we were beginning to see traffic in our U.S. stores slow. Strong competitors were entering our business. And perhaps most troublesome, where in the past Starbucks had always been forward-thinking and nimble in its decision-making and execution, like many fast-growing companies before us, we had allowed our success to make us complacent.
>
> It was obvious to me, and to our leadership team, that Starbucks needed nothing less than a full-fledged transformation to return to profitable growth. Our blueprint for change was the transformation agenda: improving the state of our business through better training, tools, and products; renewing our attention to store-level economics and operating efficiency; reigniting our emotional attachment with customers; and realigning Starbucks' organization for the long term.
>
> Since then, we have worked through the multitude of challenges required to revitalize our brand and transform our company—all in the face of the worst global economic environment of our generation. Today, I am pleased to report that we have made and continue to make significant progress in transforming Starbucks and returning the company to sustainable, profitable growth while preserving our values and guiding principles.
>
> With our progress over the past two years, we are now in a position to take advantage of the global opportunities for Starbucks.[1]

COMPANY BACKGROUND

Starbucks Coffee, Tea, and Spice

Starbucks got its start in 1971 when three academics, English teacher Jerry Baldwin, history

C-334   **Part 2**   Cases in Crafting and Executing Strategy

Exhibit 1   Selected Operating Statistics for Starbucks Stores, Fiscal Years 2005–2009

	Fiscal Years Ending				
	Sept. 27, 2009	Sept. 28, 2008	Sept. 30, 2007	Oct. 1, 2006	Oct. 2, 2005
Net Revenues at Company-Operated Retail Stores ($ millions)					
United States	$ 6,572.1	$ 6,997.7	$ 6,560.9	$ 5,495.2	$ 4,539.5
International	1,608.0	1,774.2	1,437.4	1,087.9	852.5
Operating Income at Company-Operated Retail Stores ($ millions)					
United States	$ 531.8	$ 454.2	$ 1,005.2	$ 955.2	$ 818.5
International	92.9	110.0	137.7	108.5	82.3
Percentage Change in Sales at Company-Operated Stores Open 13 Months or Longer					
United States	−6%	−5%	4%	7%	9%
International	−2%	2%	7%	8%	6%
Worldwide average	−5%	−3%	5%	7%	8%
Average Sales Revenues at Company-Operated Retail Stores					
United States	$938,000	$970,000	$1,048,000	$1,049,000	$1,004,000
United Kingdom and Ireland	$870,000	$924,000	$ 958,000	$ 925,000	$ 853,000
Canada	$835,000	$910,000	$ 918,000	$ 870,000	$ 829,000
China	$549,000	$537,000	$ 508,000	$ 460,000	$ 447,000
All other international locations	$678,000	$681,000	$ 663,000	$ 633,000	$ 605,000
Stores Opened during the Year (net of closures)					
United States					
Company-operated stores	(474)	445	1,065	810	580
Licensed stores	35	438	723	733	596
International					
Company-operated stores	89	236	286	240	177
Licensed stores	305	550	497	416	319
Total store openings (net of closures)	(45)	1,669	2,571	2,199	1,672

Sources: Management Presentation at Barclays Capital Retail and Restaurants Conference on April 28, 2010, www.starbucks.com, accessed June 8, 2010; 2009 10-K report, p. 19 and p. 76; and 2007 10-K report, p. 70.

teacher Zev Siegel, and writer Gordon Bowker—all coffee aficionados—opened Starbucks Coffee, Tea, and Spice in the touristy Pikes Place Market in Seattle. Sharing a love for fine coffees and exotic teas, the three partners believed they could build a clientele in Seattle that would appreciate the best coffees and teas, much like what had already emerged in the San Francisco Bay area. They each invested $1,350 and borrowed another

$5,000 from a bank to open the Pikes Place store. The inspiration and mentor for the Starbucks venture in Seattle was a Dutch immigrant named Alfred Peet who had opened Peet's Coffee and Tea in Berkeley, California, in 1966. Peet's store specialized in importing fine coffees and teas and dark-roasting its own beans the European way to bring out the full flavors of the beans. Customers were encouraged to learn how to grind the beans and make their own freshly brewed coffee at home. Baldwin, Siegel, and Bowker were well acquainted with Peet's expertise, having visited his store on numerous occasions and listened to him expound on quality coffees and the importance of proper bean-roasting techniques.

The Pikes Place store featured modest, hand-built, classic nautical fixtures. One wall was devoted to whole bean coffees, while another had shelves of coffee products. The store did not offer fresh-brewed coffee sold by the cup, but tasting samples were sometimes available. Initially, Siegel was the only paid employee. He wore a grocer's apron, scooped out beans for customers, extolled the virtues of fine, dark-roasted coffees, and functioned as the partnership's retail expert. The other two partners kept their day jobs but came by at lunch or after work to help out. During the start-up period, Baldwin kept the books and developed a growing knowledge of coffee; Bowker served as the "magic, mystery, and romance man."[2] The store was an immediate success, with sales exceeding expectations, partly because of interest stirred by a favorable article in the *Seattle Times*. For most of the first year, Starbucks ordered its coffee beans from Peet's, but then the partners purchased a used roaster from Holland, set up roasting operations in a nearby ramshackle building, and came up with their own blends and flavors.

By the early 1980s, the company had four Starbucks stores in the Seattle area and had been profitable every year since opening its doors. But then Zev Siegel experienced burnout and left the company to pursue other interests. Jerry Baldwin took over day-to-day management of the company and functioned as chief executive officer; Gordon Bowker remained involved as an owner but devoted most of his time to his advertising and design firm, a weekly newspaper he had founded, and a microbrewery that he was launching known as the Redhook Ale Brewery.

Howard Schultz Enters the Picture

In 1981, Howard Schultz, vice president and general manager of U.S. operations for a Swedish maker of stylish kitchen equipment and coffee-makers, decided to pay Starbucks a visit—he was curious about why Starbucks was selling so many

of his company's products. When he arrived at the Pikes Place store, a solo violinist was playing Mozart at the door (his violin case open for donations). Schultz was immediately taken by the powerful and pleasing aroma of the coffees, the wall displaying coffee beans, and the rows of coffeemakers on the shelves. As he talked with the clerk behind the counter, the clerk scooped out some Sumatran coffee beans, ground them, put the grounds in a cone filter, poured hot water over the cone, and shortly handed Schultz a porcelain mug filled with freshly brewed coffee. After taking only three sips of the brew, Schultz was hooked. He began asking questions about the company, the coffees from different parts of the world, and the different ways of roasting coffee.

Later, when he met with Jerry Baldwin and Gordon Bowker, Schultz was struck by their knowledge of coffee, their commitment to providing customers with quality coffees, and their passion for educating customers about the merits of dark-roasted coffees. Baldwin told Schultz, "We don't manage the business to maximize anything other than the quality of the coffee."[3] The company purchased only the finest arabica coffees and put them through a meticulous dark-roasting process to bring out their full flavors. Baldwin explained that the cheap robusta coffees used in supermarket blends burned when subjected to dark-roasting. He also noted that the makers of supermarket blends preferred lighter roasts because it allowed higher yields (the longer a coffee was roasted, the more weight it lost).

Schultz was also struck by the business philosophy of the two partners. It was clear that Starbucks stood not just for good coffee but also for the dark-roasted flavor profiles that the founders were passionate about. Top-quality, fresh-roasted, whole-bean coffee was the company's differentiating feature and a bedrock value. It was also clear to Schultz that Starbucks was strongly committed to educating its customers to appreciate the qualities of fine coffees. The company depended mainly on word of mouth to get more people into its stores, then built customer loyalty cup by cup as buyers gained a sense of discovery and excitement about the taste of fine coffee.

On his return trip to New York, Howard Schultz could not stop thinking about Starbucks and what it would be like to be a part of the Starbucks enterprise. Schultz recalled, "There was something magic about it, a passion and authenticity I had never experienced in business."[4] The appeal of living in the Seattle area was another strong plus. By the time he landed at Kennedy Airport, he knew in his heart he wanted to go to work for Starbucks. At the first opportunity, Schultz asked Baldwin whether there was any way he could fit into Starbucks. While he and Baldwin had established an easy, comfortable personal rapport, it still took a year, numerous meetings at which Schultz presented his ideas, and a lot of convincing to get Baldwin, Bowker, and their silent partner from San Francisco to agree to hire him. Schultz pursued a job at Starbucks far more vigorously than Starbucks pursued hiring Schultz. The owners were nervous about bringing in an outsider, especially a high-powered New Yorker who had not grown up with the values of the company. Nonetheless, Schultz continued to press his ideas about the tremendous potential of expanding the Starbucks enterprise outside Seattle and exposing people all over America to Starbucks coffee.

At a meeting with the three owners in San Francisco in the spring of 1982, Schultz once again presented his ideas and vision for opening Starbucks stores across the United States and Canada. He thought the meeting went well and flew back to New York, believing a job offer was in the bag. However, the next day Jerry Baldwin called Schultz and indicated that the owners had decided against hiring him because geographic expansion was too risky and they did not share Schultz's vision for Starbucks. Schultz was despondent, seeing his dreams of being a part of Starbucks' future go up in smoke. Still, he believed so deeply in Starbucks' potential that he decided to make a last-ditch appeal; he called Baldwin the next day and made an impassioned, reasoned case for why the decision was a mistake. Baldwin agreed to reconsider. The next morning Baldwin called Schultz and told him the job of heading marketing and overseeing the retail stores was his. In September 1982, Howard Schultz took over his new responsibilities at Starbucks.

Starbucks and Howard Schultz, 1982–1985

In his first few months at Starbucks, Schultz spent most of his waking hours in the four Seattle stores—working behind the counters, tasting different kinds of coffee, talking with customers, getting to know store personnel, and learning the retail aspects of the coffee business. By December, Jerry Baldwin concluded that Schultz was ready for the final part of his training: actually roasting the coffee. Schultz spent a week getting an education about the colors of different coffee beans, listening for the telltale second pop of the beans during the roasting process, learning to taste the subtle differences among the various roasts, and familiarizing himself with the roasting techniques for different beans.

Schultz made a point of acclimating himself to the informal dress code at Starbucks, gaining credibility and building trust with colleagues, and making the transition from the high-energy, coat-and-tie style of New York to the more casual, low-key ambience of the Pacific Northwest. Schultz made real headway in gaining the acceptance and respect of company personnel while working at the Pike Place store one day during the busy Christmas season that first year. The store was packed and Schultz was behind the counter ringing up sales of coffee when someone shouted that a shopper had just headed out the door with two coffeemakers. Without thinking, Schultz leaped over the counter and chased the thief, yelling, "Drop that stuff! Drop it!" The thief dropped both pieces and ran. Schultz returned to the store, holding the coffeemakers up like trophies. Everyone applauded. When Schultz returned to his office later that afternoon, his staff had strung up a banner that read: "Make my day."[5]

Schultz was overflowing with ideas for the company. Early on, he noticed that first-time customers sometimes felt uneasy in the stores because of their lack of knowledge about fine coffees and because store employees sometimes came across as a little arrogant or superior to coffee novices. Schultz worked with store employees on customer-friendly sales skills and developed brochures that made it easy for customers to learn about fine coffees. However, Schultz's biggest inspiration and vision for Starbucks' future came during the spring of 1983 when the company sent him to Milan, Italy, to attend an international housewares show. While walking from his hotel to the convention center, he spotted an espresso bar and went inside to look around. The cashier beside the door nodded and smiled. The barista behind the counter greeted Schultz cheerfully and began pulling a shot of espresso for one customer and handcrafting a foamy cappuccino for another, all the while conversing merrily with patrons standing at the counter. Schultz thought the barista's performance was great theater. Just down the way on a side street, he entered an even more crowded espresso bar, where the barista, which he surmised to be the owner, was greeting customers by name; people were laughing and talking in an atmosphere that plainly was comfortable and familiar. In the next few blocks, he saw two more espresso bars. That afternoon when the trade show concluded for the day, Schultz walked the streets of Milan to explore more espresso bars. Some were stylish and upscale; others attracted a blue-collar clientele. Most had few chairs, and it was common for Italian opera to be playing in the background. What struck Schultz was how popular and vibrant the Italian coffee bars were. They seemed to function as an integral community gathering place, and energy levels were typically high. Each bar had its own unique character, but they all had a barista that performed with flair and established a camaraderie with the customers.

Schultz remained in Milan for a week, exploring coffee bars and learning as much as he could about the Italian passion for coffee drinks. Schultz was particularly struck by the fact that there were 1,500 coffee bars in Milan, a city about the size of Philadelphia, and a total of 200,000 in all of Italy. In one bar, he heard a customer order a *caffelatte* and decided to try one himself—the barista made a shot of espresso, steamed a frothy pitcher of milk, poured the two together in a cup, and put a dollop of foam on the top. Schultz liked it immediately, concluding that lattes should be a feature item on any coffee bar menu even though none of the coffee experts he had talked to had ever mentioned them.

Schultz's 1983 trip to Milan produced a revelation: the Starbucks stores in Seattle completely missed the point. There was much more to the coffee business than just selling beans and getting people to appreciate grinding their own beans and brewing fine coffee in their homes. What Starbucks needed to do was serve fresh-brewed coffee, espressos and cappuccinos in its stores (in addition to beans and coffee equipment) and try to create an American version of the Italian

coffee bar culture. Going to Starbucks should be an experience, a special treat, a place to meet friends and visit. Re-creating the authentic Italian coffee bar culture in the United States could be Starbucks' differentiating factor.

Schultz Becomes Frustrated

On Schultz's return from Italy, he shared his revelation and ideas for modifying the format of Starbucks' stores with Baldwin and Bowker. But instead of winning their approval for trying out some of his ideas, Schultz encountered strong resistance. Baldwin and Bowker argued that Starbucks was a retailer, not a restaurant or coffee bar. They feared that serving drinks would put them in the beverage business and diminish the integrity of Starbucks' mission as a purveyor of fine coffees. They pointed out that Starbucks had been profitable every year and there was no reason to rock the boat in a small, private company like Starbucks. But a more pressing reason not to pursue Schultz's coffee bar concept emerged shortly—Baldwin and Bowker were excited by an opportunity to purchase Peet's Coffee and Tea. The acquisition was finalized in early 1984, and to fund it Starbucks had to take on considerable debt, leaving little in the way of financial flexibility to support Schultz's ideas for entering the beverage part of the coffee business or expanding the number of Starbucks stores. For most of 1984, Starbucks managers were dividing their time between operations in Seattle and the Peet's enterprise in San Francisco. Schultz found himself in San Francisco every other week supervising the marketing and operations of the five Peet stores. Starbucks employees began to feel neglected and, in one quarter, did not receive their usual bonus due to tight financial conditions. Employee discontent escalated to the point where a union election was called. The union won by three votes. Baldwin was shocked at the results, concluding that employees no longer trusted him. In the months that followed, he began to spend more of his energy on the Peet's operation in San Francisco.

It took Howard Schultz nearly a year to convince Jerry Baldwin to let him test an espresso bar. Baldwin relented when Starbucks opened its sixth store in April 1984. It was the first Starbucks store designed to sell beverages, and it was the first located in downtown Seattle. Schultz asked for a 1,500-square-foot space to set up a full-scale Italian-style espresso bar, but Baldwin agreed to allocating only 300 square feet in a corner of the new store. The store opened with no fanfare as a deliberate experiment to see what would happen. By closing time on the first day, some 400 customers had been served, well above the 250-customer average of Starbucks' best-performing stores. Within two months, the store was serving 800 customers per day. The two baristas could not keep up with orders during the early-morning hours, resulting in lines outside the door onto the sidewalk. Most of the business was at the espresso counter, while sales at the regular retail counter were only adequate.

Schultz was elated at the test results, expecting that Baldwin's doubts about entering the beverage side of the business would be dispelled and that he would gain approval to pursue the opportunity to take Starbucks to a new level. Every day he went into Baldwin's office to show him the sales figures and customer counts at the new downtown store. But Baldwin was not comfortable with the success of the new store, believing that it felt wrong and that espresso drinks were a distraction from the core business of marketing fine arabica coffees at retail. Baldwin rebelled at the thought that people would see Starbucks as a place to get a quick cup of coffee to go. He adamantly told Schultz, "We're coffee roasters. I don't want to be in the restaurant business. . . . Besides, we're too deeply in debt to consider pursuing this idea."[6] While he didn't deny that the experiment was succeeding, he didn't want to go forward with introducing beverages in other Starbucks stores. Schultz's efforts to persuade Baldwin to change his mind continued to meet strong resistance, although to avoid a total impasse Baldwin finally did agree to let Schultz put espresso machines in the back of one or two other Starbucks stores.

Over the next several months, Schultz made up his mind to leave Starbucks and start his own company. His plan was to open espresso bars in high-traffic downtown locations, serve espresso drinks and coffee by the cup, and try to emulate the friendly, energetic atmosphere he had encountered in Italian espresso bars. Baldwin and Bowker, knowing how frustrated Schultz had become, supported his efforts to go out on his own and agreed to let him stay in his current job and office until definitive plans were in place. Schultz left Starbucks in late 1985.

Schultz's Il Giornale Venture

With the aid of a lawyer friend who helped companies raise venture capital and go public, Schultz began seeking out investors for the kind of company he had in mind. Ironically, Jerry Baldwin committed to investing $150,000 of Starbucks' money in Schultz's coffee bar enterprise, thus becoming Schultz's first investor. Baldwin accepted Schultz's invitation to be a director of the new company, and Gordon Bowker agreed to be a part-time consultant for six months. Bowker, pumped up about the new venture, urged Schultz to make sure that everything about the new stores—the name, the presentation, the care taken in preparing the coffee—was calculated to elevate customer expectations and lead them to expect something better than competitors offered. Bowker proposed that the new company be named Il Giornale Coffee Company (pronounced *il jor NAHL ee*), a suggestion that Howard accepted. In December 1985, Bowker and Schultz made a trip to Italy, where they visited some 500 espresso bars in Milan and Verona, observing local habits, taking notes about decor and menus, snapping photographs, and videotaping baristas in action.

About $400,000 in seed capital was raised by the end of January 1986, enough to rent an office, hire a couple of key employees, develop a store design, and open the first store. But it took until the end of 1986 to raise the remaining $1.25 million needed to launch at least eight espresso bars and prove that Schultz's strategy and business model were viable. Schultz made presentations to 242 potential investors, 217 of whom said no. Many who heard Schultz's hourlong presentation saw coffee as a commodity business and thought that Schultz's espresso bar concept lacked any basis for sustainable competitive advantage (no patent on dark roast, no advantage in purchasing coffee beans, no ways to bar the entry of imitative competitors). Some noted that coffee couldn't be turned into a growth business—consumption of coffee had been declining since the mid-1960s. Others were skeptical that people would pay $1.50 or more for a cup of coffee, and the company's hard-to-pronounce name turned some off. Being rejected by so many potential investors was disheartening—some who listened to Schultz's presentation didn't even bother to call him back; others refused to take his calls. Nonetheless, Schultz maintained an upbeat attitude and displayed passion and enthusiasm in making his pitch. He ended up raising $1.65 million from about 30 investors; most of the money came from 9 people, 5 of whom became directors.

The first Il Giornale store opened in April 1986. It had 700 square feet and was located near the entrance of Seattle's tallest building. The decor was Italian, and there were Italian words on the menu. Italian opera music played in the background. The baristas wore white shirts and bow ties. All service was stand-up; there were no chairs. National and international papers were hung on rods on the wall. By closing time on the first day, 300 customers had been served—mostly in the morning hours.

But while the core idea worked well, it soon became apparent that several aspects of the format were not appropriate for Seattle. Some customers objected to the incessant opera music, others wanted a place to sit down, and many did not understand the Italian words on the menu. These "mistakes" were quickly fixed, but an effort was made not to compromise the style and elegance of the store. Within six months, the store was serving more than 1,000 customers a day. Regular customers had learned how to pronounce the company's name. Because most customers were in a hurry, it became apparent that speedy service was essential.

Six months after the first Il Giornale opened, a second store was opened in another downtown building. In April 1987, a third store was opened in Vancouver, British Columbia, to test the transferability of the company's business concept outside Seattle. Schultz's goal was to open 50 stores in five years, and he needed to dispel his investors' doubts about geographic expansion early on to achieve his growth objective. By mid-1987, sales at the three stores were running at a rate equal to $1.5 million annually.

Il Giornale Acquires Starbucks

In March 1987, Jerry Baldwin and Gordon Bowker decided to sell the whole Starbucks operation in Seattle—the stores, the roasting plant, and the Starbucks name. Bowker wanted to cash out his coffee business investment to concentrate on his other enterprises; Baldwin, who was tired of commuting between Seattle and San Francisco, wanted to concentrate on the Peet's operation. As he recalls, "My wife and I had a 30-second conversation and decided to keep Peet's. It was the original and it was better."[7]

Schultz knew immediately that he had to buy Starbucks; his board of directors agreed. Schultz and his newly hired finance and accounting manager drew up a set of financial projections for the combined operations and a financing package that included a stock offering to Il Giornale's original investors and a line of credit with local banks. While a rival plan to acquire Starbucks was put together by another Il Giornale investor, Schultz's proposal prevailed and within weeks Schultz had raised the $3.8 million needed to buy Starbucks. The acquisition was completed in August 1987. The new name of the combined companies was Starbucks Corporation. Howard Schultz, at the age of 34, became Starbucks' president and CEO.

STARBUCKS AS A PRIVATE COMPANY, 1987–1992

The following Monday morning, Howard returned to the Starbucks offices at the roasting plant, greeted all the familiar faces, and accepted their congratulations. Then he called the staff together for a meeting on the roasting plant floor:

> All my life I have wanted to be part of a company and a group of people who share a common vision. . . . I'm here today because I love this company. I love what it represents. . . . I know you're concerned. . . . I promise you I will not let you down. I promise you I will not leave anyone behind. . . . In five years, I want you to look back at this day and say "I was there when it started. I helped build this company into something great."[8]

Schultz told the group that his vision was for Starbucks to become a national company with values and guiding principles that employees could be proud of. He indicated that he wanted to include people in the decision-making process and that he would be open and honest with them.

Schultz believed that building a company that valued and respected its people, that inspired them, and that shared the fruits of success with those who contributed to the company's long-term value was essential, not just an intriguing option. His aspiration was for Starbucks to become the most respected brand name in coffee and for the company to be admired for its corporate responsibility. In the next few days and weeks, Schultz came to see that the unity and morale at Starbucks had deteriorated badly in the 20 months he had been at Il Giornale. Some employees were cynical and felt unappreciated. There was a feeling that prior management had abandoned them and a wariness about what the new regime would bring. Schultz decided to make building a new relationship of mutual respect between employees and management a priority.

The business plan Schultz had presented investors called for the new 9-store company to open 125 stores in the next five years—15 the first year, 20 the second, 25 the third, 30 the fourth, and 35 the fifth. Revenues were projected to reach $60 million in 1992. But the company lacked experienced management. Schultz had never led a growth effort of such magnitude and was just learning what the job of CEO was all about, having been the president of a small company for barely two years. Dave Olsen, a Seattle coffee bar owner whom Schultz had recruited to direct store operations at Il Giornale, was still learning the ropes in managing a multistore operation. Ron Lawrence, the company's controller, had worked as a controller for several organizations. Other Starbucks employees had only the experience of managing or being a part of a six-store organization. When Starbucks' key roaster and coffee buyer resigned, Schultz put Dave Olsen in charge of buying and roasting coffee. Lawrence Maltz, who had 20 years' experience in business and 8 years' experience as president of a profitable public beverage company, was hired as executive vice president and charged with heading operations, finance, and human resources.

In the next several months, a number of changes were instituted. To symbolize the merging of the two companies and the two cultures, a new logo was created that melded the designs of the Starbucks logo and the Il Giornale logo. The Starbucks stores were equipped with espresso machines and remodeled to look more Italian than Old World nautical. Il Giornale green replaced the traditional Starbucks brown. The result was a new type of store—a cross between a retail coffee bean store and an espresso bar/café—that became Starbucks' signature.

By December 1987, the mood of the employees at Starbucks had turned upbeat. They were buying into the changes that Schultz was making, and trust began to build between management and employees. New stores were on the verge of opening in Vancouver and Chicago. One Starbucks store employee, Daryl Moore, who had started working at Starbucks in 1981 and who had voted against unionization in 1985, began to question the need for a union with his fellow employees. Over the next few weeks, Moore began a move to decertify the union. He carried a decertification letter around to Starbucks' stores securing the signatures of employees who no longer wished to be represented by the union. He got a majority of store employees to sign the letter and presented it to the National Labor Relations Board. The union representing store employees was decertified. Later, in 1992, the union representing Starbucks' roasting plant and warehouse employees was also decertified.

Market Expansion Outside the Pacific Northwest

Starbucks' entry into Chicago proved far more troublesome than management anticipated. The first Chicago store opened in October 1987, and three more stores were opened over the next six months. Customer counts at the stores were substantially below expectations. Chicagoans did not take to dark-roasted coffee as fast as Schultz had anticipated. The first downtown store opened onto the street rather than into the lobby of the building where it was located; in the winter months, customers were hesitant to go out in the wind and cold to acquire a cup of coffee. It was expensive to supply fresh coffee to the Chicago stores out of the Seattle warehouse (the company solved the problem of freshness and quality assurance by putting freshly roasted beans in special FlavorLock bags that used vacuum packaging techniques with a one-way valve to allow carbon dioxide to escape without allowing air and moisture in). Rents were higher in Chicago than in Seattle, and so were wage rates. The result was a squeeze on store profit margins. Gradually, customer counts improved, but Starbucks lost money on its Chicago stores until, in 1990, prices were raised to reflect higher rents and labor costs, more experienced store mangers were hired, and a critical mass of customers caught on to the taste of Starbucks products.

Portland, Oregon, was the next market entered, and Portland coffee drinkers took to Starbucks products quickly. By 1991, the Chicago stores had become profitable and the company was ready for its next big market entry. Management decided on California because of its host of neighborhood centers and the receptiveness of Californians to innovative, high-quality food. Los Angeles was chosen as the first California market to enter, principally because of its status as a trendsetter and its cultural ties to the rest of the country. L.A. consumers embraced Starbucks quickly, and the *Los Angeles Times* named Starbucks as the best coffee in America before the first store opened. The entry into San Francisco proved more troublesome because San Francisco had an ordinance against converting stores to restaurant-related uses in certain prime urban neighborhoods; Starbucks could sell beverages and pastries to customers at stand-up counters but could not offer seating in stores that had formerly been used for general retailing. However, the city council was soon convinced by café owners and real estate brokers to change the code. Still, Starbucks faced strong competition from Peet's and local espresso bars in the San Francisco market.

Starbucks' store expansion targets proved easier to meet than Schultz had originally anticipated, and he upped the numbers to keep challenging the organization. Starbucks opened 15 new stores in fiscal 1988, 20 in 1989, 30 in 1990, 32 in 1991, and 53 in 1992—producing a total of 161 stores, significantly above his original 1992 target of 125 stores.

From the outset, the strategy was to open only company-owned stores; franchising was avoided so as to keep the company in full control of the quality of its products and the character and location of its stores. But company owner-

ship of all stores required Starbucks to raise new venture capital to cover the cost of new store expansion. In 1988, the company raised $3.9 million; in 1990, venture capitalists provided an additional $13.5 million; and, in 1991, another round of venture capital financing generated $15 million. Starbucks was able to raise the needed funds despite posting losses of $330,000 in 1987, $764,000 in 1988, and $1.2 million in 1989. While the losses were troubling to Starbucks' board of directors and investors, Schultz's business plan had forecast losses during the early years of expansion. At a particularly tense board meeting where directors sharply questioned him about the lack of profitability, Schultz said:

> Look, we're going to keep losing money until we can do three things. We have to attract a management team well beyond our expansion needs. We have to build a world-class roasting facility. And we need a computer information system sophisticated enough to keep track of sales in hundreds and hundreds of stores.[9]

Schultz argued for patience as the company invested in the infrastructure to support continued growth well into the 1990s. He contended that hiring experienced executives ahead of the growth curve, building facilities far beyond current needs, and installing support systems laid a strong foundation for rapid, profitable growth down the road. His arguments carried the day with the board and with investors, especially since revenues were growing by approximately 80 percent annually and customer traffic at the stores was meeting or exceeding expectations.

Starbucks became profitable in 1990. Profits had increased every year since 1990 except for fiscal year 2000 (because of a $58.8 million in investment write-offs in four dot-com enterprises) and for fiscal year 2008 (when the sharp global economic downturn hit the company's bottom line very hard). Because of the economic downturn in 2008–2009, Howard Schultz believed that new strategic initiatives and rejuvenated strategy execution efforts were very much needed at Starbucks. Exhibit 2 provides a summary of the company's financial performance for fiscal years 2005–2009. Exhibit 3 shows the long-term performance of the company's stock price; the stock had split 2-for-1 five times.

Exhibit 2   **Financial Summary for Starbucks Corporation, Fiscal Years 2005–2009 ($ billions, except for per share amounts)**

	Fiscal Years Ending*				
	Sept. 27, 2009	Sept. 28, 2008	Sept. 30, 2007	Oct. 1, 2006	Oct. 2, 2005
Results of Operations Data					
Net revenues:					
Company-operated retail store revenues	$8,180.1	$ 8,771.9	$7,998.3	$ 6,583.1	$ 5,391.9
Specialty revenues:					
Licensing	1,222.3	1,171.6	1,026.3	860.6	673
Foodservice and other	372.2	439.5	386.9	343.2	304.4
Total specialty revenues	1,594.5	1,611.1	1,413.2	1,203.8	977.4
Total net revenues	$9,774.6	$10,383.0	$ 9,411.5	$7,786.9	$6,369.3
Cost of sales, including occupancy costs	4,324.9	4,645.3	3,999.1	3,178.8	2,605.2
Store operating expenses	3,425.1	3,745.3	3,215.9	2,687.8	2,165.9
Other operating expenses	264.4	330.1	294.2	253.7	192.5
Depreciation and amortization expenses	534.7	549.3	467.2	387.2	340.2
General and administrative expenses	453.0	456.0	489.2	479.4	361.6
Restructuring charges	332.4	266.9	—	—	—
Total operating expenses	9,334.5	9,992.7	8,465.6	6,986.9	5,665.4
Income from equity investees	121.9	113.6	108.0	93.9	76.6
Operating income	$ 562.0	$ 503.9	$1,053.9	$ 894.0	$ 780.5
Earnings before cumulative effect of change in accounting principle	390.8	315.5	672.6	581.5	494.4
Cumulative effect of accounting change for asset retirement obligations, net of taxes	—	—	—	17.2	—
Net earnings	$ 390.8	$ 315.5	$ 672.6	$ 564.3	$ 494.4
Net earnings per common share—diluted	$0.52	$0.43	$0.87	$0.71	$0.61
Balance Sheet Data					
Current assets	$2,035.8	$ 1,748.0	$1,696.5	$1,529.8	$1,209.3
Current liabilities	1,581.0	2,189.7	2,155.6	1,935.6	1,227.0
Total assets	5,576.8	5,672.6	5,343.9	4,428.9	3,513.7
Short-term borrowings	—	713	710.3	700	277
Long-term debt (including current portion)	549.5	550.3	550.9	2.7	3.6
Shareholders' equity	$3,045.7	$ 2,490.9	$2,284.1	$2,228.5	$2,090.3
Cash Flow Data					
Net cash provided by operating activities	$1,389.0	$1,258.7	$ 1,331.2	$ 1,131.6	$922.9
Capital expenditures (net additions to property, plant and equipment)	$445.6	$984.5	$1,080.3	$771.2	$643.3

*The company's fiscal year ended on the Sunday closest to September 30.

Source: Starbucks, 2009, 2007 and 2005 10-K reports.

Exhibit 3   **The Performance of Starbucks' Stock, 1993–2010**

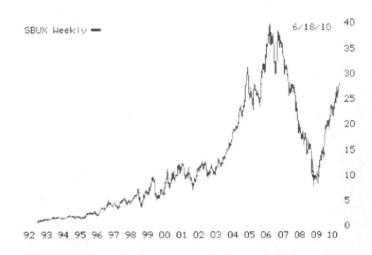

Source: Wall Street Journal, http://online.wsj.com, accessed June 18, 2010.

STARBUCKS STORES: DESIGN, AMBIENCE, AND EXPANSION OF LOCATIONS

Store Design

Starting in 1991, Starbucks created its own in-house team of architects and designers to ensure that each store would convey the right image and character. Stores had to be custom-designed because the company didn't buy real estate or build its own freestanding structures; rather, each space was leased in an existing structure, making each store differ in size and shape. Most stores ranged in size from 1,000 to 1,500 square feet and were located in office buildings, downtown and suburban retail centers, airport terminals, university campus areas, and busy neighborhood shopping areas convenient for pedestrian foot traffic and/or drivers. Only a select few were in suburban malls.

A "stores of the future" project team was formed in 1995 to raise Starbucks' store design to a still higher level and come up with the next generation of Starbucks stores. The team came

up with four store designs—one for each of the four stages of coffeemaking: growing, roasting, brewing, and aroma—each with its own color combinations, lighting scheme, and component materials. Within each of the four basic store templates, Starbucks could vary the materials and details to adapt to different store sizes and settings (downtown buildings, college campuses, neighborhood shopping areas). In late 1996, Starbucks began opening new stores based on one of four formats and color schemes.

But as the number of stores increased rapidly between 2000 and 2003, greater store diversity and layout quickly became necessary. Some stores had special seating areas to help make Starbucks a desirable gathering place where customers could meet and chat or simply enjoy a peaceful interlude in their day. Flagship stores in high-traffic, high-visibility locations had fireplaces, leather chairs, newspapers, couches, and lots of ambience. The company also experimented with drive-through windows in locations where speed and convenience were important to customers and with kiosks in supermarkets, building lobbies, and other public places. In recent years, Starbucks had begun emphasizing drive-through retail stores in order to provide a greater degree of access and convenience for nonpedestrian customers. At the end of fiscal 2009, Starbucks had around 2,650 drive-through locations.[10]

In June 2009, Starbucks announced a new global store design strategy. Each new store was to be a reflection of the environment in which it operated and was to be environmentally friendly. In 2010, Starbucks began an effort to achieve Leadership in Energy and Environmental Design (LEED) certification for all new company-owned stores. (LEED certification was a program that used independent third parties to certify that a building incorporated green building design, construction, operations, and maintenance solutions.)[11] Core characteristics of each new store included celebration of local materials and craftsmanship, a focus on reused and recycled elements, exposure of structural integrity and authentic roots, elevation of coffee and removal of unnecessary distractions, storytelling and customer engagement through all five senses, and flexibility to meet the needs of many customer types.[12] Exhibit 4 shows the diverse nature of Starbucks stores.

To better control average store opening costs, the company centralized buying, developed standard contracts and fixed fees for certain items, and consolidated work under those contractors who displayed good cost-control practices. The retail operations group outlined exactly the minimum amount of equipment each core store needed so that standard items could be ordered in volume from vendors at 20 to 30 percent discounts, then delivered just in time to the store site either from company warehouses or the vendor. Modular designs for display cases were developed. The layouts for new and remodeled stores were developed on a computer, with software that allowed the costs to be estimated as the design evolved. All this cut store opening and remodeling costs significantly and shortened the process to about 18 weeks.

Store Ambience

Starbucks management viewed each store as a billboard for the company and as a contributor to building the company's brand and image. The company went to great lengths to make sure that store fixtures, merchandise displays, colors, artwork, banners, music, and aromas all blended to create a consistent, inviting, stimulating environment that evoked the romance of coffee; that signaled the company's passion for coffee; that enhanced the mood and ambience of the store; and that rewarded customers with ceremony, stories, surprise, and a satisfying experience. The thesis was that every detail mattered in making Starbucks stores a welcoming and pleasant "third place" (apart from home and work) where people could meet friends and family, enjoy a quiet moment alone with a newspaper or book, or simply spend quality time relaxing.

To try to keep the coffee aromas in the stores pure, Starbucks banned smoking and asked employees to refrain from wearing perfumes or colognes. Prepared foods were kept covered so that customers would smell coffee only. Colorful banners and posters were used to keep the look of Starbucks stores fresh and to highlight seasons and holidays. Company designers came up with artwork for commuter mugs and T-shirts in different cities that were in keeping with each city's personality (peach-shaped coffee mugs for Atlanta, pictures of Paul Revere for Boston and the Statue of Liberty for New York).

In August 2002, Starbucks teamed up with T-Mobile USA to experiment with providing Internet access and enhanced digital entertainment to patrons at more than 1,200 Starbucks locations. The objective was to heighten the "third place" Starbucks experience, entice customers into perhaps buying a second latte or espresso while they caught up on e-mail, listened to digital music, put the finishing touches on a presentation, or surfed the Internet. Since the August 2002 introduction of Wi-Fi at Starbucks, wireless Internet service had been added at most company-operated stores in the United States. In an effort to better bridge Starbucks' "third place" coffeehouse experience with digital and social media, Starbucks announced that, beginning July 1, 2010, it would provide free Wi-Fi one-click Internet service through AT&T in all company-operated stores in the United States. There were also plans for a new online customer experience called the Starbucks Digital Network, in partnership with Yahoo, to debut in the fall of 2010 in U.S. company-operated Starbucks stores. This online experience would provide customers with free unrestricted access—via laptop, e-reader, or smartphone—to various paid sites and services such as the *Wall Street Journal*'s site

Exhibit 4   **Scenes from Starbucks Stores**

(www.wsj.com), exclusive content and previews, free downloads, and local community news and activities.

Store Expansion Strategy

In 1992 and 1993, Starbucks developed a three-year geographic expansion strategy to target areas that not only had favorable demographic profiles but also could be serviced and supported by the company's operations infrastructure. For each targeted region, Starbucks selected a large city to serve as a "hub"; teams of professionals were located in hub cities to support the goal of opening 20 or more stores in the hub in the first two years. Once a number of stores were opened in a hub, then additional stores were opened in smaller, surrounding "spoke" areas in the region. To oversee the expansion process, Starbucks had zone vice presidents who oversaw the store expansion process in a geographic region and instilled the Starbucks culture in the newly opened stores.

In recent years, Starbucks' strategy in major metropolitan cities had been to blanket major cities with stores, even if some stores cannibalized a nearby store's business. While a new store might draw 30 percent of the business of an existing store two or so blocks away, management believed that a "Starbucks everywhere" strategy cut down on delivery and management costs, shortened customer lines at individual stores, and increased foot traffic for all the stores in an area. In 2002, new stores generated an average of $1.2 million in first-year revenues, compared with $700,000 in 1995 and only $427,000 in 1990. The steady increases in new-store revenues were due partly to growing popularity of premium coffee drinks, partly to Starbucks' growing reputation, and partly to expanded product offerings. But the strategy of blanketing metropolitan areas with stores had cannibalized sales of existing stores to such an extent that average sales per store in the United States had dropped to around $1 million annually. Starbucks' long-term profitability target for its retail stores in the United States was an operating profit margin in the high teens—the operating margin was 14.3 percent in fiscal 2007, but declining store sales and depressed economic conditions had driven the margins down to 6.0 percent in fiscal 2008 and 7.5 percent in fiscal 2009.

One of Starbucks' core competencies was identifying good retailing sites for its new stores. The company was regarded as having the best real estate team in the coffee bar industry and a sophisticated system for identifying not only the most attractive individual city blocks but also the exact store location that was best; it also worked hard at building good relationships with local real estate representatives in areas where it was opening multiple store locations.

Licensed Retail Stores In 1995, Starbucks began entering into licensing agreements for store locations in areas where it did not have ability to locate its own outlets. Two early licensing agreements were with Marriott Host International to operate Starbucks retail stores in airport locations and with Aramark Food and Services to put Starbucks stores on university campuses and other locations operated by Aramark. Very quickly, Starbucks began to make increased use of licensing, both domestically and internationally. Starbucks preferred licensing to franchising because licensing permitted tighter controls over the operations of licensees.

Starbucks received a license fee and a royalty on sales at all licensed locations and supplied the coffee for resale at these locations. All licensed stores had to follow Starbucks' detailed operating procedures, and all managers and employees who worked in these stores received the same training given to managers and employees in company-operated Starbucks stores. As of 2009, there were 4,364 licensed stores in the United States and 3,439 licensed stores internationally.

International Expansion In markets outside the continental United States (including Hawaii), Starbucks had a two-pronged store expansion: either open company-owned and -operated stores or else license a reputable and capable local company with retailing know-how in the target host country to develop and operate new Starbucks stores. In most countries, Starbucks used a local partner/licensee to help it recruit talented individuals, set up supplier relationships, locate suitable store sites, and cater to local market conditions. Starbucks looked for partners/licensees that had strong retail/restaurant experience, had values and a corporate culture compatible with Starbucks, were committed to good customer service, possessed talented management and strong financial resources, and had demonstrated brand-building skills. In those foreign countries where business risks were deemed relatively high, most if not all Starbucks stores were licensed rather than being company-owned and operated. As of September 2009, Starbucks had company-operated and licensed stores in 50 countries (see Exhibit 5) and expected to open 200 new stores internationally in fiscal 2010.

Starbucks' long-term profitability target for its international operations was an operating profit margin in the mid-to-high teens. But the margins in recent years had been far below the

Exhibit 5   Company-Operated and Franchised Starbucks Stores

A. Number of Starbucks Store Locations Worldwide, 1987–March 2010 (selected years)

End of Fiscal Year*	Company-Operated Store Locations		Licensed Store Locations		Worldwide Total
	United States	International	United States	International	
1987	17	0	0	0	17
1990	84	0	0	0	84
1995	627	0	49	0	676
2000	2,446	530	173	352	3,501
2005	4,918	1,217	2,435	1,671	10,241
2006	5,728	1,457	3,168	2,087	12,440
2007	6,793	1,743	3,891	2,584	15,011
2008	7,238	1,979	4,329	3,134	16,680
2009	6,764	2,068	4,364	3,439	16,635
March 28, 2010	6,736	2,076	4,385	3,467	16,664

B. International Starbucks Store Locations at End of Fiscal Year 2009

International Locations of Company-Operated Starbucks Stores		International Locations of Licensed Starbucks Stores					
		Americas		Asia-Pacific		Europe/Africa/Middle East	
Canada	775	Canada	262	Japan	875	Turkey	123
United Kingdom	666	Mexico	261	South Korea	288	United Arab Emirates	91
China	191	Other	69	China	283	Spain	76
Germany	144			Taiwan	222	Greece	69
Thailand	131			Philippines	160	Saudi Arabia	68
Singapore	64			Malaysia	118	Kuwait	62
Australia	23			Indonesia	74	France	52
Other	74			New Zealand	42	Switzerland	47
Total	2,068					United Kingdom	46
						Other	151
						Licensed total worldwide	3,439

*Starbucks' fiscal year ended on the Sunday closest to September 30.
Source: Starbucks, 10-K reports, various years, and company records.

target: 8.1 percent in fiscal 2007, 5.2 percent in fiscal 2008, and 4.5 percent in fiscal 2009.

STARBUCKS' STRATEGY TO EXPAND ITS PRODUCT OFFERINGS AND ENTER NEW MARKET SEGMENTS

In the mid-1990s, thinking it was time for Starbucks to move out into mainstream markets, Howard Schultz led what proved to be an ongoing series of initiatives to expand Starbucks' product offerings beyond its retail stores and to pursue sales of Starbucks products in a wider variety of distribution channels and market segments. The strategy was to make Starbucks products more accessible to both existing and new customers where they worked, traveled, shopped, and dined and to find and promote new occasions for enjoying Starbucks products. The strategic objectives were to capitalize on Starbucks' growing brand awareness and brand-name strength and create a broader foundation for sustained long-term growth in revenues and profits.

The first initiative involved the establishment of an in-house specialty sales group to begin marketing Starbucks coffee products to restaurants, airlines, hotels, universities, hospitals, business offices, country clubs, and select retailers. Early users of Starbucks coffee included Horizon Airlines, a regional carrier based in Seattle, and United Airlines. There was much internal debate at Starbucks about whether it made sense for Starbucks coffee to be served on all United flights (since there was different coffeemaking equipment on different planes) and the possible damage to the integrity of the Starbucks brand if the quality of the coffee served did not measure up. It took seven months of negotiations for Starbucks and United to arrive at a mutually agreeable way to handle quality control on United's various types of planes. The specialty sales group also won accounts at Hyatt, Hilton, Sheraton, Radisson, and Westin hotels, resulting in packets of Starbucks coffee being in each room with coffeemaking equipment. Starbucks entered into an agreement with Wells Fargo to provide coffee service at some of the bank's locations in California. Later, the specialty sales group began working with leading institutional foodservice distributors, including Sysco Corporation and US Foodservice, to handle the distribution of Starbucks products to hotels, restaurants, office coffee distributors, educational and health care institutions, and other such enterprises. In fiscal 2009, Starbucks generated revenues of $372.2 million from providing whole bean and ground coffees and assorted other Starbucks products to some 21,000 food service accounts.

The second initiative came in 1994 when PepsiCo and Starbucks entered into a joint venture (now called the North American Coffee Partnership) to create new coffee-related products in bottles or cans for mass distribution through Pepsi channels. Howard Schultz saw the venture with PepsiCo as a major paradigm shift with the potential to cause Starbucks' business to evolve in heretofore unimaginable directions. The joint venture's first new product, Mazagran, a lightly flavored carbonated coffee drink, was a failure. Then, at a meeting with Pepsi executives, Schultz suggested developing a bottled version of Frappuccino, a new cold coffee drink that Starbucks had begun serving at its retail stores in the summer of 1995 and that quickly became a big hot-weather seller. Pepsi executives were enthusiastic. After months of experimentation, the joint venture product research team came up with a shelf-stable version of Frappuccino that tasted quite good. It was tested in West Coast supermarkets in the summer of 1996; sales ran 10 times projections, with 70 percent being repeat business. Sales of Frappuccino ready-to-drink beverages reached $125 million in 1997 and achieved national supermarket penetration of 80 percent. Starbucks' management believed that the market for Frappuccino would ultimately exceed $1 billion. The company began selling ready-to-drink Frappuccino products in Japan, Taiwan, and South Korea in 2005 chiefly through agreements with leading local distributors; the ready-to-drink beverage market in these countries represented more than $10 billion in annual sales.[13] In 2007, the PepsiCo-Starbucks partnership introduced a line of chilled Starbucks Doubleshot espresso drinks in the United States. Also in 2007, PepsiCo and Starbucks entered into a second joint venture called the International Coffee Partnership (ICP) for the purpose of introducing Starbucks-related beverages in country markets outside North America; one of the ICP's early moves was to begin marketing Frappuccino in China.[14] As of 2010, sales of Frappuccino products worldwide had reached $2 billion annually.[15]

In 2008, Starbucks partnered with Suntory to begin selling chilled ready-to-drink Doubleshot drinks in Japan. In 2010, Starbucks partnered with Arla Foods to begin selling Doubleshot products and Starbucks Discoveries chilled cup coffees in retail stores (as well as in Starbucks retail stores) across the United Kingdom.

In October 1995, Starbucks partnered with Dreyer's Grand Ice Cream to supply coffee extract for a new line of coffee ice cream made and distributed by Dreyer's under the Starbucks brand. By July 1996, Starbucks coffee-flavored ice cream was the number-one-selling superpremium brand in the coffee segment. In 2008, Starbucks discontinued its arrangement with Dreyer's and entered into an exclusive agreement with Unilever to manufacture, market, and distribute Starbucks-branded ice creams in the United States and Canada. Unilever was considered the global leader in ice cream, with annual sales of about $6 billion; its ice cream brands included Ben & Jerry's, Breyers, and Good Humor. Seven flavors of Starbucks ice cream and two flavors of novelty bars were marketed in 2010. Pints were available in the freezer sections at supermarkets for a suggested retail price of $3.99; the novelty bars sold for a suggested retail price of $2.49 and were also available in many convenience stores.

In 1997, a Starbucks store manager who had worked in the music industry and selected the music Starbucks played as background in its stores suggested that Starbucks begin selling the background music on tapes (and later on CDs as they become the preferred format). The manager had gotten compliments from customers wanting to buy the music they heard and suggested to senior executives that there was a market for the company's handpicked music. Research through two years of comment cards turned up hundreds asking Starbucks to sell the music it played in its stores. The Starbucks tapes/CDs proved a significant seller as an addition to the company's product line. In 2000, Starbucks acquired Hear Music, a San Francisco–based company, to give it added capability in enhancing its music CD offerings. In 2004, Starbucks introduced Hear Music media bars, a service that offered custom CD burning at select Starbucks stores. Later, Starbucks began offering customers the option of downloading music from the company's 200,000+ song library and, if they wished, having the downloaded songs burned onto a CD for purchase.

In the spring of 2008, Starbucks, in partnership with Apple's iTunes, began offering a Pick of the Week music card at its 7,000 stores in the United States that allowed customers to download each week's music selection at iTunes.[16] In 2010, Starbucks was continuing to offer CDs with handpicked music and new CDs featuring particular artists, all managed by Starbucks Entertainment in conjunction with Concord Music Group (which began managing the Hear Music Record Label in 2008); the CDs were typically priced at $12.95. Starbucks also had established a relationship with the William Morris Agency to identify books that it could offer for sale in its stores. Over the years, Starbucks' successes in music and books had included eight Grammy Awards and three number one books on the *New York Times* best-seller list.

In 1998, Starbucks licensed Kraft Foods to market and distribute Starbucks whole bean and ground coffees in grocery and mass-merchandise channels across the United States. Kraft managed all distribution, marketing, advertising, and promotions and paid a royalty to Starbucks based on a percentage of net sales. Product freshness was guaranteed by Starbucks' FlavorLock packaging, and the price per pound paralleled the prices in Starbucks' retail stores. Flavor selections in supermarkets were more limited than the varieties at Starbucks stores. The licensing relationship with Kraft was later expanded to include the marketing and distribution of Starbucks coffees in the United Kingdom and Europe. Going into 2010, Starbucks coffees were available in some 33,500 grocery and warehouse clubs in the United States and 5,500 retail outlets outside the United States; Starbucks' revenues from these sales were approximately $370 million in fiscal 2009.[17]

In 1999, Starbucks purchased Tazo Tea for $8.1 million. Tazo Tea, a tea manufacturer and distributor based in Portland, Oregon, was founded in 1994 and marketed its teas to restaurants, food stores, and tea houses. Starbucks proceeded to introduce hot and iced Tazo Tea drinks in its retail stores. As part of a long-term campaign to expand the distribution of its line of superpremium Tazo teas, Starbucks expanded its agreement with Kraft to market and distribute Tazo teas worldwide. In August 2008, Starbucks entered into an agreement with PepsiCo and Unilever (Lipton Tea was one of Unilever's leading brands) to manufacture, market, and distribute Starbucks' superpremium Tazo Tea ready-to-drink beverages (including iced teas, juiced teas, and herbal-infused teas) in the United States and Canada. The Tazo line of ready-to-drink beverages was to become part of an existing venture between PepsiCo and Unilever (the Pepsi/Lipton Tea partnership) that was the leading North American distributor of ready-to-drink teas.

In 2001, Starbucks introduced the Starbucks Card, a reloadable card that allowed customers to pay for their purchases with a quick swipe at the cash register and also to earn and redeem rewards. In 2009, about 15 percent of customer purchases at Starbucks stores were made on Starbucks cards.

In 2003, Starbucks acquired Seattle's Best Coffee, an operator of Seattle's Best coffee shops and marketer of Seattle's Best whole bean and ground coffees, for $70 million. Starbucks continued to operate Seattle's Best as a separate subsidiary. As of May 2008, there were more than 540 Seattle's Best cafés in the United States (a number of which were in Borders book and music stores) and 86 Seattle's Best Coffee Express espresso bars. The Seattle's Best product line included more than 30 whole bean and ground coffees (including flavored, organic, and Fair Trade Certified coffees), espresso beverages, signature handcrafted JavaKula blended beverages, OvenSong bakery food and sandwiches, and select merchandise. Shortly after the acquisition, Starbucks expanded its licensing arrangement with Kraft Foods to include marketing and distributing Seattle's Best whole bean and ground coffees in grocery and mass merchandise channels in North America, with Starbucks to receive a royalty on all such sales. In 2009, Seattle's Best whole bean and ground coffee blends were available nationwide in supermarkets and were being served at more than 15,000 food service locations (college campuses, restaurants, hotels, airlines, and cruise lines). A new Seattle's Best line of ready-to-drink iced lattes was introduced in April 2010 in major grocery and convenience stores in the western United States; the manufacture, marketing, and distribution of the new Seattle's Best beverages was managed by PepsiCo as part of the long-standing Starbucks-PepsiCo joint venture for ready-to-drink Frappuccino products. In May 2010, Starbucks announced that it would relaunch Seattle's Best Coffee with new distinctive red packaging and a red logo, boost efforts to open more franchised Seattle's Best cafés, and expand the availability of Seattle's Best coffees to 30,000 distribution points by October 2010. By July 2010, freshly brewed and iced Seattle's Best Coffee drinks were being sold at 7,250 Burger King outlets in the United States, 9,000 Subway locations, and some 299 AMC movie theaters in five countries.

In 2004 Starbucks teamed with Jim Beam Brands to invent a Starbucks Coffee Liqueur that would be sold be sold in bars, liquor stores, and restaurants; projections were for systemwide gross sales of more than $8 million annually. Launched in February 2005, Starbucks Coffee Liqueur was the number-one-selling new spirit product year-to-date through August 2005, according to Nielsen. In October 2005, again collaborating with Jim Beam Brands, Starbucks introduced Starbucks Cream Liqueur, a blend of cream, spirits, and a hint of Starbucks coffee. There were an estimated 22 million cordial consumers in the U.S. market, making the cream liqueur category nearly three times the size of coffee liqueur category. Both Starbucks Coffee Liqueur and Starbucks Cream Liqueur were packaged in 750 milliliter bottles priced at $22.99.

In April 2005, Starbucks acquired Ethos Water for $8 million in cash. The acquisition was made to expand the line of beverages in Starbucks stores in the United States. Following the acquisition, the brand also became known for its campaign to raise $10 million by donating $0.05 of the retail price of each bottle sold to a charitable organization working to increase access to clean drinking water and conduct sanitation and hygiene education programs in developing countries in Africa and Asia; in 2010, more than $6 million had been raised.[18] The production, distribution, and marketing of Ethos water products was handled by PepsiCo, as part of its long-standing joint venture with Starbucks.

In response to customer requests for more wholesome food and beverage options and also to bring in business from non–coffee drinkers, Starbucks in 2008 began offering fruit cups, yogurt parfaits, skinny lattes, banana walnut bread (that was nearly 30 percent real banana), a 300-calorie farmer's market salad with all-natural dressing, and a line of "better-for-you" smoothies called Vivanno Nourishing Blends. Each Vivanno smoothie averaged 250 calories and consisted of one serving of fruit, 16 grams of protein, and 5 grams of fiber.[19] Additionally, in 2009, healthier, lower-calorie selections were included in the bakery cases at Starbucks stores, and the recipes for several other food items on the menu at Starbucks stores were reformulated to include whole grains and dried fruits and to cut back on or eliminate the use of artificial flavorings, dyes, high-fructose corn syrup, and artificial preservatives.[20]

In 2008, Starbucks introduced a new coffee blend called Pike Place Roast that would be brewed every day, all day in every Starbucks store.[21] Before then, Starbucks rotated coffees through its brewed lineup, sometimes switching them weekly, sometimes daily. While some customers liked the ever-changing variety, the feedback from a majority of customers indicated a preference for a consistent brew that customers could count on when they came into a Starbucks store. This reinvention of brewed coffee returned the company to the practice of grinding the beans in the store. Pike Place Roast was brewed in small batches in 30-minute intervals to ensure that customers were provided the freshest coffee possible. The Pike Place Roast was created by Starbucks' master blenders and coffee quality team using input from nearly 1,000 customers—it was smoother than any other Starbucks coffee and tasted great either black or with cream and sugar.

In the fall of 2009, Starbucks introduced Starbucks VIA Ready Brew—packets of roasted coffee in an instant form. VIA was made with a proprietary microground technology that Starbucks claimed represented a breakthrough.[22] Simply adding a packet of VIA to a cup of hot or cold water produced an instant coffee with a rich, full-bodied taste that closely replicated the taste, quality, and flavor of traditional freshly brewed coffee. Initially, VIA was introduced in Starbucks stores in the United States and Canada and select food service accounts; Starbucks stores held a four-day Starbucks VIA Taste Challenge

promotional during which customers were invited to compare the difference between Starbucks VIA and fresh-brewed Starbucks coffee. During the 2009 holiday season, Starbucks VIA Ready Brew was one of the top-selling coffee products at Amazon.com. Encouraged by favorable customer response, in mid-2010 Starbucks expanded the distribution of VIA to include 25,000 grocery store, mass-merchandise store, and drugstore accounts, including Kroger, Safeway, Walmart, Target, Costco, and CVS. VIA was available in three roasts—Colombian, Italian Roast, and Decaffeinated Italian Roast; the suggested retail price for Starbucks VIA was $2.95 for three servings and $7.49 for eight servings. Starbucks executives saw VIA as a promising vehicle for entering the instant coffee market and attracting a bigger fraction of on-the-go and at-home coffee drinkers. Instant coffee made up a significant fraction of the coffee purchases in the United Kingdom (80 percent), Japan (53 percent), Russia (85 percent), and other countries where Starbucks stores were located—in both the UK and Japan, sales of instant coffee exceeded $4 billion annually. Globally, the instant and single-serve coffee category was a $23 billion market. In March 2010, Starbucks made VIA available in all of its Starbucks stores in the UK. In April 2010, Starbucks introduced VIA in all of Japan's 870 Starbucks stores under the name Starbucks VIA Coffee Essence.[23]

The company's overall retail sales mix in 2009 was 76 percent beverages, 18 percent food items, 3 percent coffeemaking equipment and other merchandise, and 3 percent whole bean coffees.[24] However, the product mix in each store varied, depending on the size and location of each outlet. Larger stores carried a greater variety of whole coffee beans, gourmet food items, teas, coffee mugs, coffee grinders, coffeemaking equipment, filters, storage containers, and other accessories. Smaller stores and kiosks typically sold a full line of coffee beverages, a limited selection of whole bean and ground coffees and Tazo teas, and a few coffee-drinking accessories. Moreover, menu offerings at Starbucks stores were typically adapted to local cultures; for instance, the menu offerings at stores in North America included a selection of muffins, but stores in France had no muffins and instead featured locally made French pastries.

Starbucks' Consumer Products Group

All distribution channels for Starbucks products outside both licensed and company-operated retail stores were collectively referred to by Starbucks executives as "specialty operations." In 2010, Starbucks formed its Consumer Products Group (CPG) to manage all specialty operations activities. CPG was responsible for selling a selection of whole bean and ground coffees as well as a selection of premium Tazo teas outside Starbucks retail stores through licensing and distribution arrangements with Kraft, PepsiCo, Unilever, and others that covered both the United States and international markets. CPG also oversaw production and sales of ready-to-drink beverages (including bottled Frappuccino beverages, Starbucks Doubleshot espresso drinks, and Discoveries chilled cup coffee) as well as Starbucks superpremium ice creams and Starbucks liqueurs through the company's marketing and distribution agreements and joint ventures with PepsiCo, Unilever, and others. And it managed the sales of various Starbucks products to both food service accounts and the vast majority of the company's partnerships and licensing arrangements with prominent third parties.

Exhibit 6 shows the recent performance of the Consumer Products Group. Starbucks executives considered CPG's specialty operations attractive from the standpoint of both long-term growth and profitability. In fiscal 2007–2009, the company's operating profit margins from specialty operations were higher than the long-term target of 35 percent and vastly superior to the operating profit margins for the company's U.S. and international operations, as the following table shows:

	Operating Profit Margins		
	FY 2009	FY 2008	FY 2007
Consumer Products Group	39.6%	37.3%	35.9%
U.S. operations	7.5	6.0	14.3
International operations	4.8	5.2	8.1

Advertising

So far, Starbucks had spent relatively little money on advertising, preferring instead to build the brand cup by cup with customers and depend on word of mouth and the appeal of its storefronts. Advertising expenditures were $126.3 million in fiscal 2009, versus $129.0 million in fiscal 2008, $103.5 million in 2007, and $107.5 million in 2006. Starbucks stepped up advertising efforts in 2008 to combat the strategic initiatives of McDonald's and several other fast-food chains to begin offering premium coffees and coffee drinks at prices below those charged by Starbucks. In 2009, McDonald's reportedly spent more than $100 million on television, print, radio, billboard, and online ads promoting its new line of McCafé coffee drinks. Starbucks countered with the

Exhibit 6   Performance of Starbuck's Consumer Products Group, Fiscal Years 2007–2009

	Fiscal Year		
Consumer Product Group Operations	2009	2008	2007
Licensing revenues	$427.2	$392.6	$366.3
Foodservice revenues	322.4	355.0	326.1
Total revenues	$749.6	$747.6	$692.4
Operating income	$296.3	$279.2	$248.9
Operating income as a percent of total revenues	39.5%	37.3%	35.9%

Source: Starbucks, 2009 10-K report, p. 76.

biggest advertising campaign the company had ever undertaken.[25]

Vertical Integration

Howard Schultz saw Starbucks as having a unique strategy compared to the strategies pursued by its many coffeehouse competitors. He observed:

> People sometimes fail to realize that almost unlike any retailer or restaurant, we are completely vertically integrated. We source coffee from 30 countries. We have a proprietary roasting process. We distribute to company owned stores, and finally serve the coffee. Others are resellers of commodity-based coffees.[26]

HOWARD SCHULTZ'S EFFORTS TO MAKE STARBUCKS A GREAT PLACE TO WORK

Howard Schultz deeply believed that Starbucks' success was heavily dependent on customers having a very positive experience in its stores. This meant having store employees who were knowledgeable about the company's products, who paid attention to detail in preparing the company's espresso drinks, who eagerly communicated the company's passion for coffee, and who possessed the skills and personality to deliver consistent, pleasing customer service. Many of the baristas were in their 20s and worked part-time, going to college on the side or pursuing other career activities. The challenge to Starbucks, in Schultz's view, was how to attract, motivate, and reward store employees in a manner that would make Starbucks a company that people would want to work for and that would generate enthusiastic commitment and higher levels of customer service. Moreover, Schultz wanted to send all Starbucks employees a message that would cement the trust that had been building between management and the company's workforce.

Instituting Health Care Coverage for All Employees

One of the requests that employees had made to the prior owners of Starbucks was to extend health insurance benefits to part-time workers. Their request had been turned down, but Schultz believed that expanding health insurance coverage to include part-timers was something the company needed to do. His father had recently passed away from cancer and he knew from having grown up in a family that struggled to make ends meet how difficult it was to cope with rising medical costs. In 1988, Schultz went to the board of directors with his plan to expand the company's health insurance plans to include part-timers who worked at least 20 hours per week. He saw the proposal not as a generous gesture but as a core strategy to win employee loyalty and commitment to the company's mission. Board members resisted because the company was unprofitable and the added costs of the extended coverage would only worsen the company's bottom line. But Schultz argued passionately that it was the right thing to do and wouldn't be as expensive as it seemed. He observed that if the new benefit reduced turnover, which he believed was likely, then it would reduce the costs of hiring and training—which equaled about $3,000 per new hire; he further pointed out that it cost $1,500 a year to provide an employee with full benefits. Part-timers, he argued, were vital to Starbucks, constituting two-thirds of the company's workforce. Many were baristas who knew the favorite drinks of regular customers; if the barista left, that connection with the customer was broken. Moreover, many part-time employees were called on to open the stores early, sometimes at 5:30 or 6:00 a.m.; others had to work until closing, usually 9:00 p.m. or later. Providing these employees with health insurance benefits, he argued, would signal that the company honored their value and contribution.

The board approved Schultz's plan, and starting in late 1988, part-timers working 20 or more hours were offered the same health coverage as full-time employees. Starbucks paid 75 percent of an employee's health insurance premium; the employee paid 25 percent. Over the years, Starbucks extended its health coverage to include preventive care, prescription drugs, dental care, eye care, mental health, and chemical dependency. Coverage was also offered for unmarried partners in a committed relationship. Since most Starbucks employees were young and comparatively healthy, the company had been able to provide broader coverage while keeping monthly payments relatively low. Even when the company fell on lean times in 2008–2009, Starbucks refrained from making cuts in employee health insurance benefits; company expenditures for employee health insurance were $300 million in fiscal 2009, more than the company spent on its purchases of coffee beans.[27]

A Stock Option Plan for Employees

By 1991, the company's profitability had improved to the point where Schultz could pursue a stock option plan for all employees, a program he believed would have a positive, long-term effect on the success of Starbucks.[28] Schultz wanted to turn all Starbucks employees into partners, give them a chance to share in the success of the company, and make clear the connection between their contributions and the company's market value. Even though Starbucks was still a private company, the plan that emerged called for granting stock options to every full-time and part-time employee in proportion to his or her base pay. In May 1991, the plan, dubbed Bean Stock, was presented to the board. Though board members were concerned that increasing the number of shares might unduly dilute the value of the shares of investors who had put up hard cash, the plan received unanimous approval. The first grant was made in October 1991, just after the end of the company's fiscal year in September; each partner was granted stock options worth 12 percent of base pay. When the Bean Stock program was initiated, Starbucks dropped the term *employee* and began referring to all of its people as *partners* because every member of Starbucks' workforce became eligible for stock option awards after six months of employment and 500 paid work hours.

Starbucks went public in June 1992, selling its initial offering at a price of $17 per share. Starting in October 1992 and continuing through October 2004, Starbucks granted each eligible employee a stock option award with a value equal to 14 percent of base pay. Beginning in 2005, the plan was modified to tie the size of each employee's stock option awards to three factors: (1) Starbucks' success and profitability for the fiscal year, (2) the size of an employee's base wages, and (3) the price at which the stock option could be exercised. The value of the stock options exercised by Starbucks partners was $44 million in fiscal 2009, $50 million in fiscal 2008, and $274 million in fiscal 2007. As of September 27, 2009, Starbucks partners held 63.6 million shares in stock option awards that had a weighted-average contractual life of 6.7 years; these shares had a weighted-average exercise price of $14.75 and an aggregate value of $442.4 million.[29]

Starbucks Stock Purchase Plan for Employees

In 1995, Starbucks implemented an employee stock purchase plan that gave partners who had been employed for at least 90 days an opportunity to purchase company stock through regular payroll deductions. Partners who enrolled could devote anywhere from 1 to 10 percent of their base earnings (up to a maximum of $25,000) to purchasing shares of Starbucks stock. After the end of each calendar quarter, each participant's contributions were used to buy Starbucks stock at a discount of 5 percent of the closing price on the last business day of the each calendar quarter (the discount was 15 percent until March 2009).

Since inception of the plan, some 23.5 million shares had been purchased by partners; roughly one-third of Starbucks partners participated in the stock purchase plan during the 2000–2009 period.

The Workplace Environment

Starbucks' management believed that the company's competitive pay scales and comprehensive benefits for both full-time and part-time partners allowed it to attract motivated people with above-average skills and good work habits. An employee's base pay was determined by the pay scales prevailing in the geographic region where an employee worked and by the person's job skills, experience, and job performance. About 90 percent of Starbucks' partners were full-time or part-time baristas, paid on an hourly basis. After six months of employment, baristas could expect to earn $8.50 to $9.50 per hour. In 2009, experienced full-time baristas in the company's U.S. stores earned an average of about $37,800; store managers earned an average of $44,400.[30] Voluntary turnover at Starbucks was 13 percent in 2009.[31] Starbucks executives believed that efforts to make the company an attractive, caring place to work were responsible for its relatively low turnover rates. Starbucks received 225,000 job applications in 2008 and 150,000 job applications in 2009.

Surveys of Starbucks partners conducted by *Fortune* magazine in the course of selecting companies for inclusion on its annual list "100 Best Companies to Work For" indicated that full-time baristas liked working at Starbucks because of the camaraderie, while part-timers were particularly pleased with the health insurance benefits (those who enrolled in Starbucks' most economical plan for just routine health care paid only $6.25 per week).[32] Starbucks had been named to *Fortune*'s list in 1998, 1999, 2000, and every year from 2002 through 2010. In 2010, Starbucks was ranked 93rd, down from 24th in 2009 and 7th in 2008.

Starbucks' management used annual Partner View surveys to solicit feedback from its workforce, learn their concerns, and measure job satisfaction. The 2002 survey revealed that many employees viewed the benefits package as only "average," prompting the company to increase its match of 401(k) contributions for those who had

been with the company more than three years and to have these contributions vest immediately. In a survey conducted in fiscal 2008, 80 percent of Starbucks partners reported being satisfied.[33]

Schultz's approach to offering employees good compensation and a comprehensive benefits package was driven by his belief that sharing the company's success with the people who made it happen helped everyone think and act like an owner, build positive long-term relationships with customers, and do things efficiently. Schultz's rationale, based on his father's experience of going from one low-wage, no-benefits job to another, was that if you treated your employees well, they in turn would treat customers well.

Exhibit 7 contains a summary of Starbucks' fringe benefit program.

Employee Training and Recognition

To accommodate its strategy of rapid store expansion, Starbucks put in systems to recruit, hire,

Exhibit 7 Starbucks' Fringe Benefit Program, 2010

- Medical insurance
- Sick time
- Dental and vision care
- Paid vacations (up to 120 hours annually for hourly workers with five or more years of service at retail stores and up to 200 hours annually for salaried and nonretail hourly employees with five or more years of service)
- Six paid holidays
- One paid personal day every six months for salaried and nonretail hourly partners
- A 30 percent discount on purchases of beverages, food, and merchandise at Starbucks stores
- Mental health and chemical dependency coverage
- 401(k) retirement savings plan—the company matched from 25% to 150%, based on length of service, of each employee's contributions up to the first 4% of compensation
- Short- and long-term disability
- Stock purchase plan—eligible employees could buy shares at a discounted price through regular payroll deductions
- Life insurance
- Short- and long-term disability insurance
- Accidental death and dismemberment insurance
- Adoption assistance
- Financial assistance program for partners that experience a financial crisis
- Stock option plan (Bean stock)
- Pre-tax payroll deductions for commuter expenses
- Free coffee and tea products each week
- Tuition reimbursement program

Source: Starbucks, "Careers," www.starbucks.com, accessed June 7, 2010.

and train baristas and store managers. Starbucks' vice president for human resources used some simple guidelines in screening candidates for new positions: "We want passionate people who love coffee. . . . We're looking for a diverse workforce, which reflects our community. We want people who enjoy what they're doing and for whom work is an extension of themselves."[34]

All partners/baristas hired for a retail job in a Starbucks store received at least 24 hours training in their first two to four weeks. The topics included classes on coffee history, drink preparation, coffee knowledge (four hours), customer service (four hours), and retail skills, plus a four-hour workshop called "Brewing the Perfect Cup." Baristas spent considerable time learning about beverage preparation—grinding the beans, steaming milk, learning to pull perfect (18- to 23-second) shots of espresso, memorizing the recipes of all the different drinks, practicing making the different drinks, and learning how to customize drinks to customer specifications. There were sessions on cash register operations, how to clean the milk wand on the espresso machine, explaining the Italian drink names to customers, selling home espresso machines, making eye contact with customers and interacting with them, and taking personal responsibility for the cleanliness of the store. And there were rules to be memorized: milk must be steamed to at least 150 degrees Fahrenheit but never more than 170 degrees; every espresso shot not pulled within 23 seconds must be tossed; never let coffee sit in the pot more than 20 minutes; always compensate dissatisfied customers with a Starbucks coupon that entitled them to a free drink.

Management trainees attended classes for 8 to 12 weeks. Their training went much deeper, covering not only coffee knowledge and information imparted to baristas but also details of store operations, practices and procedures as set forth in the company's operating manual, information systems, and the basics of managing people. Starbucks' trainers were all store managers and district managers with on-site experience. One of their major objectives was to ingrain the company's values, principles, and culture and to pass on their knowledge about coffee and their passion about Starbucks.

When Starbucks opened stores in a new market, it sent a Star Team of experienced managers and baristas to the area to lead the store opening effort and to conduct one-on-one training following the company's formal classes and basic orientation sessions at the Starbucks Coffee School in San Francisco. From time to time, Starbucks conducted special training programs, including a coffee masters program for store employees, leadership training for store managers, and career programs for partners in all types of jobs.

To recognize partner contributions, Starbucks had created a partner recognition program consisting of 18 different awards and programs. Examples included Coffee Master awards, Certified Barista awards, Spirit of Starbucks awards for exceptional achievement by a partner, a Manager of the Quarter for store manager leadership, Green Apron Awards for helping create a positive and welcoming store environment, Green Bean Awards for exceptional support for company's environmental mission, and Bravo! Awards for exceeding the standards of Starbucks customer service, significantly increasing sales, or reducing costs.

STARBUCKS' VALUES, BUSINESS PRINCIPLES, AND MISSION

During the early building years, Howard Schultz and other Starbucks senior executives worked to instill some key values and guiding principles into the Starbucks culture. The cornerstone value in their effort "to build a company with soul" was that the company would never stop pursuing the perfect cup of coffee by buying the best beans and roasting them to perfection. Schultz was adamant about controlling the quality of Starbucks products and building a culture common to all stores. He was rigidly opposed to selling artificially flavored coffee beans, saying that "we will not pollute our high-quality beans with chemicals"; if a customer wanted hazelnut-flavored coffee, Starbucks would provide it by adding hazelnut syrup to the drink rather than by adding hazelnut flavoring to the beans during roasting. Running flavored beans through the grinders would result in chemical residues being left behind to alter the flavor of beans ground afterward; plus, the chemical smell given off by artificially flavored beans was absorbed by other beans in the store.

Starbucks' management was also emphatic about the importance of employees paying attention to what pleased customers. Employees were trained to go out of their way and to take heroic measures, if necessary, to make sure customers were fully satisfied. The theme was "just say yes" to customer requests. Further, employees were encouraged to speak their minds without fear of retribution from upper management—senior executives wanted employees to be straight with them, being vocal about what Starbucks was doing right, what it was doing wrong, and what changes were needed. The intent was for employees to be involved in and contribute to the process of making Starbucks a better company.

Starbucks' Mission Statement

In early 1990, the senior executive team at Starbucks went to an off-site retreat to debate the company's values and beliefs and draft a mission statement. Schultz wanted the mission statement to convey a strong sense of organizational purpose and to articulate the company's fundamental beliefs and guiding principles. The draft was submitted to all employees for review, and several changes were made based on employee comments. The resulting mission statement and guiding principles are shown in Exhibit 8. In 2008, Starbucks partners from all across the company met for several months to refresh the mission statement and rephrase the underlying guiding principles; the revised mission statement and guiding principles are also shown in Exhibit 8.

STARBUCKS' COFFEE PURCHASING STRATEGY

Coffee beans were grown in 70 tropical countries and were the second-most-traded commodity in the world after petroleum. Most of the world's coffee was grown by some 25 million small farmers, most of whom lived on the edge of poverty. Starbucks personnel traveled regularly to coffee-producing countries, building relationships with growers and exporters, checking on agricultural conditions and crop yields, and searching out varieties and sources that would meet Starbucks' exacting standards of quality and flavor. The coffee-purchasing group, working with Starbucks

personnel in roasting operations, tested new varieties and blends of green coffee beans from different sources. Sourcing from multiple geographic areas not only allowed Starbucks to offer a greater range of coffee varieties to customers but also spread the company's risks regarding weather, price volatility, and changing economic and political conditions in coffee-growing countries.

Starbucks' coffee sourcing strategy had three key elements:

- Make sure that the prices Starbucks paid for green (unroasted) coffee beans were high enough to ensure that small farmers were able to cover their production costs and provide for their families.
- Use purchasing arrangements that limited Starbucks' exposure to sudden price jumps due to weather, economic and political conditions in the growing countries, new agreements establishing export quotas, and periodic efforts to bolster prices by restricting coffee supplies.
- Work directly with small coffee growers, local coffee-growing cooperatives, and other types of coffee suppliers to promote coffee cultivation methods that protected biodiversity and were environmentally sustainable.

Pricing and Purchasing Arrangements

Commodity-grade coffee was traded in a highly competitive market as an undifferentiated product. However, high-altitude arabica coffees of the quality purchased by Starbucks were bought on a negotiated basis at a substantial premium above commodity coffee. The prices of the top-quality coffees sourced by Starbucks depended on supply and demand conditions at the time of the purchase and were subject to considerable volatility due to weather, economic and political conditions in the growing countries, new agreements establishing export quotas, and periodic efforts to bolster prices by restricting coffee supplies.

Starbucks typically used fixed-price purchase commitments to limit its exposure to fluctuating coffee prices in upcoming periods and, on occasion, purchased coffee futures contracts to provide price protection. In years past, there had been times when unexpected jumps in coffee

Exhibit 8   Starbucks' Mission Statement, Values, and Business Principles

Mission Statement, 1990–October 2008

Establish Starbucks as the premier purveyor of the finest coffee in the world while maintaining our uncompromising principles as we grow.

The following six guiding principles will help us measure the appropriateness of our decisions:

- Provide a great work environment and treat each other with respect and dignity.
- Embrace diversity as an essential component in the way we do business.
- Apply the highest standards of excellence to the purchasing, roasting, and fresh delivery of our coffee.
- Develop enthusiastically satisfied customers all of the time.
- Contribute positively to our communities and our environment.
- Recognize that profitability is essential to our future success.

Mission Statement, October 2008 Forward

Our Mission: To inspire and nurture the human spirit—one person, one cup, and one neighborhood at a time.

Here are the principles of how we live that every day:

Our Coffee

It has always been, and will always be, about quality. We're passionate about ethically sourcing the finest coffee beans, roasting them with great care, and improving the lives of people who grow them. We care deeply about all of this; our work is never done.

Our Partners

We're called partners, because it's not just a job, it's our passion. Together, we embrace diversity to create a place where each of us can be ourselves. We always treat each other with respect and dignity. And we hold each other to that standard.

Our Customers

When we are fully engaged, we connect with, laugh with, and uplift the lives of our customers—even if just for a few moments. Sure, it starts with the promise of a perfectly made beverage, but our work goes far beyond that. It's really about human connection.

Our Stores

When our customers feel this sense of belonging, our stores become a haven, a break from the worries outside, a place where you can meet with friends. It's about enjoyment at the speed of life—sometimes slow and savored, sometimes faster. Always full of humanity.

Our Neighborhood

Every store is part of a community, and we take our responsibility to be good neighbors seriously. We want to be invited in wherever we do business. We can be a force for positive action— bringing together our partners, customers, and the community to contribute every day. Now we see that our responsibility—and our potential for good—is even larger. The world is looking to Starbucks to set the new standard, yet again. We will lead.

Our Shareholders

We know that as we deliver in each of these areas, we enjoy the kind of success that rewards our shareholders. We are fully accountable to get each of these elements right so that Starbucks—and everyone it touches—can endure and thrive.

Source: Starbucks, "Our Starbucks Mission," www.starbucks.com, accessed March 7, 2010.

prices had put a squeeze on Starbucks' margins, forcing an increase in the prices of the beverages and beans sold at retail. During fiscal 2008, Starbucks more than doubled its volume of its fixed-price purchase commitments compared with fiscal 2007 because of the risk of rising prices for green coffee beans. Starbucks bought 367 million pounds of green coffee beans in fiscal 2009, paying an average of $1.47 per pound. At the end of fiscal 2009, the company had purchase commitments totaling $238 million, which, together with existing inventory, were expected to provide an adequate supply of green coffee through fiscal 2010.[35]

Starbucks and Fair Trade Certified Coffee

A growing number of small coffee growers were members of democratically run cooperatives that were registered with the Fair Trade Labeling Organizations International; these growers could sell their beans directly to importers, roasters, and retailers at favorable guaranteed fair trade prices. The idea behind guaranteed prices for fair trade coffees was to boost earnings for small coffee growers enough to allow them to invest in their farms and communities, develop the business skills needed to compete in the global market for coffee, and afford basic health care, education, and home improvements.

Starbucks began purchasing Fair Trade Certified coffee in 2000, steadily increasing its purchasing and marketing of such coffees in line with growing awareness of what Fair Trade Certified coffees were all about and consumer willingness to pay the typically higher prices for fair trade coffees. In 2008, Starbucks announced that it would double its purchases of Fair Trade Certified coffees in 2009, resulting in total purchases of 39 million pounds in 2009 (versus 19 million pounds in 2008 and 10 million pounds in 2005) and making Starbucks the largest purchaser of Fair Trade Certified coffee in the world. Starbucks marketed Fair Trade Certified coffees at most of its retail stores and through other locations that sold Starbucks coffees.

Best-Practice Coffee Cultivation and Environmental Sustainability

Since 1998, Starbucks had partnered with Conservation International's Center for Environmental Leadership to promote environmentally sustainable best practices in coffee cultivation methods and to develop specific guidelines—called Coffee and Farmer Equity (C.A.F.E.) Practices—to help farmers grow high-quality coffees in ways that were good for the planet. The C.A.F.E. Practices covered four areas: product quality, the price received by farmers/growers, safe and humane working conditions (including compliance with minimum wage requirements and child labor

provisions), and environmental responsibility.[36] In addition, Starbucks operated Farmer Support Centers in Costa Rica and Rwanda that were staffed with agronomists and experts on environmentally responsible coffee growing methods; staff members at these two centers worked with coffee farming communities to promote best practices in coffee production and improve both coffee quality and production yields. During 2008–2009, approximately 80 percent of the coffee beans purchased by Starbucks came from suppliers whose coffee-growing methods met C.A.F.E. standards. In those instances where Starbucks sourced its coffee beans from non-grower C.A.F.E. Practices suppliers, it required suppliers to submit evidence of payments made through the coffee supply chain to demonstrate how much of the price Starbucks paid for green coffee beans got to the farmer/grower.

A growing percentage of the coffees that Starbucks purchased were grown organically (i.e., without the use of pesticides, herbicides, or chemical fertilizers); organic cultivation methods resulted in clean ground water and helped protect against degrading of local ecosystems, many of which were fragile or in areas where biodiversity was under severe threat. Starbucks purchased 14 million pounds of certified organic coffee in fiscal 2009.

COFFEE ROASTING OPERATIONS

Starbucks considered the roasting of its coffee beans to be something of an art form, entailing trial-and-error testing of different combinations of time and temperature to get the most out of each type of bean and blend. Recipes were put together by the coffee department, once all the components had been tested. Computerized roasters guaranteed consistency. Highly trained and experienced roasting personnel monitored the process, using both smell and hearing, to help check when the beans were perfectly done—coffee beans make a popping sound when ready. Starbucks' standards were so exacting that roasters tested the color of the beans in a blood-cell analyzer and discarded the entire batch if the reading wasn't on target. After roasting and cooling, the coffee was immediately vacuum-sealed in bags that preserved freshness for up to 26 weeks. As a matter of policy, however, Starbucks removed coffees on its shelves after three months and, in the case of coffee used to prepare beverages in stores, the shelf life was limited to seven days after the bag was opened.

Starbucks had roasting plants in Kent, Washington; York, Pennsylvania; Minden, Nevada; Charleston, South Carolina; and The Netherlands. In addition to roasting capability, these plants also had additional space for warehousing and shipping coffees. In keeping with Starbucks' corporate commitment to reduce its environmental footprint, the new state-of-the-art roasting plant in South Carolina had been awarded LEED Silver certification for New Construction by the U.S. Green Building Council. Twenty percent of materials used in the construction of the building were from recycled content and more than 75 percent of the waste generated during construction was recycled. In addition, the facility used state-of-the-art light and water fixtures and was partly powered by wind energy. Some of the green elements in the South Carolina plant were being implemented in the other roasting plants as part of the company's initiative to achieve LEED certification for all company-operated facilities by the end of 2010.[37] In May 2010, Starbucks announced the opening of its first LEED-certified store in Asia. Located in Fukuoka, Japan, the new store was designed to serve as an extension of the existing landscape and to preserve the surrounding trees.[38]

STARBUCKS' CORPORATE SOCIAL RESPONSIBILITY STRATEGY

Howard Schultz's effort to "build a company with soul" included a long history of doing business in ways that were socially and environmentally responsible. A commitment to do the right thing had been central to how Starbucks operated as a company since Howard Schultz first became CEO in 1987. The specific actions comprising Starbucks' social responsibility strategy had varied over the years, but the intent of the strategy was consistently one of contributing positively to the communities in which Starbucks had stores, being a good environmental steward, and conducting its business in ways that earned the trust and respect of customers, partners/employees, suppliers, and the general public.

The Starbucks Foundation was set up in 1997 to orchestrate the company's philanthropic activities. Starbucks stores participated regularly in local charitable projects and community improvement activities. For years, the company had engaged in efforts to reduce, reuse, and recycle waste, conserve on water and energy usage, and generate less solid waste. Customers who brought their own mugs to stores were given a $0.10 discount on beverage purchases—in 2009, some 26 million beverages were served in customers' mugs. Coffee grounds, which were a big portion of the waste stream in stores, were packaged and given to customers, parks, schools, and plant nurseries as a soil amendment. Company personnel purchased paper products with high levels of recycled content and unbleached fiber. Stores participated in Earth Day activities each year with in-store promotions and volunteer efforts to educate employees and customers about the impacts their actions had on the environment. Suppliers were encouraged to provide the most energy-efficient products within their category and eliminate excessive packaging; Starbucks had recently instituted a set of Supplier Social Responsibility Standards covering the suppliers of all the manufactured goods and services used in the company's operations. No genetically modified ingredients were used in any food or beverage products that Starbucks served, with the exception of milk (U.S. labeling requirements do not require milk producers to disclose the use of hormones aimed at increasing the milk production of dairy herds). In 2005, Starbucks made a $5 million, five-year commitment to long-term relief and recovery efforts for victims of hurricanes Rita and Katrina and committed $5 million to support educational programs in China. In 2010, the Starbucks Foundation donated $1 million to the American Red Cross efforts to provide aid to those suffering the devastating effects of the earthquake in Haiti; in addition, Starbucks customers were invited to make cash donations to the Haitian relief effort at store registers.[39]

In 2008–2010, Starbucks' corporate social responsibility strategy had four main elements:

1. *Ethically sourcing all of the company's products.* This included promoting responsible growing practices for the company's coffees, teas, and cocoa and striving to buy the manufactured products and services it needed from suppliers that had a demonstrated commitment to social and environmental responsibility. Starbucks had a 2015 goal of purchasing 100 percent of its coffees through sources there were either Fair Trade Certified or met C.A.F.E. Practices guidelines.

2. *Community involvement.* This included engaging in a wide variety of community service activities, Starbucks Youth Action Grants to engage young people in community improvement projects (in fiscal 2009, Starbucks made 71 grants totaling $2.1 million), a program to provide medicine to people in Africa with HIV, the Ethos Water Fund, and donations by the Starbucks Foundation. The company had a goal of getting Starbucks partners and customers to contribute more than 1 million hours of community service annually by 2015; service contributions totaled 246,000 hours in 2008 and 186,000 hours in 2009.

3. *Environmental stewardship.* Initiatives here included a wide variety of actions to increase recycling, reduce waste, be more energy-efficient and use renewable energy sources, conserve water resources, make all company facilities as green as possible by using environmentally friendly building materials and energy-efficient designs, and engage in more efforts to address climate change. The company had immediate objectives of achieving LEED certification globally for all new company-operated stores beginning in late 2010, reducing energy consumption in company-owned stores by 25 percent by the end of fiscal 2010, and purchasing renewable energy equivalent to 50 percent of the electricity used in company-owned stores by the end of fiscal 2010. Management believed that the company was on track to achieve all three targets.

In 2009, Starbucks became a member of the Business for Innovative Climate Change and Energy Policy coalition, which sought to spur a clean energy economy and mitigate global warming by advocating strong legislation by the U.S. Congress. Starbucks was also collaborating with Earthwatch Institute on replanting rain forests, mapping water resources and biodiversity indicators, and sharing sustainable agriculture practices with coffee growers. Starbucks had goals to implement front-of-store recycling in all company-owned stores by 2015, to ensure that 100 percent of its cups were reusable or recyclable by 2015, to serve 25 percent of the beverages made in its stores in reusable containers by 2015, and to reduce water consumption in company-owned stores by 25 percent by 2015. In 2009 the company made progress toward achieving all these goals but still faced significant challenges in implementing recycling at its more than 16,000 stores worldwide because of wide variations in municipal recycling capabilities.

4. *Farmer loans.* Because many of the tens of thousands of small family farms with less than 30 acres that grew coffees purchased by Starbucks often lacked the money to make farming improvements and/or cover all expenses until they sold their crops, Starbucks provided funding to organizations that made loans to small coffee growers. Over the years, Starbucks had committed more than $15 million to a variety of coffee farmer loan funds. The company boosted its farmer loan commitments from $12.5 million to $14.5 million in 2009 and had a goal to commit a total of $20 million by 2015.

In 2010, Starbucks was named to *Corporate Responsibility Magazine*'s list "The 100 Best Corporate Citizens" for the 10th time. The "100 Best Corporate Citizens" list was based on more than 360 data points of publicly available information in seven categories: Environment, Climate Change, Human Rights, Philanthropy, Employee Relations, Financial Performance, and Governance. In addition, Starbucks had received over 25 awards from a diverse group of organizations for its philanthropic, community service, and environmental activities.

TOP MANAGEMENT CHANGES: CHANGING ROLES FOR HOWARD SCHULTZ

In 2000, Howard Schultz decided to relinquish his role as CEO, retain his position as chairman of the company's board of directors, and assume the newly created role of chief strategic officer. Orin Smith, a Starbucks executive who had been with the company since its early days, was named CEO. Smith retired in 2005 and was replaced as CEO by Jim Donald, who had been president of Starbucks' North American division. In 2006, Donald proceeded to set a long-term objective of having 40,000 stores worldwide and launched a program of rapid store expansion in an effort to achieve that goal.

But investors and members of Starbucks' board of directors (including Howard Schultz) became uneasy about Donald's leadership of the company when customer traffic in Starbucks' U.S. stores began to erode in 2007, new store openings worldwide were continuing at the rate of six per day, and Donald kept pressing for increased efficiency in store operations at the expense of good customer service. Investors were distressed with the company's steadily declining stock price during 2007. Schultz had lamented in a 2007 internal company e-mail (which was leaked to the public) that the company's aggressive growth had led to "a watering down of the Starbucks experience."[40] In January 2008, Starbucks' board asked Howard Schultz to return to his role as CEO and lead a major restructuring and revitalization initiative.

HOWARD SCHULTZ'S TRANSFORMATION AGENDA FOR STARBUCKS, 2008–2010

Immediately upon his return as Starbucks CEO, Schultz undertook a series of moves to revamp the company's executive leadership team and change the roles and responsibilities of several key executives.[41] A former Starbucks executive was hired for the newly created role of chief creative officer responsible for elevating the in-store experience of customers and achieving new levels of innovation and differentiation.

Because he believed that Starbucks in recent years had become less passionate about customer relationships and the coffee experience that had fueled the company's success, Schultz further decided to launch a major campaign to retransform Starbucks into the company he had envisioned it ought to be and to push the company to new plateaus of differentiation and innovation—the transformation effort instantly became the centerpiece of his return as company CEO. Schultz's transformation agenda for Starbucks had three main themes: strengthen the core, elevate the experience, and invest and grow. Specific near-term actions that Schultz implemented to drive his transformation of Starbucks in 2008–2010 included the following:

- Slowing the pace of new store openings in the United States and opening a net of 75 new stores internationally.
- Closing 900 underperforming company-operated stores in the United States, nearly 75 percent of which were within three miles of an existing Starbucks store. It was expected that these closings would boost sales and traffic at many nearby stores.
- Raising the projected return on capital requirements for proposed new store locations.
- Restructuring the company's store operations in Australia to focus on three key cities and surrounding areas—Brisbane, Melbourne, and Sydney—and to close 61 underperforming store locations (mostly located in other parts of Australia).
- Coming up with new designs for future Starbucks stores. The global store design strategy was aimed at promoting a reinvigorated customer experience by reflecting the character of each store's surrounding neighborhood and making customers feel truly at home when visiting their local store. All of the designs had to incorporate environmentally friendly materials and furnishings.
- Enhancing the customer experience at Starbucks stores, including the discontinuance of serving warmed breakfast sandwiches in North American stores (because the scent of

warmed sandwiches interfered with the coffee aroma) and a program to develop best-in-class baked goods and other new menu items that would make Starbucks a good source of a healthy breakfast for people on the go and better complement its coffee and espresso beverages. These efforts to improve the menu offerings at Starbucks stores were directly responsible for (1) the recent additions of fruit cups, yogurt parfaits, skinny lattes, the farmer's market salad, Vivanno smoothies, and healthier bakery selections, (2) the reformulated recipes to cut back on or eliminate the use of artificial flavorings, dyes, high-fructose corn syrup, and artificial preservatives, and (3) all-day brewing of Pikes Place Roast.

- A program to share best practices across all stores worldwide.

- Additional resources and tools for store employees, including laptops, an Internet-based software for scheduling work hours for store employees, and a new point-of-sale system for all stores in the United States, Canada, and the United Kingdom.

- Rigorous cost-containment initiatives to improve the company's bottom line, including a 1,000-person reduction in the staffing of the company's organizational support infrastructure to trim administrative expenses at the company's headquarters and regional offices.

- Renewed attention to employee training and reigniting enthusiasm on the part of store employees to please customers. In February 2008, Schultz ordered that 7,100 U.S. stores be temporarily closed for three regularly operating business hours (at 5:30 p.m. local time) for the purpose of conducting a special training session for store employees. The objectives were to give baristas hands-on training to improve the quality of the drinks they made, help reignite the emotional attachment of store employees to customers (a long-standing tradition at Starbucks stores), and refocus the attention of store employees on pleasing customers. Schultz viewed the training session as a way to help the company regain its "soul of the past" and improve the in-store Starbucks experience for customers.[42] When several major shareholders called Schultz to

get his take on why he was closing 7,100 stores for three hours, he told them, "I am doing the right thing. We are retraining our people because we have forgotten what we stand for, and that is the pursuit of an unequivocal, absolute commitment to quality."[43]

Schultz's insistence on more innovation had also spurred the recent introduction of the Starbucks VIA instant coffees.

Howard Schultz believed that the turning point in his effort to transform Starbucks came when he decided to hold a leadership conference for 10,000 store managers in New Orleans in early 2008. According to Schultz:

I knew that if I could remind people of our character and values, we could make a difference. The conference was about galvanizing the entire leadership of the company—being vulnerable and transparent with our employees about how desperate the situation was, and how we had to understand that everyone must be personally accountable and responsible for every single customer interaction. We started the conference with community service. Our efforts represent the largest single block of community support in the history of New Orleans, contributing more than 54,000 volunteer hours and investing more than $1 million in local projects like painting, landscaping, and building playgrounds.

If we had not had New Orleans, we wouldn't have turned things around. It was real, it was truthful, and it was about leadership. An outside CEO would have come into Starbucks and invariably done what was expected, which was cut the thing to the bone. We didn't do that. Now we did cut $581 million of costs out of the company. The cuts targeted all areas of the business, from supply chain efficiencies to waste reduction to rightsizing our support structure. But 99 percent were not consumer-facing, and in fact, our customer satisfaction scores began to rise at this time and have continued to reach unprecedented levels. We reinvested in our people, we reinvested in innovation, and we reinvested in the values of the company.

In 2010, as part of Schultz's "invest and grow" aspect of transforming Starbucks, the company was formulating plans to open "thousands of new stores" in China over time.[44] Japan had long been Starbucks' biggest foreign market outside North America, but Howard Schultz said that "Asia clearly represents the most significant growth opportunity on a go-forward basis."[45]

Schultz also indicated that Starbucks was anxious to begin opening stores in India and Vietnam, two country markets that Starbucks believed were potentially lucrative.

Exhibit 9 is a letter that Howard Schultz sent to customers on the day he reassumed the position of Starbucks' chief executive officer. Exhibit 10 is a letter that Howard Schultz sent to all Starbucks partners three weeks after he returned as company CEO.

STARBUCKS' FUTURE PROSPECTS

In April 2010, halfway through the fiscal year, Howard Schultz continued to be pleased with the company's progress in returning to a path of profitable, long-term growth. Following five consecutive quarters of declining sales at stores open 13 months or longer (beginning with the first quarter of fiscal 2008), sales at Starbucks' company-operated stores worldwide had improved in each of the most recent five consecutive quarters—see Exhibit 11. Moreover, traffic (as measured by the number of cash register transactions) increased by 3 percent in the company's U.S. stores in the second quarter of fiscal 2010, the first positive increase in the last 13 quarters. Net revenues increased 8.6 percent in the second quarter of fiscal 2010 compared with the same quarter in fiscal 2009, while net income jumped from $25.0 million in the second quarter of fiscal 2009 to $217.3 million in the second quarter of fiscal 2010.

Exhibit 9   Letter from Howard Schultz to Starbucks Customers, January 7, 2008

To Our Customers:

Twenty-five years ago, I walked into Starbucks' first store and I fell in love with the coffee I tasted, with the passion of the people working there, and with how it looked, smelled and felt. From that day, I had a vision that a store can offer a welcoming experience for customers, be part of their community, and become a warm "third place" that is part of their lives everyday and that it can provide a truly superior cup of coffee.

Based on that vision, I, along with a very talented group of people, brought Starbucks to life. We did it by being creative, innovative and courageous in offering coffee products that very few in America had ever tasted; by celebrating the interaction between us and our customers; by developing a store design unlike any that existed before; and by bringing on board an exceptionally engaged group of partners (employees) who shared our excitement about building a different kind of company.

In doing this, we developed a culture based on treating each other, our customers and our coffee growers with respect and dignity. This includes embracing diversity, committing ourselves to ethical sourcing practices, providing health care and stock options to all of our eligible full- and part-time partners, supporting the communities we serve, and, most of all, ensuring that we are a company you can be proud to support.

I am writing today to thank you for the trust you have placed in us and to share with you my personal commitment to ensuring that every time you visit our stores you get the distinctive Starbucks Experience that you have come to expect, marked by the consistent delivery of the finest coffee in the world. To ensure this happens, in addition to my role as chairman, I am returning to the position of chief executive officer to help our partners build upon our heritage and our special relationship with you, and lead our company into the future.

We have enormous opportunity and exciting plans in place to make the Starbucks Experience as good as it has ever been and even better. In the coming months, you will see this come to life in the way our stores look, in the way our people serve you, in the new beverages and products we will offer. That is my promise to you. Everyone at Starbucks looks forward to sharing these initiatives with you.

Onward,

Howard Schultz

Exhibit 10   Communication from Howard Schultz to All Starbucks Partners, February 4, 2008

What I Know to Be True

Dear Partners,

As I sit down to write this note (6:30 a.m. Sunday morning) I am enjoying a spectacular cup of Sumatra, brewed my favorite way—in a French press.

It has been three weeks since I returned to my role as CEO of the company I love. We have made much progress as we begin to transform and innovate and there is much more to come. But this is not a sprint—it is a marathon—it always has been. I assure you that when all is said and done, we will, as we always have, succeed at our highest potential. We will not be deterred from our course—we are and will be a great, enduring company, known for inspiring and nurturing the human spirit.

During this time, I have heard from so many of you; in fact, I have received more than 2,000 emails. I can feel your passion and commitment to the company, to our customers and to one another. I also thank you for all your ideas and suggestions . . . keep them coming. No one knows our business and our customers better than you. I have visited with you in many of your stores, as well as stopping by to see what our competitors are doing as well.

It's been just a few days since my last communications to you, but I wanted to share with you

what I know to be true:

- Since 1971, we have been ethically sourcing and roasting the highest quality *Arabica* coffee in the world, and today there is not a coffee company on earth providing higher quality coffee to their customers than we are. Period!

- We are in the people business and always have been. What does that mean? It means you make the difference. You are the Starbucks brand. We succeed in the marketplace and distinguish ourselves by each and every partner embracing the values, guiding principles and culture of our company and bringing it to life one customer at a time.

  Our stores have become the Third Place in our communities—a destination where human connections happen tens of thousands of times a day. We are not in the coffee business serving people. We are in the people business serving coffee. You are the best people serving the best coffee and I am proud to be your partner. There is no other place I would rather be than with you right here, right now!

- We have a renewed clarity of purpose and we are laser-focused on the customer experience. We have returned to our core to reaffirm our coffee authority and we will have some fun doing it. We are not going to embrace the status quo. Instead, we will be curious, bold and innovative in our actions and, in doing so, we will exceed the expectation of our customers.

- There will be cynics and critics along the way, all of whom will have an opinion and a point of view. This is not about them or our competitors, although we must humbly respect the changing landscape and the many choices facing every consumer. We will be steadfast in our approach and in our commitment to the *Starbucks Experience*—what we know to be true. However, this is about us and our customers. We are in control of our destiny. Trust the coffee and trust one another.

- I will lead us back to the place where we belong, but I need your help and support every step of the way. My expectations of you are high, but higher of myself.

- I want to hear from you. I want to hear about your ideas, your wins, your concerns, and how we can collectively continue to improve. Please feel free to reach out to me. I have been flooded with emails, but believe me, I am reading and responding to all of them.

As I said, I am proud to be your partner. I know this to be true.

Onward . . .

Howard

P.S. Everything that we do, from this point on (from the most simple and basic), matters.

Master the fundamentals. Experience Starbucks.

Source: Starbucks, press release, February 4, 2008, www.starbucks.com, accessed June 17, 2010.

Exhibit 11   Quarterly Sales Trends at Starbucks Company-Operated Stores, Quarter 1 of Fiscal 2008 through Quarter 2 of Fiscal 2010

Sales at Company-Operated Starbucks Stores	Five Quarters of Deteriorating Sales				
	Q1 2008	Q2 2008	Q3 2008	Q4 2008	Q1 2009
United States	(1%)	(4%)	(5%)	(8%)	(10%)
International	5%	3%	2%	0%	(3%)

Sales at Company-Operated Starbucks Stores	Five Quarters of Improving Sales				
	Q2 2009	Q3 2009	Q4 2009	Q1 2010	Q2 2010
United States	(8%)	(6%)	(1%)	4%	7%
International	(3%)	(2%)	0%	4%	7%

In commenting on the company's earnings for the second quarter of fiscal 2010, Schultz said:

> Starbucks second quarter results demonstrate the impact of innovation and the success of our efforts to dramatically transform our business over the last two years. Much credit goes to our partners all around the world who continue to deliver an improved experience to our customers. In addition, new products like Starbucks VIA, the opening of exciting new stores in Asia, Europe and the U.S., and expanded distribution outside our retail stores all represent opportunities for future growth.[46]

In March 2010, Starbucks announced its first-ever cash dividend of $0.10 per share to be paid quarterly starting with the second quarter of fiscal 2010.

The company's updated targets for full-year 2010 were as follows:

- Mid-single-digit revenue growth worldwide, driven by mid-single-digit sales growth at company-operated stores open at least 13 months.
- Opening approximately 100 net new stores in the United States and approximately 200 net new stores in international markets. Both the U.S. and international net new additions were expected to be primarily licensed stores.
- Earnings per share in the range of $1.19 to $1.22.
- Non-GAAP earnings per share in the range of $1.19 to $1.22, excluding approximately $0.03 of expected restructuring charges and including approximately $0.04 from the extra week in the fiscal fourth quarter, as fiscal 2010 was a 53-week year for Starbucks.
- Capital expenditures are expected to be approximately $500 million for the full year.
- Cash flow from operations of at least $1.5 billion, and free cash flow of more than $1 billion.

Long term, the company's objective was to maintain Starbucks' standing as one of the most recognized and respected brands in the world. To achieve this, Starbucks executives planned to continue disciplined global expansion of its company-operated and licensed retail store base, introduce relevant new products in all its channels, and selectively develop new channels of distribution.

Schultz's long-term vision for Starbucks had seven key elements:

- Be the undisputed coffee authority.
- Engage and inspire Starbucks partners.
- Ignite the emotional attachment with our customers.
- Expand our global presence—while making each store the heart of the local neighborhood.
- Be a leader in ethical sourcing and environmental impact.
- Create innovative growth platforms worthy of our coffee.
- Deliver a sustainable economic model.

Schultz believed that Starbucks still had enormous growth potential. In the United States, Starbucks had only a 3 percent share of the estimated

37 billion cups of coffee served to on-the-go coffee drinkers, only a 4 percent share of the 25 billion cups of coffee served at home, and only a 13 percent share of the 3.7 billion cups of coffee served in restaurants and coffeehouses.[47] Internationally, Starbucks' shares of these same segments were smaller. According to Schultz:

> The size of the prize is still huge. We sell less than 10 percent of the coffee consumed in the U.S. and less than 1 percent outside the U.S.

The momentum will come from international. Slower growth in the U.S., accelerating growth overseas. The response to the Starbucks brand has been phenomenal in our international markets.[48]

Nonetheless, since his return as CEO in January 2008, Schultz had been mum about whether and when the company would aggressively pursue former CEO Jim Donald's lofty goal of having 40,000 stores worldwide.

ENDNOTES

[1] Starbucks, 2009 annual report, "Letter to Shareholders," p.1.

[2] Howard Schultz and Dori Jones Yang, *Pour Your Heart into It* (New York: Hyperion, 1997), p. 33.

[3] Ibid., p. 34.

[4] Ibid., p. 36.

[5] As told in ibid., p. 48.

[6] Ibid., pp. 61–62.

[7] As quoted in Jennifer Reese, "Starbucks: Inside the Coffee Cult," *Fortune*, December 9, 1996, p.193.

[8] Schultz and Yang, *Pour Your Heart Into It*, pp. 101–2.

[9] Ibid., p. 142.

[10] Starbucks, 2009 annual report, p. 3.

[11] Starbucks, "Global Responsibility Report," 2009, p. 13.

[12] "Starbucks Plans New Global Store Design," *Restaurants and Institutions*, June 25, 2009, www.rimag.com, accessed December 29, 2009.

[13] Starbucks, press releases, May 31, 2005, and October 25, 2005.

[14] Starbucks, press release, November 1, 2007.

[15] As stated by Howard Schultz in an interview with *Harvard Business Review* editor-in-chief Adi Ignatius; the interview was published in the July–August 2010 of the *Harvard Business Review*, pp. 108–15.

[16] Starbucks, "Starbucks and iTunes Bring Complimentary Digital Music and Video Offerings with Starbucks Pick of the Week," April 15, 2008, http://news.starbucks.com/article_display.cfm?article_id=93, accessed June 8, 2010.

[17] Starbucks, 2009 annual report, p. 5.

[18] Starbucks, "Starbucks Foundation," www.starbucks.com, accessed June 18, 2010.

[19] Starbucks, press release, July 14, 2008.

[20] Starbucks, press release, June 30, 2009.

[21] Starbucks, press release, April 7, 2008.

[22] Starbucks, press release, February 19, 2009.

[23] Starbucks, press release, April 13, 2010.

[24] Starbucks, 2009 annual report, p. 4.

[25] Claire Cain Miller, "New Starbucks Ads Seek to Recruit Online Fans," *New York Times*, May 18, 2009, www.nytimes.com, accessed January 3, 2010.

[26] Andy Server, "Schultz' Plan to Fix Starbucks," *Fortune*, January 18, 2008, www.fortune.com, accessed June 21, 2010.

[27] Beth Cowitt, "Starbucks CEO: We Spend More on Healthcare Than Coffee," *Fortune*, June 7, 2010, http://money.cnn.com/2010/06/07/news/companies/starbucks_schultz_healthcare.fortune/index.html, accessed June 8, 2010.

[28] As related in Schultz and Yang, *Pour Your Heart Into It*, pp. 131–36.

[29] Starbucks, 2009 10-K report, p. 68.

[30] "100 Best Companies to Work For," *Fortune*, http://money.cnn.com/magazines/fortune/bestcompanies/2010/snapshots/93.html, accessed June 9, 2010.

[31] Ibid.

[32] Starbucks, press release, May 21, 2009, www.starbucks.com, accessed June 14, 2010.

[33] Starbucks, "Global Responsibility Report," 2008.

[34] Kate Rounds, "Starbucks Coffee," *Incentive* 167, no. 7, p. 22.

[35] Starbucks, 2009 10-K report, p. 6.

[36] Starbucks, "Corporate Responsibility," www.starbucks.com, accessed June 18, 2010.

[37] Starbucks, press release, February 19, 2009.

[38] Starbucks, press release, May 26, 2010.

[39] Starbucks, press release, January 18, 2010.

[40] "Shakeup at Starbucks," January 7, 2008, www.cbsnews.com, accessed June 16, 2010.

[41] Transcript of Starbucks Earnings Conference Call for Quarters 1 and 3 of fiscal year 2008, http://seekingalpha.com, accessed June 16, 2010.

[42] "Coffee Break for Starbucks' 135,000 Baristas," CNN, http://money.cnn.com, February 26, 2008, accessed December 28, 2009, and "Starbucks Takes a 3-Hour Coffee Break," *New York Times*, February 27, 2008, www.nytimes.com, accessed June 15, 2010.

[43] Quoted in Adi Ignatius, "We Had to Own the Mistakes," *Harvard Business Review* 88, no. 7/8 (July–August 2010), p. 111.

[44] Mariko Sanchanta, "Starbucks Plans Major China Expansion," *Wall Street Journal*, April 13, 2010, http://online.wsj.com, accessed June 10, 2010.

[45] Ibid.

[46] Starbucks, press release, April 21, 2010.

[47] Management presentation to Barclays Capital Retail and Restaurants Conference, April 28, 2010, www.starbucks.com, accessed June 21, 2010.

[48] Server, "Schultz' Plan to Fix Starbucks."

CASE 20

Southwest Airlines in 2010: Culture, Values, and Operating Practices

Arthur A. Thompson
The University of Alabama

John E. Gamble
The University of South Alabama

In 2010, Southwest Airlines was the market share leader in domestic air travel in the United States; it transported more passengers from U.S. airports to U.S. destinations than any other airline, and it offered more regularly scheduled domestic flights than any other airline. Southwest also had the enviable distinction of being the only major U.S. air carrier that was consistently profitable. The U.S. airline industry had lost money in 15 of the 30 years from 1980 through 2009, with combined annual losses exceeding combined annual profits by $43.2 billion. Yet Southwest had reported a profit every year since 1973, chiefly because of its zealous pursuit of low operating costs, low fares, and customer-pleasing service.

From humble beginnings as a quirky but scrappy underdog that flew mainly to secondary airports (rather than high-traffic airports like Chicago O'Hare, Dallas–Fort Worth, Atlanta Hartsfield, and New York's LaGuardia and Kennedy airports), Southwest had climbed up through the industry ranks to become a major competitive force in the domestic segment of the U.S. airline industry. It had weathered industry downturns, dramatic increases in the prices of jet fuel, cataclysmic falloffs in airline traffic due to terrorist attacks and economy-wide recessions, and fare wars and other attempts by rivals to undercut its business, all the while adding more and more flights to more and more airports. Since 2000, the number of passengers flying Southwest had increased by more than 28 million annually, whereas passenger traffic on domestic routes had declined at such carriers as American Airlines, Delta, Continental, United, and US Airways—see Exhibit 1.

COMPANY BACKGROUND

In late 1966, Rollin King, a San Antonio entrepreneur who owned a small commuter air service, marched into Herb Kelleher's law office with a plan to start a low-cost/low-fare airline that would shuttle passengers between San Antonio, Dallas, and Houston.[1] Over the years, King had heard many Texas businesspeople complain about the length of time that it took to drive between the three cities and the expense of flying the airlines currently serving these cities. His business concept for the airline was simple: attract passengers by flying convenient schedules, get passengers to their destination on time, make sure they have a good experience, and charge fares competitive with travel by automobile. Kelleher, skeptical that King's business idea was viable, dug into the possibilities during the next few weeks and concluded that a new airline was feasible; he agreed to handle the necessary legal work and also to invest $10,000 of his own funds in the venture.

In 1967, Kelleher filed papers to incorporate the new airline and submitted an application to the Texas Aeronautics Commission for the new company to begin serving Dallas, Houston, and San Antonio.[2] But rival airlines in Texas pulled every string they could to block the new airline from commencing operations, precipitating a contentious four-year parade of legal and regulatory proceedings. Herb Kelleher led the fight on the company's behalf, eventually prevailing in

Exhibit 1   **Total Number of Domestic and International Passengers Traveling on Selected U.S. Airlines, 2000–2009 (in thousands)**

	Total Number of Enplaned Passengers (including both passengers paying for tickets and passengers traveling on frequent flyer awards)						
Carrier	2000	2002	2004	2006	2007	2008	2009
American Airlines							
Domestic	68,319	77,489	72,648	76,813	76,581	71,539	66,142
International	17,951	16,580	18,858	21,313	21,562	21,233	19,578
Total	86,270	94,069	91,506	98,126	98,143	92,772	85,720
Continental Air Lines[1]							
Domestic	36,591	31,653	31,529	35,795	37,117	34,501	31,915
International	8,747	8,247	9,146	10,994	11,859	12,418	12,031
Total	45,338	39,900	40,675	46,789	48,976	46,919	43,946
Delta Air Lines[2]							
Domestic	97,965	83,747	79,374	63,496	61,599	59,276	55,627
International	7,596	7,036	7,416	10,020	11,435	12,339	12,118
Total	105,561	90,783	86,790	73,516	73,034	71,615	67,745
JetBlue Airways							
Domestic	1,128	5,672	11,616	18,098	20,528	20,479	20,008
International	—	—	116	408	777	1,345	2,370
Total	1,128	5,672	11,732	18,506	21,305	21,824	22,378
Northwest Airlines[2]							
Domestic	48,462	43,314	45,959	45,141	43,812	38,449	32,542
International	8,228	7,454	7,576	7,831	8,042	10,323	8,323
Total	56,690	50,768	53,535	52,972	51,854	48,772	40,865
Southwest Airlines (Domestic only, has no international flights)	**72,568**	**72,459**	**81,121**	**96,330**	**101,948**	**101,921**	**101,338**
United Air Lines[1]							
Domestic	72,450	57,830	60,081	57,229	56,402	51,661	45,571
International	10,625	9,532	9,490	10,770	11,011	11,409	10,454
Total	83,075	67,362	69,571	67,999	67,413	63,071	56,025
US Airways[3]							
Domestic	56,667	43,480	37,810	31,886	51,895	48,504	44,515
International	3,105	3,679	4,598	4,609	4,978	6,272	6,460
Total	59,772	47,159	42,408	36,495	56,873	54,776	50,975

[1]Continental and United agreed to merge in May 2010; the deal became effective on October 1, 2010.

[2]Delta Air Lines and Northwest Airlines announced their intent to merge in October 2008; however, the merger did not clear all regulatory hurdles until 2010 and combined reporting did not begin until 2010.

[3]US Airways and America West merged in September 2005; beginning in 2007, traffic data for US Airways includes the results of the merger.

Source: U.S. Department of Transportation, Bureau of Transportation Statistics, Air Carrier Statistics, Form T-100.

June 1971 after winning two appeals to the Texas Supreme Court and a favorable ruling from the U.S. Supreme Court. Kelleher recalled, "The constant proceedings had gradually come to enrage me. There was no merit to our competitors' legal assertions. They were simply trying to use their superior economic power to squeeze us dry so we would collapse before we ever got into business. I was bound and determined to show that Southwest Airlines was going to survive and was going into operation."[3]

In January 1971, Lamar Muse was brought in as Southwest's CEO to get operations under way. Muse was an aggressive, self-confident airline veteran who knew the business well and who had the entrepreneurial skills to tackle the challenges of building the airline from scratch and then competing head-on with the major carriers. Through private investors and an initial public offering of stock in June 1971, Muse raised $7 million in new capital to purchase planes and equipment and provide cash for start-up. Boeing agreed to supply three new 737s from its inventory, discounting its price from $5 million to $4 million and financing 90 percent of the $12 million deal. Muse was able to recruit a talented senior staff that included a number of veteran executives from other carriers. He particularly sought out people who were innovative, wouldn't shirk from doing things differently or unconventionally, and were motivated by the challenge of building an airline from scratch. Muse wanted his executive team to be willing to think like mavericks and not be lulled into instituting practices at Southwest that imitated what was done at other airlines.

Southwest's Struggle to Gain a Market Foothold

In June 1971, Southwest initiated its first flights with a schedule that soon included 6 round-trips between Dallas and San Antonio and 12 round-trips between Houston and Dallas. But the introductory $20 one-way fares to fly the Golden Triangle, well below the $27 and $28 fares charged by rivals, attracted disappointingly small numbers of passengers. Southwest's financial resources were stretched so thin that the company bought fuel for several months on Lamar Muse's personal credit card. Money for parts and tools was so tight that, on occasion, company personnel got on the phone with acquaintances at rival airlines operating at the terminal and arranged to borrow what was needed. Nonetheless, morale and enthusiasm remained high; company personnel displayed can-do attitudes and

adeptness at getting by on whatever resources were available.

To try to gain market visibility and drum up more passengers, Southwest decided it had to do more than run ads in the media publicizing its low fares:

- Southwest decided to have its flight hostesses dress in colorful hot pants and white knee-high boots with high heels. Recruiting ads for Southwest's first group of hostesses were headlined "Attention, Raquel Welch: You can have a job if you measure up." Two thousand applicants responded, and those selected for interviews were asked to come dressed in hot pants to show off their legs—the company wanted to hire long-legged beauties with sparkling personalities. More than 30 of Southwest's first graduating class of 40 flight attendants consisted of young women who were cheerleaders and majorettes in high school and thus had experience performing in front of people while skimpily dressed.

- A second attention-getting action was to give passengers free alcoholic beverages during daytime flights. Most passengers on these flights were business travelers. Management's thinking was that many passengers did not drink during the daytime and that with most flights being less than an hour's duration it would be cheaper to simply give the drinks away rather than collect the money.

- Taking a cue from being based at Dallas Love Field, Southwest began using the tag line "Now There's Somebody Else Up There Who Loves You." The routes between Houston, Dallas, and San Antonio became known as the Love Triangle. Southwest's planes were referred to as Love Birds, drinks became Love Potions, peanuts were called Love Bites, drink coupons were Love Stamps, and tickets were printed on Love Machines. The "Love" campaign set the tone for Southwest's approach to its customers and company efforts to make flying Southwest an enjoyable, fun, and differentiating experience. (Later, when the company went public, it chose LUV as its stock-trading symbol.)

- In order to add more flights without buying more planes, the head of Southwest's ground operations came up with a plan for ground crews to off-load passengers and baggage, refuel the plane, clean the cabin and restock the galley, on-load passengers and baggage, do the necessary preflight checks and paperwork, and push away from the gate in 10 minutes. The 10-minute turn became one of Southwest's signatures during the 1970s and 1980s. (In later years, as passenger volume grew and many flights were filled to capacity, the turnaround time gradually expanded to 25 minutes—because it took more time to unload and load a plane with 125 passengers, as compared with a half-full plane with just 60–65 passengers. Even so, the 25-minute average turnaround time at Southwest during the 2000–2009 period was shorter than the 30- to 50-minute turnaround times typical at other major airlines.)

- In late November 1971, Lamar Muse came up with the idea of offering a $10 fare to passengers on the Friday-night Houston–Dallas flight. With no advertising, the 112-seat flight sold out. This led Muse to realize that Southwest was serving two quite distinct types of travelers in the Golden Triangle market: (1) business travelers who were more time-sensitive than price-sensitive and wanted weekday flights at times suitable for conducting business and (2) price-sensitive leisure travelers who wanted lower fares and had more flexibility about when to fly.[4] He came up with a two-tier on-peak/off-peak pricing structure in which all seats on weekday flights departing before 7:00 P.M. were priced at $26 and all seats on other flights were priced at $13. Passenger traffic increased significantly—and system-wide on-peak/off-peak pricing soon became standard across the whole airline industry.

- In 1972, the company decided to move its flights in Houston from the newly opened Houston Intercontinental Airport (where it was losing money and where it took 45 minutes to get to downtown) to the abandoned Houston Hobby Airport located much closer to downtown Houston. Despite being the only carrier to fly into Houston Hobby, the results were spectacular—business travelers who flew to Houston frequently from Dallas and San Antonio found the Houston Hobby location far more convenient, and passenger traffic doubled almost immediately.

- In early 1973, in an attempt to fill empty seats on its San Antonio–Dallas flights, Southwest cut its regular $26 fare to $13 for all seats, all days, and all times. When Braniff International, at that time one of Southwest's major rivals, announced $13 fares of its own, Southwest retaliated with a two-page ad, run in the Dallas newspapers, headlined "Nobody is going to shoot Southwest Airlines out of the sky for a lousy $13" and containing copy saying Braniff was trying to run Southwest out of business. The ad announced that Southwest would not only match Braniff's $13 fare but that it would also give passengers the choice of buying a regular-priced ticket for $26 and receiving a complimentary fifth of Chivas Regal scotch, Crown Royal Canadian whiskey, or Smirnoff vodka (or, for nondrinkers, a leather ice bucket). More than 75 percent of Southwest's Dallas-Houston passengers opted for the $26 fare, although the percentage dropped as the two-month promotion wore on and corporate controllers began insisting that company employees use the $13 fare. The local and national media picked up the story of Southwest's offer, proclaiming the battle as a David-versus-Goliath struggle in which the upstart Southwest did not stand much of a chance against the much larger and well-established Braniff; grassroots sentiment in Texas swung to Southwest's side.

All these moves paid off. The resulting gains in passenger traffic enabled allowed Southwest to report its first-ever annual profit in 1973.

More Legal and Regulatory Hurdles

During the rest of the 1970s, Southwest found itself embroiled in another round of legal and regulatory battles. One involved Southwest's refusal to move its flights from Dallas Love Field, located 10 minutes from downtown, to the newly opened Dallas–Fort Worth (DFW) Regional Airport, which was 30 minutes from downtown Dallas. Local officials were furious because they were counting on fees from Southwest's flights in and out of DFW to help service the debt on the bonds issued to finance the construction of DFW. Southwest's position was that it was not required to move because it had not agreed to do so or been ordered to do so by the Texas Aeronautics Commission—moreover, the company's headquarters were located at Love Field. The courts eventually ruled that Southwest's operations could remain at Love Field.

A second battle ensued when rival airlines protested Southwest's application to begin serving several smaller cities in Texas; their protest was based on arguments that these markets were already well served and that Southwest's entry would result in costly overcapacity. Southwest countered that its low fares would allow more people to fly and grow the market. Again, Southwest prevailed and its views about low fares expanding the market proved accurate. In the year before Southwest initiated service, 123,000 passengers flew from Harlingen Airport in the Rio Grande Valley to Houston, Dallas, or San Antonio; in the 11 months following Southwest's initial flights, 325,000 passengers flew to the same three cities.

Believing that Braniff and Texas International were deliberately engaging in tactics to harass Southwest's operations, Southwest convinced the U.S. government to investigate what it considered predatory tactics by its chief rivals. In February 1975, Braniff and Texas International were indicted by a federal grand jury for conspiring to put Southwest out of business—a violation of the Sherman Antitrust Act. The two airlines pleaded "no contest" to the charges, signed cease-and-desist agreements, and were fined a modest $100,000 each.

When Congress passed the Airline Deregulation Act in 1978, Southwest applied to the Civil Aeronautics Board (now the Federal Aviation Agency) to fly between Houston and New Orleans. The application was vehemently opposed by local government officials and airlines operating out of DFW because of the potential for passenger traffic to be siphoned away from DFW. The opponents solicited the aid of Fort Worth congressman Jim Wright, then the majority leader of the U.S. House of Representatives, who took the matter to the floor of the House of Representatives; a rash of lobbying and maneuvering ensued. What emerged came to be known as the Wright Amendment of 1979: no airline may provide nonstop or through-plane service from Dallas Love Field to any city in any state except for locations in Texas, Louisiana, Arkansas, Oklahoma, and New Mexico. Southwest was prohibited from advertising, publishing schedules or fares, or checking baggage for travel from Dallas Love Field to any city it served outside the five-state "Wright Zone." The Wright Amendment continued in effect until 1997, when Alabama, Mississippi, and Kansas were added to the Wright Zone; in 2005, Missouri was added to the Wright Zone. In 2006, after a heated battle in Congress, legislation was passed and signed into law that repealed the Wright Amendment beginning in 2014.

The Emergence of a Combative Can-Do Culture at Southwest

The legal, regulatory, and competitive battles that Southwest fought in its early years produced a strong esprit de corps among Southwest personnel and a drive to survive and prosper despite the odds. With newspaper and TV stories reporting Southwest's difficulties regularly, employees were fully aware that the airline's existence was constantly on the line. Had the company been forced to move from Love Field, it would most likely have gone under, an outcome that employees, Southwest's rivals, and local government officials understood well. According to Southwest's former president Colleen Barrett, the obstacles thrown in Southwest's path by competitors and local officials were instrumental in building Herb Kelleher's passion for Southwest Airlines and ingraining a combative, can-do spirit into the corporate culture:

> They would put twelve to fifteen lawyers on a case and on our side there was Herb. They almost wore him to the ground. But the more arrogant they were, the more determined Herb got that this airline was going to go into the air—and stay there.
>
> The warrior mentality, the very fight to survive, is truly what created our culture.[5]

When Lamar Muse resigned in 1978, Southwest's board wanted Herb Kelleher to take over as chairman and CEO. But Kelleher enjoyed practicing law and, while he agreed to become chairman of the board, he insisted that someone else be CEO. Southwest's board appointed Howard Putnam, a group vice president of marketing services at United Airlines, as Southwest's president and CEO in July 1978. Putnam asked Kelleher to become more involved in Southwest's day-to-day operations, and over the next three years, Kelleher got to know many of the company's personnel and observe them in action. Putnam announced his resignation in the fall of 1981 to become president and chief operating officer at Braniff International. This time, Southwest's board succeeded in persuading Kelleher to take on the additional duties of CEO and president.

Sustained Growth and the Emergence of a New Industry Leader, 1981–2009

When Herb Kelleher took over in 1981, Southwest was flying 27 planes to 14 destination cities and had $270 million in revenues and 2,100 employees. Over the next 20 years, Southwest Airlines prospered under Kelleher's leadership. When Kelleher stepped down as CEO in mid-2001, the company had 350 planes flying to 58 U.S. airports, annual revenues of $5.6 billion, more than 30,000 employees, and 64 million fare-paying passengers annually. Under the two CEOs who succeeded Kelleher, Southwest continued its march to becoming the market share leader in domestic air travel; by 2009, it was earning annual revenues of $10.4 billion, employing 34,874 people, flying 537 planes to 69 airports in 36 states, and transporting some 86 million fare-paying passengers and some 100 million passengers (including those traveling on frequent flyer awards) annually. In the process, the company won more industry Triple Crown Awards for best on-time record, best baggage handling, and fewest customer complaints than any other U.S. airline.

Exhibit 2 provides a five-year summary of Southwest's financial and operating performance. Exhibit 3 provides selected financial and operating data for major U.S. air carriers during 1995–2009.

Exhibit 2   Summary of Southwest Airlines' Financial and Operating Performance, 2005–2009

	Years Ended December 31				
	2009	**2008**	**2007**	**2006**	**2005**
Financial Data ($ millions, except per share data)					
Operating revenues	$10,350	$11,023	$ 9,861	$ 9,086	$ 7,584
Operating expenses	10,088	10,574	9,070	8,152	6,859
Operating income	262	449	791	934	725
Other expenses (income) net	98	171	(267)	144	(54)
Income before taxes	164	278	1,058	790	779
Provision for income taxes	65	100	413	291	295
Net Income	$ 99	$ 178	$ 645	$ 499	$ 484
Net income per share, basic	$0.13	$0.24	$0.85	$0.63	$0.61
Net income per share, diluted	.13	.24	.84	.61	.60
Cash dividends per common share	$0.018	$0.018	$0.018	$0.018	$0.018
Total assets at period-end	$14,269	$14,068	$16,772	$13,460	$14,003
Long-term obligations at period-end	$ 3,325	$ 3,498	$ 2,050	$ 1,567	$ 1,394
Stockholders' equity at period-end	$ 5,466	$ 4,953	$ 6,941	$ 6,449	$ 6,675

Exhibit 2   (Concluded)

	Years Ended December 31				
	2009	2008	2007	2006	2005
Operating Data					
Revenue passengers carried	86,310,229	88,529,234	88,713,472	83,814,823	77,693,875
Enplaned passengers[1]	101,338,228	101,920,598	101,910,809	96,276,907	88,379,900
Revenue passenger miles (RPMs) (000s)	74,456,710	73,491,687	72,318,812	67,691,289	60,223,100
Available seat miles (ASMs) (000s)	98,001,550	103,271,343	99,635,967	92,663,023	85,172,795
Load factor[2]	76.0%	71.2%	72.6%	73.1%	70.7%
Average length of passenger haul (miles)	863	830	815	808	775
Average aircraft stage length (miles)	639	636	629	622	607
Trips flown	1,125,111	1,191,151	1,160,699	1,092,331	1,028,639
Average passenger fare	$114.61	$119.16	$106.60	$104.40	$93.68
Passenger revenue yield per RPM	13.29¢	14.35¢	13.08¢	12.93¢	12.09¢
Operating revenue yield per ASM	10.56¢	10.67¢	9.90¢	9.81¢	8.90¢
Operating expenses per ASM	10.29¢	10.24¢	9.10¢	8.80¢	8.05¢
Fuel costs per gallon (average)	$2.12	$2.44	$1.80	$1.64	$1.13
Fuel consumed, in gallons (millions)	1,428	1,511	1,489	1,389	1,287
Full-time equivalent employees at year-end	34,726	35,499	34,378	32,664	31,729
Size of fleet at year-end[3]	537	537	520	481	445

[1]Includes passengers traveling on free travel award tickets.
[2]Revenue passenger miles divided by available seat miles.
[3]Includes leased aircraft.
Source: Southwest Airlines, 2009 10-K report, p. 23.

HERB KELLEHER: SOUTHWEST'S CELEBRATED CEO

Herb Kelleher majored in philosophy at Wesleyan University in Middletown, Connecticut, graduating with honors. He earned his law degree at New York University, again graduating with honors and also serving as a member of the law review. After graduation, he clerked for a New Jersey Supreme Court justice for two years and then joined a law firm in Newark. Upon marrying a woman from Texas and becoming enamored with Texas, he moved to San Antonio, where he became a successful lawyer and came to represent Rollin King's small aviation company.

When Herb Kelleher took on the role of Southwest's CEO in 1981, he made a point of visiting with maintenance personnel to check on how well the planes were running and of talking with the flight attendants. Kelleher did not do much managing from his office, preferring instead to be out among the troops as much as he could. His style was to listen and observe and to offer

Case 20   Southwest Airlines in 2010: Culture, Values, and Operating Practices   C-283

Exhibit 3   Selected Operating and Financial Data for Major U.S. Airline Carriers, 1995–2009 (selected years)

	1995	2000	2005	2007	2008	2009
Passengers (in millions)	559.0	666.2	738.3	769.6	743.3	703.9
Flights (in thousands)	8,062	9,035	11,564	11,399	10,841	10,373
Revenue passenger miles (in billions)	603.4	692.8	778.6	829.4	812.4	769.5
Available seat miles (in billions)	807.1	987.9	1,002.7	1,037.7	1,021.3	957.2
Load factor	67.0	72.4	77.7	79.9	79.5	80.4
Passenger revenues (in millions)	$69,470	$93,622	$93,500	$107,678	$111,542	$91,331
Operating profit (loss) (in millions)	$5,852	$6,999	$427	$9,344	($3,348)	$2,409
Net profit (loss) excluding one-time charges and gains (in millions)	$2,283	$2,486	($5,782)	$4,998	($9,464)	($2,799)
Total employees	546,987	679,967	562,467	560,997	556,920	536,200

Sources: Air Transport Association, *2010 Economic Report*, pp. 8, 19, 23, and 30; *2009 Economic Report*, p. 19; Air Transport Association, *2008 Economic Report*, p. 19; and Air Transport Association, *2005 Economic Report*, p. 7.

encouragement. Kelleher attended most graduation ceremonies of flight attendant classes, and he often appeared to help load bags on "Black Wednesday," the busy travel day before Thanksgiving. He was held in the highest regard by Southwest employees and knew thousands of their names. When he attended a Southwest employee function, he was swarmed like a celebrity.

Kelleher had an affinity for bold-print Hawaiian shirts, owned a tricked-out motorcycle, and made no secret of his passion for cigarettes and Wild Turkey whiskey. He loved to make jokes and engage in pranks and corporate antics, prompting some people to refer to him as the "clown prince" of the airline industry. He once appeared at a company gathering dressed in an Elvis costume and had arm-wrestled a South Carolina company executive at a public event in Dallas for rights to use "Just Plane Smart" as an advertising slogan.[6] Kelleher was well known inside and outside the company for his combativeness, particularly when it came to beating back competitors. On one occasion, he reportedly told a group of veteran employees, "If someone says they're going to smack us in the face—knock them out, stomp them out, boot them in the ditch, cover them over, and move on to the next thing. That's the Southwest spirit at work."[7] On another occasion, he said, "I love battles. I think it's part of the Irish in me. It's like what Patton said, 'War is hell and I love it so.' That's how I feel. I've never gotten tired of fighting."[8]

While Southwest was deliberately combative and flamboyant in some aspects of its operations, when it came to the financial side of the business Kelleher insisted on fiscal conservatism, a strong balance sheet, comparatively low levels of debt, and zealous attention to bottom-line profitability. While believing strongly in being prepared for adversity, Kelleher had an aversion to Southwest personnel spending time drawing up all kinds of formal strategic plans, saying, "Reality is chaotic; planning is ordered and logical. The meticulous nit-picking that goes on in most strategic planning processes creates a mental straightjacket that becomes disabling in an industry where things change radically from one day to the next." Kelleher wanted Southwest managers to think ahead, have contingency plans, and be ready to act when it appeared that the future held significant risks or when new conditions suddenly appeared and demanded prompt responses.

Kelleher was a strong believer in the principle that employees—not customers—came first:

> You have to treat your employees like your customers. When you treat them right, then they will treat your outside customers right. That has been a very powerful competitive weapon for us. You've got to take the time to listen to people's ideas. If you just tell somebody no, that's an act of power and, in my opinion, an abuse of power. You don't want to constrain people in their thinking.[9]

Another indication of the importance that Kelleher placed on employees was the message he had penned in 1990 that was prominently displayed in the lobby of Southwest's headquarters in Dallas:

> The people of Southwest Airlines are "the creators" of what we have become—and of what we will be.
>
> Our people transformed an idea into a legend. That legend will continue to grow only so long as it is nourished—by our people's indomitable spirit, boundless energy, immense goodwill, and burning desire to excel.
>
> Our thanks—and our love—to the people of Southwest Airlines for creating a marvelous family and a wondrous airline.

In June 2001, Herb Kelleher stepped down as CEO but continued on in his role as chairman of Southwest's board of directors and the head of the board's executive committee; as chairman, he played a lead role in Southwest's strategy, expansion to new cities and aircraft scheduling, and governmental and industry affairs. In May 2008, after more than 40 years of leadership at Southwest, Kelleher retired as chairman; he was, however, scheduled to remain a full-time Southwest employee until July 2013.

EXECUTIVE LEADERSHIP AT SOUTHWEST, 2001–2010

In June 2001, responding to anxious investor concerns about the company's leadership succession plans, Southwest Airlines began an orderly transfer of power and responsibilities from Herb Kelleher, age 70, to two of his most trusted protégés: James F. Parker, 54, Southwest's general counsel, succeeded Kelleher as Southwest's CEO, and Colleen Barrett, 56, Southwest's executive vice president–customers and self-described keeper of Southwest's pep-rally corporate culture, became president and chief operating officer.

James Parker, CEO from 2001 to 2004

James Parker's association with Herb Kelleher went back 23 years, to the time when they were colleagues at Kelleher's old law firm. Parker moved over to Southwest from the law firm in February 1986. Parker's profile inside the company as Southwest's vice president and general counsel had been relatively low, but he was Southwest's chief labor negotiator, and much of the credit for Southwest's good relations with employee unions belonged to him. Prior to his appointment as CEO, Parker had been a member of the company's executive planning committee; his experiences ranged from properties and facilities to technical services team to the company's alliances with vendors and partners. Parker and Kelleher were said to think much alike, and Parker was regarded as having a good sense of humor, although he did not have as colorful and flamboyant a personality as Kelleher. Parker was seen as an honest, straight-arrow kind of person who had a strong grasp of Southwest's culture and market niche and who could be nice or tough, depending on the situation. When his appointment was announced, Parker said:

> There is going to be no change of course insofar as Southwest is concerned. We have a very experienced leadership team. We've all worked together for a long time. There will be evolutionary changes in Southwest, just as there have always been in our history. We're going to stay true to our business model of being a low-cost, low-fare airline.[10]

Parker retired unexpectedly, for personal reasons, in July 2004, stepping down as CEO and vice chairman of the board and also resigning from the company's board of directors. He was succeeded by Gary C. Kelly.

Colleen Barrett, Southwest's President from 2001 to 2008

Colleen Barrett began working with Kelleher as his legal secretary in 1967 and had been with Southwest since 1978. As executive vice president–customers, Barrett had a high profile among Southwest employees and spent most of her time on culture building, morale building, and customer service; her goal was to ensure that employees felt good about what they were doing and felt empowered to serve the cause of Southwest Airlines.[11] She and Kelleher were regarded as Southwest's guiding lights, and some analysts said she was essentially functioning as the company's chief operating officer (COO) prior to her formal appointment as president. Much of the credit for the company's strong record of customer service and its strong-culture work climate belonged to Barrett.

Barrett had been the driving force behind lining the hallways at Southwest's headquarters with photos of company events and trying to create a family atmosphere at the company. Believing it was important to make employees feel cared about and important, Barrett had put together a network of contacts across the company to help her stay in touch with what was happening with employees and their families. When network members learned about events that were worthy of acknowledgment, the word quickly got to Barrett—the information went into a database, and an appropriate greeting card or gift was sent. Barrett had a remarkable ability to give gifts that were individualized and that connected her to the recipient.[12]

Barrett was the first woman appointed as president and COO of a major U.S. airline. In October 2001, *Fortune* ranked Colleen Barrett 20th on its list of the 50 most powerful women in American business. Barrett retired as president in July 2008, but was scheduled to remain as a full-time Southwest employee until 2013.

Gary C. Kelly, Southwest's CEO from 2004 Onward

Gary Kelly was appointed vice chairman of the board of directors and CEO of Southwest effective July 15, 2004. Prior to that time, Kelly was executive vice president and chief financial officer (CFO) from 2001 to 2004, and vice president–finance and CFO from 1989 to 2001. He joined Southwest in 1986 as its controller. In 2008, effective with the retirement of Kelleher and Barrett, Kelly assumed the titles of chairman of the board, CEO, and president.

When Kelly was named CEO in 2004, Herb Kelleher said:

> Gary Kelly is one of our brightest stars, well respected throughout the industry and well known, over more than a decade, to the media, analyst, and investor communities for his excellence. As part of our Board's succession planning, we had already focused on Gary as Jim Parker's successor, and that process has simply been accelerated by Jim's personal decision to retire. Under Gary's

leadership, Southwest has achieved the strongest balance sheet in the American airline industry; the best fuel hedging position in our industry; and tremendous progress in technology.[13]

During his tenure as CEO, Kelly and other top-level Southwest executives had sharpened and fine-tuned Southwest's strategy in a number of areas, continued to expand operations (adding both more flights and initiating service to new airports), and worked to maintain the company's low-cost advantage over its domestic rivals.

Kelly saw four factors as keys to Southwest's recipe for success:[14]

- Hire great people, treat 'em like family.
- Care for our Customers warmly and personally, like they're guests in our home.
- Keep fares and operating costs lower than anybody else by being safe, efficient, and operationally excellent.
- Stay prepared for bad times with a strong balance sheet, lots of cash, and a stout fuel hedge.

To help Southwest be a standout performer on these four key success factors, Kelly had established five strategic objectives for Southwest:[15]

- Be the best place to work.
- Be the safest, most efficient, and most reliable airline in the world.
- Offer customers a convenient flight schedule with lots of flights to lots of places they want to go.
- Offer customers the best overall travel experience.
- Do all of these things in a way that maintains a low cost structure and the ability to offer low fares.

During 2008–2009, Kelly initiated a slight revision of Southwest's mission statement and also spearheaded a vision statement that called for a steadfast focus on a triple bottom line of Performance, People, and Planet—see Exhibit 4.

SOUTHWEST AIRLINES' STRATEGY

From day one, Southwest had pursued a low-cost/low-price/no-frills strategy. Its signature low

C-286   **Part 2** Cases in Crafting and Executing Strategy

Exhibit 4   Southwest Airline's Mission, Vision, and Triple Bottom Line Commitment to Performance, People, and Planet

THE MISSION OF SOUTHWEST AIRLINES

The mission of Southwest Airlines is dedication to the highest quality of Customer Service delivered with a sense of warmth, friendliness, individual pride, and Company Spirit.

TO OUR EMPLOYEES

We are committed to provide our Employees a stable work environment with equal opportunity for learning and personal growth. Creativity and innovation are encouraged for improving the effectiveness of Southwest Airlines. Above all, Employees will be provided the same concern, respect, and caring attitude within the organization that they are expected to share externally with every Southwest Customer.

TO OUR COMMUNITIES

Our goal is to be the hometown airline of every community we serve, and because those communities sustain and nurture us with their support and loyalty, it is vital that we, as individuals and in groups, embrace each community with the SOUTHWEST SPIRIT of involvement, service, and caring to make those communities better places to live and work.

TO OUR PLANET

We strive to be a good environmental steward across our system in all of our hometowns, and one component of our stewardship is efficiency, which by its very nature, translates to eliminating waste and conserving resources. Using cost-effective and environmentally beneficial operating procedures (including facilities and equipment), allows us to reduce the amount of materials we use and, when combined with our ability to reuse and recycle material, preserves these environmental resources.

TO OUR STAKEHOLDERS

Southwest's vision for a sustainable future is one where there will be a balance in our business model between Employees and Community, the Environment, and our Financial Viability. In order to protect our world for future generations, while meeting our commitments to our Employees, Customers, and Stakeholders, we will strive to lead our industry in innovative efficiency that conserves natural resources, maintains a creative and innovative workforce, and gives back to the Communities in which we live and work.

Source: Southwest Airlines, "One Report, 2009," www.southwest.com, accessed August 20, 2010.

fares made air travel affordable to a wide segment of the U.S. population—giving substance to its tag line "The Freedom to Fly." It employed a relatively simple fare structure, with all of the fare options plainly displayed at the company's website. The lowest fares were usually nonrefundable but could be applied to future travel on Southwest Airlines without incurring a change fee (rival airlines charged a change fee of $100 to $175), and the company's advance purchase requirements on tickets were more lenient than those of its rivals. Many Southwest flights had some seats available at deeply discounted fares, provided they were purchased online at the company's website.

In November 2007, Southwest introduced a new Business Select fare to attract economy-minded business travelers; Business Select customers had early boarding privileges, received extra Rapid Rewards (frequent flyer credits), and a free cocktail. In 2008, rival airlines instituted a series of add-on fees—including a fuel surcharge for each flight, fees for checking bags, fees for processing frequent flyer travel awards, fees for buying a ticket in person at the airport or calling a toll-free number to speak with a ticket agent to make a reservation, fees for changing a previously purchased ticket to a different flight, and fees for in-flight snacks and beverages—to help defray skyrocketing costs for jet fuel (which had climbed from about 15 percent of operating expenses in 2000 to 40 percent of operating expenses in mid-2008). Southwest, however, choose to forgo à la carte pricing and stuck with an all-inclusive fare price. During 2009, Southwest ran an ad campaign called "Bags Fly Free" to publicize the cost savings of flying Southwest rather than paying the $20 to $50 fees that rival airlines charged for a first or second checked bag.

When advance reservations were weak for particular weeks or times of the day or on certain routes, Southwest made a regular practice of initiating special fare promotions to stimulate ticket sales on flights that otherwise would have had numerous empty seats. For instance, the company had used fare sales to combat slack air travel during much of the recession of 2008–2009.

The combined effect of Southwest's "Bags Fly Free" ads and periodic fare sales resulted in company-record load factors for every month from July through December 2009. (A load factor was the percentage of all available seats on all flights that were occupied by fare-paying passengers.) Southwest continued to run the "Bags Fly Free" ads during the first half of 2010. In June 2010, to celebrate its 39 years of flying, Southwest instituted a two-day special promotion of $39 one-way fares for travel up to 450 miles, $79 one-way fares for travel between 451 and 1,000 miles, and $119 one-way fares for travel between 1,001 and 1,500 miles; the fares were good for travel from September 8, 2010, through November 17, 2010 to select destinations.

Southwest was a shrewd practitioner of the concept of price elasticity, proving in one market after another that the revenue gains from increased ticket sales and the volume of passenger traffic would more than compensate for the revenue erosion associated with low fares. When Southwest entered the Florida market with an introductory $17 fare from Tampa to Fort Lauderdale, the number of annual passengers flying that route jumped 50 percent, to more than 330,000. In Manchester, New Hampshire, passenger counts went from 1.1 million in 1997, the year prior to Southwest's entry, to 3.5 million in 2000, and average one-way fares dropped from just over $300 to $129. Southwest's success in stimulating higher passenger traffic at airports across the United States via low fares and frequent flights had been coined the "Southwest effect" by personnel at the U.S. Department of Transportation. Exhibit 5 shows the cities and airports Southwest served in May 2010. Southwest began service to Boston, New York (LaGuardia), Minneapolis–St. Paul, and Milwaukee in 2009. Management had announced plans for Southwest to begin service to Newark, New Jersey and two South Carolina airports—Charleston and Greenville-Spartanburg—in 2011.

Unlike the hub-and-spoke route systems of rival airlines (where operations were concentrated at a limited number of hub cities and most destinations were served via connections through the hub), Southwest's route system had been carefully designed to concentrate on flights between pairs of cities 150 to 700 miles apart that handled enough passenger traffic to allow Southwest to offer a sizable number of daily flights. As a general rule, Southwest did not initiate service to an airport unless it envisioned the potential for originating at least 8 flights a day there and saw opportunities to add more flights over time—in Denver, for example, Southwest had boosted the number of daily departures from 13 in January 2006 (the month in which service to and from Denver was initiated) to 79 daily departures in May 2008 and to 129 departures in May 2010. Southwest's point-to-point route system minimized connections, delays, and total trip time—its emphasis on nonstop flights between pairs of cities allowed about 75 percent of Southwest's passengers to fly nonstop to their destination. While a majority of Southwest's flights involved actual in-air flight times of less than 90 minutes, in recent years the company had added a significant number of nonstop flights to more distant airports where its low fares could generate profitable amounts of passenger traffic.

Southwest's frequent flyer program, Rapid Rewards, was based on trips flown rather than mileage. Rapid Rewards customers received one credit for each one-way trip or two credits for each round-trip flown and could also earn credits by using the services of Southwest's car rental, hotel, and credit card partners. There were two principal types of travel awards:

- *Standard Awards*—these were for Rapid Rewards members who accumulated one free round-trip after the accumulation of 16 credits within 24 consecutive months. Standard Awards were valid for one free round-trip to any destination available on Southwest Airlines, had to be used within 12 months, and were subject to seat restrictions and blackout dates around certain major holidays.

- *Companion Passes*—these were for Rapid Rewards members who accumulated 100 credits within a 12-month period; these passes provided unlimited free round-trip travel to any destination available on Southwest for a designated companion of a qualifying Rapid Rewards Member who purchased a ticket or

Exhibit 5   Airports and Cities Served by Southwest Airlines, May 2010

Southwest's Top 10 Airports			
	Daily Departures	Number of Gates	Nonstop Cities Served
Chicago Midway	224	29	51
Las Vegas	223	19	57
Baltimore/Washington	181	20	44
Phoenix	177	24	44
Houston (Hobby)	135	17	30
Dallas (Love Field)	131	15	15
Denver	129	14	42
Los Angeles (LAX)	116	11	20
Oakland	114	13	20
Orlando	104	12	33

Other Airports Served by Southwest Airlines			
Albany	Fort Myers/Naples	Minneapolis/St. Paul	Reno/Tahoe
Albuquerque	Harlingen/South Padre Island	Nashville	Sacramento
Amarillo		New Orleans	St. Louis
Austin	Hartford/Springfield	New York (LaGuardia)	Salt Lake City
Birmingham	Indianapolis	Norfolk	San Antonio
Boise	Long Island (MacArthur)	Oklahoma City	San Francisco
Boston Logan	Jackson, MS	Omaha	San Jose
Buffalo	Jacksonville	Ontario, CA	Seattle/Tacoma
Burbank, CA	Kansas City	Orange County, CA	Spokane
Cleveland	Little Rock	Panama City, FL	Tampa
Columbus, OH	Louisville	Philadelphia	Tucson
Corpus Christi, TX	Lubbock	Pittsburgh	Tulsa
Detroit Metro	Manchester, NH	Portland, OR	Washington, DC (Dulles)
El Paso	Midland/Odessa, TX	Providence	West Palm Beach
Fort Lauderdale	Milwaukee	Raleigh-Durham	

Source: Southwest Airlines, www.southwest.com, accessed August 5, 2010.

used a free travel award ticket. The Rapid Rewards member and designated companion had to travel together on the same flight. Companion Passes were valid for 12 months after issuance and were not subject to seat restrictions or blackout dates.

In addition, Rapid Rewards members who flew 32 qualifying flights within a 12-month period received priority boarding privileges for a year. Southwest customers redeemed 2.4 million free ticket awards during 2009 and 2.8 million free ticket awards in both 2007 and 2008. Free travel award usage accounted for about 8 percent of

Southwest's total revenue passenger miles flown during 2007–2009. Since the inception of Rapid Rewards in 1987, approximately 16 percent of all fully earned awards had expired without being used.

Customer Service and Customer Satisfaction

Southwest's approach to delivering good customer service and creating customer satisfaction was predicated on presenting a happy face to passengers, displaying a fun-loving attitude, and doing things in a manner calculated to make sure passengers had a positive flying experience. The company made a special effort to employ gate personnel who enjoyed interacting with customers, had good interpersonal skills, and displayed cheery, outgoing personalities. A number of Southwest's gate personnel let their wit and sense of humor show by sometimes entertaining those in the gate area with trivia questions or contests such as "Who has the biggest hole in their sock?" Apart from greeting passengers coming onto planes and assisting them in finding open seats and stowing baggage, flight attendants were encouraged to be engaging, converse and joke with passengers, and go about their tasks in ways that made passengers smile. On some flights, attendants sang announcements to passengers on takeoff and landing. On one flight while passengers were boarding, an attendant with bunny ears popped out of an overhead bin exclaiming "Surprise!" The repertoires to amuse passengers varied from flight crew to flight crew.

During their tenure, both Herb Kelleher and Colleen Barrett had made a point of sending congratulatory notes to employees when the company received letters from customers complimenting particular Southwest employees; complaint letters were seen as learning opportunities for employees and reasons to consider making adjustments. Employees were provided the following policy guidance regarding how far to go in trying to please customers:

> No Employee will ever be punished for using good judgment and good old common sense when trying to accommodate a Customer—no matter what our rules are.[16]
>
> When you empower People to make a positive difference every day, you allow them to decide. Most guidelines are written to be broken as long as the Employee is leaning toward the Customer. We follow the Golden Rule and try to do the right thing and think about our Customer.[17]

Southwest executives believed that conveying a friendly, fun-loving spirit to customers was the key to competitive advantage. As one Southwest manager put it, "Our fares can be matched; our airplanes and routes can be copied. But we pride ourselves on our customer service."[18]

In 2007, Southwest did an "extreme gate makeover" to improve the airport experience of customers. The makeover included adding (1) a business-focused area with padded seats, tables with power outlets, power stations with stools, and a flat-screen TV with news programming, and (2) a family-focused area with smaller tables and chairs, power stations for charging electrical devices, and kid-friendly programming on a flat-screen TV.

Marketing and Promotion

Southwest was continually on the lookout for novel ways to tell its story, make its distinctive persona come alive, and strike a chord in the minds of air travelers. Many of its print ads and billboards were deliberately unconventional and attention-getting so as to create and reinforce the company's maverick, fun-loving, and combative image. Some previous campaigns had used the slogans "The Low-Fare Airline" and "The All-Time On-Time Airline"; others had touted the company's Triple Crown Awards. One of the company's billboard campaigns highlighted the frequency of the company's flights with such headlines as "Austin Auften," "Phoenix Phrequently," and "L.A. A.S.A.P." Each holiday season since 1985, Southwest had run a "Christmas Card" ad on TV featuring children and their families from the Ronald McDonald Houses and Southwest employees. Fresh advertising campaigns were launched periodically—Exhibit 6 shows four representative ads.

In 2002, Southwest began changing the look of its planes, updating its somewhat drab gold-orange-red scheme to a much fresher and brighter canyon blue/red/gold/orange scheme—see Exhibit 7.

Southwest tended to advertise far more heavily than any other U.S. carrier. According to The Nielsen Company, during the first six months of 2009, Southwest boosted its ad spending by 20 percent, to $112.6 million, to hammer home its "Bags Fly Free" message. Passenger traffic at Southwest subsequently rose, while passenger volumes went in the opposite direction at Southwest's five largest competitors—Delta, American, United, Continental, and US Airways, all of which had recently introduced or increased fees for checked baggage. Passenger travel on Southwest's domestic flights rose by more than 28 million passengers annually from 2000 through 2009, whereas passenger volume on domestic flights

Exhibit 6   **Four Samples of Southwest's Ads**

Exhibit 7   Southwest's New Look and Aircraft Equipped with Winglets

Old Color Scheme
(Plane without winglets)

New Color Scheme
(plane with winglets)

was down by 88 million passengers annually at Delta, American, United, Continental, and US Airways during this same period.

Other Strategy Elements

Southwest's strategy included several other elements:

- *Gradual expansion into new geographic markets.* Southwest generally added one or two new cities to its route schedule annually, preferring to saturate the market for daily flights to the cities/airports it currently served before entering new markets. In selecting new cities, Southwest looked for city pairs that could generate substantial amounts of both business and leisure traffic. Management believed that having numerous flights flying the same routes appealed to business travelers looking for convenient flight times and the ability to catch a later flight if they unexpectedly ran late.

- *Adding flights in areas where rivals were cutting back service.* When rivals cut back flights to cities that Southwest served, Southwest often moved in with more flights of its own, believing its lower fares would attract more passengers. When Midway Airlines ceased operations in November 1990, Southwest moved in overnight and quickly instituted flights to Chicago's Midway Airport. Southwest was a first-mover in adding flights on routes where rivals had cut their offerings following the terrorist attacks of September 11, 2001 (9/11).

When American Airlines closed its hubs in Nashville and San Jose, Southwest immediately increased the number of its flights into and out of both locations. When US Airways trimmed its flight schedule for Philadelphia and Pittsburgh, Southwest promptly boosted its flights into and out of those airports. Southwest initiated service to Denver when United, beset with financial difficulties, cut back operations at its big Denver hub.

- *Curtailing flights on marginally profitable routes where numerous seats often went unfilled and shifting planes to routes with good growth opportunities.* Management was attracted to this strategy element because it enabled Southwest to grow revenues and profits without having to add so many new planes to its fleet. This strategy was aggressively pursued in 2008–2009 as a means of coping with industry-wide declines in passenger air travel during the recession. Management canceled the planned additions to the size of its aircraft fleet in 2009, cut the number of flights in markets where ticket bookings were weak, and redeployed the capacity to support entry into four new markets with promising long-term growth potential: New York's LaGuardia Airport, Minneapolis–St. Paul International Airport, Boston's Logan International Airport, and Milwaukee's General Mitchell International Airport.

- *Putting strong emphasis on safety, high-quality maintenance, and reliable operations.*

Southwest management believed the company's low-fare strategy, coupled with frequent flights and friendly service, delivered "more value for less money" to customers rather than "less value for less money." Kelleher said, "Everybody values a very good service provided at a very reasonable price."[19]

SOUTHWEST'S EFFORTS TO EXECUTE ITS LOW-FARE STRATEGY

Southwest management fully understood that low fares necessitated zealous pursuit of low operating costs and had, over the years, instituted a number of practices to keep its costs below those of rival carriers:

- The company operated only one type of aircraft—Boeing 737s—to minimize the size of spare parts inventories, simplify the training of maintenance and repair personnel, improve the proficiency and speed with which maintenance routines could be done, and simplify the task of scheduling planes for particular flights. Furthermore, as the launch customer for Boeing's 737-300, 737-500, and 737-700 models, Southwest acquired its new aircraft at favorable prices. See Exhibit 8 for statistics on Southwest's aircraft fleet.

- Southwest was the first major airline to introduce ticketless travel (eliminating the need to print and process paper tickets) and also the first to allow customers to make reservations and purchase tickets at the company's website (thus bypassing the need to pay commissions to travel agents for handling the ticketing process and reducing staffing requirements at Southwest's reservation centers). Selling a ticket on its website cost Southwest roughly $1, versus $3 to $4 for a ticket booked through its own internal reservation system and as much as $15 for tickets for business travelers purchased through travel agents and professional business travel partners. Ticketless travel accounted for more than 95 percent of all sales in 2007, and nearly 74 percent of Southwest's revenues were generated through sales at its website.

- The company stressed flights into and out of airports in medium-sized cities and less congested airports in major metropolitan areas (Chicago Midway, Detroit Metro, Houston

Exhibit 8 Southwest's Aircraft Fleet as of March 31, 2010

Type of Aircraft	Number	Seats	Comments
Boeing 737–300	173	137	Southwest was Boeing's launch customer for this model.
Boeing 737–500	25	122	Southwest was Boeing's launch customer for this model.
Boeing 737–700	343	137	Southwest was Boeing's launch customer for this model.
	541		

Other Fleet-Related Facts

Average age of aircraft fleet—10.5 years

Average aircraft trip length—633 miles, with an average duration of 1 hour and 54 minutes

Average aircraft utilization—6.5 flights per day and 12 hours and 15 minutes of flight time

Fleet size—1990: 106 1995: 224 2000: 344 2009: 537

Firm orders for new aircraft—2010: 10 2011: 10 2012: 13 2013–2016: 58

Source: Southwest Airlines, www.southwest.com, accessed August 5, 2010, and 2009 10-K report, p. 18.

Hobby, and Dallas Love Field). This strategy helped produce better-than-average on-time performance and reduce the fuel costs associated with planes sitting in line on crowded taxiways or circling airports waiting for clearance to land. It further allowed the company to avoid paying the higher landing fees and terminal gate costs at such high-traffic airports as Atlanta's Hartsfield International, Chicago's O'Hare, and Dallas–Fort Worth (DFW) where landing slots were controlled and rationed to those airlines willing to pay the high fees. Southwest's strategy of serving less congested airports also helped minimize total travel time for passengers—driving to the airport, parking, ticketing, boarding, and flight time. However, in recent years, to help sustain growth in passenger traffic and revenues, Southwest had initiated service to airports in several large metropolitan cities where air traffic congestion was a frequent problem—such as Los Angeles (LAX), Boston (Logan International, beginning in 2009), New York (LaGuardia), Denver, San Francisco, and Philadelphia.

- Southwest's point-to-point scheduling of flights was more cost-efficient than the hub-and-spoke systems used by rival airlines. Hub-and-spoke systems involved passengers on many different flights coming in from spoke locations (or perhaps another hub) to a central airport or hub within a short span of time and then connecting to an outgoing flight to their destination—a spoke location or another hub). Most flights arrived at and departed from a hub across a two-hour window, creating big peak-valley swings in airport personnel workloads and gate utilization—airport personnel and gate areas were very busy when hub operations were in full swing and then were underutilized in the interval awaiting the next round of inbound/outbound flights. In contrast, Southwest's point-to-point routes permitted scheduling aircraft so as to minimize the time aircraft were at the gate, currently approximately 25 minutes, thereby reducing the number of aircraft and gate facilities that would otherwise be required. Furthermore, with a relatively even flow of incoming/outgoing flights and gate

traffic, Southwest could staff its terminal operations to handle a fairly steady workload across a day, whereas hub-and-spoke operators had to staff their operations to serve three to four daily peak periods.

- To economize on the amount of time it took terminal personnel to check passengers in and to simplify the whole task of making reservations, Southwest dispensed with the practice of assigning each passenger a reserved seat. Instead, for many years, passengers were given color-coded plastic cards with the letters A, B, or C when they checked in at the boarding gate. Passengers then boarded in groups, according to the color/letter on their card, sitting in whatever seat was open when they got on the plane—a procedure described by some as a "cattle call." Passengers who were particular about where they sat had to arrive at the gate early to get boarding cards and then had to position themselves near the front when it was their group's turn to board. In 2002, Southwest abandoned the use of plastic cards and began printing a big, bold A, B, or C on the boarding pass when the passenger checked in at the ticket counter; passengers then boarded in groups according to their assigned letter. In 2007–2008, in order to significantly reduce the time that passengers spent standing in line waiting for their group to board, Southwest introduced an enhanced boarding method that automatically assigned each passenger a specific number within the passenger's boarding group at the time of check-in; passengers then boarded the aircraft in that numerical order. All passengers could check in online up to 24 hours before departure time and print out a boarding pass, thus bypassing counter check-in (unless they wished to check baggage).

- Southwest flight attendants were responsible for cleaning up trash left by deplaning passengers and otherwise getting the plane presentable for passengers to board for the next flight. Rival carriers had cleaning crews come on board to perform this function until they incurred heavy losses in 2001–2005 and were forced to institute stringent cost-cutting measures that included abandoning use of cleaning crews and copying Southwest's practice.

- Southwest did not have a first-class section on any of its planes and had no fancy frequent flyer clubs at terminals.

- Southwest offered passengers no baggage transfer services to other carriers—passengers with checked baggage who were connecting to other carriers to reach their destination were responsible for picking up their luggage at Southwest's baggage claim and then getting it to the check-in facilities of the connecting carrier. (Southwest only booked tickets involving its own flights; customers connecting to flights on other carriers had to book such tickets either through travel agents or the connecting airline.)

- Starting in 2001, Southwest began converting from cloth to leather seats; the team of Southwest employees who investigated the economics of the conversion concluded that an all-leather interior would be more durable and easier to maintain, more than justifying the higher initial costs.

- Southwest was a first-mover among major U.S. airlines in employing fuel hedging and derivative contracts to counteract rising prices for crude oil and jet fuel. From 1998 through 2008, the company's fuel hedging activities produced fuel savings of about $4 billion over what it would have spent had it paid the industry's average price for jet fuel. But unexpectedly large declines in jet fuel prices in late 2008 and 2009 resulted in reported losses of $408 million on the fuel hedging contracts that the company had in place during 2009. Southwest's fuel hedging strategy involved modifying the amount of its future fuel requirements that were hedged based on management's judgments about the forward market prices of crude oil and jet fuel.

- To enhance the performance and efficiency of its aircraft fleet, Southwest had recently added vertical winglets on the wing tips of most all its planes and begun ordering new planes equipped with winglets (see Exhibit 7). These winglets reduced lift drag, allowed aircraft to climb more steeply and reach higher flight levels quicker, improved cruising performance, helped extend engine life and reduce maintenance costs, and reduced fuel burn. In 2007, Southwest entered into an agreement with Naverus, the worldwide leader in performance-based navigation systems, to develop and implement new flight procedures for Southwest planes that would result in lower fuel consumption and greenhouse gas emissions, better on-time reliability, and increased safety in bad weather and at airports situated in mountainous terrain.

- Southwest regularly upgraded and enhanced its management information systems to speed data flows, improve operating efficiency, lower costs, and upgrade its customer service capabilities. In 2001, Southwest implemented use of new software that significantly decreased the time required to generate optimal crew schedules and help improve on-time performance. In 2007–2008, Southwest invested in next-generation technology and software to improve its ticketless system and its back-office accounting, payroll, and human resource information systems. During 2009, the company replaced or enhanced its point of sale, electronic ticketing and boarding, and revenue accounting systems. During 2010, it completed an initiative to convert to a new SAP enterprise resource planning application that would replace its general ledger, accounts payable, accounts receivable, payroll, benefits, cash management, and fixed asset systems; the conversion was designed to increase data accuracy and consistency, and to lower administrative support costs.

For many decades, Southwest's operating costs had been lower than those of American, Continental, Delta, Northwest, United, US Airways, and other major U.S. airline carriers. Recently, JetBlue, an airline that began operations in 2000 and had grown rapidly with a low-cost, low-fare strategy that was similar to Southwest's strategy, had been able to achieve operating costs that were below those of Southwest—see Exhibit 9 for cost comparisons among the major U.S. airlines during the 1995–2010 period. Exhibit 10 shows a detailed breakdown of Southwest's operating costs based on the number of available seats rather than the number of passenger-occupied seats.

Exhibit 9   Comparative Operating Cost Statistics, Major U.S. Airlines, 1995–First Quarter 2010 (selected years)

	Salaries/Fringe Benefits		Fuel and Oil	Maintenance	Rentals	Landing Fees	Advertising	General and Administrative	Other Operating Expenses	Total Operating Expenses
	Pilots/Copilots	All Employees								
American Airlines										
1995	0.94¢	5.59¢	1.53¢	1.34¢	0.59¢	0.22¢	0.19¢	1.14¢	3.65¢	14.25¢
2000	1.16	5.77	2.04	1.90	0.48	0.23	0.18	0.58	3.30	14.48
2005	0.90	4.65	3.67	1.42	0.41	0.32	0.10	0.95	3.66	15.18
2008	0.87	4.81	6.19	1.72	0.37	0.31	0.12	1.91	4.12	19.54
2009	0.91	5.30	4.10	1.88	0.42	0.35	0.13	1.56	3.47	17.20
Q1 2010	0.98	5.63	4.64	2.16	0.46	0.38	0.14	1.50	3.85	18.76
Continental Air Lines										
1995	0.95¢	3.69¢	1.67¢	1.50¢	1.25¢	0.27¢	0.25¢	0.56¢	3.68	12.87¢
2000	1.25	4.43	2.18	1.42	1.17	0.24	0.09	0.59	3.57	13.70
2005	0.79	3.85	3.42	1.18	0.91	0.34	0.13	0.82	5.74	16.38
2008	0.77	3.63	5.90	1.26	0.81	0.33	0.11	1.06	6.04	19.14
2009	0.82	3.89	3.43	1.37	0.79	0.33	0.13	0.98	5.25	16.16
Q1 2010	0.90	4.21	3.75	1.40	0.83	0.35	0.14	1.03	5.80	17.49
Delta Air Lines (merged with Northwest Airlines in 2009 and began combined reporting in January 2010)										
1995	1.27¢	4.97¢	1.70¢	1.16¢	0.71¢	0.30¢	0.18¢	0.43¢	4.07¢	13.53¢
2000	1.27	5.08	1.73	1.41	0.54	0.22	0.12	0.74	3.03	12.85
2005	0.93	4.31	3.68	1.10	0.38	0.22	0.16	0.84	6.01	16.68
2008	0.76	3.55	5.99	1.08	0.20	0.21	0.10	0.82	7.85	19.79
2009	0.86	4.04	4.72	1.28	0.19	0.25	0.14	1.10	6.78	18.52
Q1 2010	1.02	4.46	4.60	1.48	0.13	0.31	0.09	0.52	6.96	18.54
JetBlue Airways										
2005	0.51¢	2.31¢	2.42¢	0.68¢	0.38¢	0.25¢	0.16¢	0.51¢	1.44¢	8.13¢
2008	0.74	2.86	5.35	0.86	0.49	0.33	0.18	0.53	2.06	12.67
2009	0.86	3.20	3.64	0.98	0.48	0.40	0.19	0.62	2.13	11.64
Q1 2010	0.97	3.62	3.93	1.04	0.48	0.40	0.14	0.88	2.30	12.80

Costs Incurred per Revenue Passenger Mile (in cents)*

(Continued)

Exhibit 9 *(Concluded)*

	Salaries/Fringe Benefits		Fuel and Oil	Maintenance	Rentals	Landing Fees	Advertising	General and Administrative	Other Operating Expenses	Total Operating Expenses
	Pilots/Copilots	All Employees								
Northwest Airlines (merged with Delta and began combined reporting in January 2010)										
1995	1.21¢	4.84¢	1.73¢	1.39¢	0.58¢	0.37¢	0.20¢	0.52¢	3.14¢	12.77¢
2000	1.01	4.76	2.35	1.55	0.53	0.31	0.17	0.55	2.77	12.99
2005	0.94	5.07	4.01	1.54	0.57	0.38	0.12	0.58	5.13	17.40
2008	0.73	3.77	7.33	1.30	0.26	0.34	0.08	0.86	6.49	20.43
2009	0.98	4.34	3.79	1.18	0.18	0.32	0.06	1.41	5.22	16.49
Southwest Airlines										
1995	0.92¢	3.94¢	1.56¢	1.21¢	0.79¢	0.35¢	0.41¢	1.09¢	1.56¢	10.91¢
2000	0.86	4.22	1.95	1.22	0.48	0.31	0.35	1.42	0.96	10.91
2005	1.18	4.70	2.44	1.17	0.31	0.34	0.29	0.73	1.23	11.21
2008	1.31	4.81	5.04	1.45	0.26	0.39	0.27	0.84	1.30	14.36
2009	1.33	4.88	4.08	1.43	0.30	0.41	0.27	0.84	1.30	13.53
Q1 2010	1.46	5.27	4.78	1.45	0.34	0.48	0.26	0.95	1.47	14.98
United Air Lines										
1995	0.86¢	4.73¢	1.51¢	1.51¢	0.90¢	0.29¢	0.17¢	0.53¢	2.92¢	12.58¢
2000	1.15	5.75	1.98	1.84	0.73	0.28	0.21	0.76	3.09	14.65
2005	0.62	3.72	3.53	1.60	0.35	0.30	0.16	0.60	5.09	15.35
2008	0.69	4.18	7.02	1.88	0.37	0.31	0.06	1.16	5.00	19.97
2009	0.70	4.06	3.39	1.87	0.35	0.37	0.04	0.90	5.06	16.03
Q1 2010	0.73	4.59	4.15	1.92	0.35	0.41	0.05	0.97	5.52	17.95
US Airways (merged with America West in September 2005 and began combined reporting in 2007)										
1995	1.55¢	7.53¢	1.59¢	2.09¢	1.05¢	0.29¢	0.13¢	0.73¢	4.32¢	17.73¢
2000	1.36	7.59	2.44	2.30	0.97	0.28	0.19	1.10	4.81	19.68
2005	0.78	3.74	3.89	1.50	1.06	0.31	0.06	0.66	7.27	18.49
2008	0.80	3.92	5.94	1.94	1.22	0.24	0.02	2.63	7.59	23.50
2009	0.78	3.97	3.20	1.90	1.23	0.27	0.03	1.06	6.77	18.42
Q1 2010	0.84	4.49	4.07	1.99	1.35	0.28	0.03	1.26	7.48	20.94

Table caption header: **Costs Incurred per Revenue Passenger Mile (in cents)***

*Costs per passenger revenue mile represent the costs per ticketed passenger per mile flown; the figures are derived by dividing the company's total expenses in each of the cost categories by the total number of miles flown by all ticketed passengers—thus, if there are 100 ticketed passengers on a flight that travels 500 miles, the number of passenger revenue miles for that flight is 100 x 500, or 50,000).

Source: U.S. Department of Transportation, Bureau of Transportation Statistics, Air Carrier Statistics Form 298C Summary Data and Form 41, Schedules P-6, P-12, P-51, and P-52.

Exhibit 10   **Southwest Airline's Operating Expenses per Available Seat Mile, 1995–2009 (selected years)**

	Costs per Available Seat Mile (in cents)								
Expense Category	2009	2008	2007	2006	2005	2004	2002	2000	1995
Salaries, wages, bonuses, and benefits	3.54¢	3.23¢	3.22¢	3.29¢	3.27¢	3.18	2.89¢	2.81¢	2.40¢
Fuel and oil	3.11	3.60	2.70	2.31	1.58	1.30	1.11	1.34	1.01
Maintenance materials and repairs	0.73	0.70	0.62	0.51	0.52	0.60	0.57	0.63	0.60
Aircraft rentals	0.19	0.15	0.16	0.17	0.19	0.23	0.27	0.33	0.47
Landing fees and other rentals	0.73	0.64	0.56	0.53	0.53	0.53	0.50	0.44	0.44
Depreciation	0.63	0.58	0.56	0.56	0.55	0.56	0.52	0.47	0.43
Other expenses	1.36	1.34	1.28	1.43	1.41	1.37	1.55	1.71	1.72
Total	10.29¢	10.24¢	9.10¢	8.80¢	8.05¢	7.70¢	7.41¢	7.73¢	7.07¢

Note: Figures in this exhibit differ from those for Southwest in Exhibit 9 because the cost figures in Exhibit 9 are based on *cost per passenger revenue mile,* whereas the cost figures in this exhibit are based on *costs per available seat mile.* Costs per revenue passenger mile represent the costs per ticketed passenger per mile flown, whereas costs per available seat mile are the *costs per seat per mile flown (irrespective of whether the seat was occupied or not).*

Source: Southwest Airlines, 10-K reports and annual reports, various years.

SOUTHWEST'S PEOPLE MANAGEMENT PRACTICES AND CULTURE

Whereas the litany at many companies was that customers come first, at Southwest the operative principle was that "employees come first and customers come second." The high strategic priority placed on employees reflected management's belief that delivering superior service required employees who not only were passionate about their jobs but also knew that the company was genuinely concerned for their well-being and committed to providing them with job security. Southwest's thesis was simple: Keep employees happy—then they will keep customers happy.

In Southwest's 2000 annual report, senior management explained why employees were the company's greatest asset:

> Our people are warm, caring and compassionate and willing to do whatever it takes to bring the Freedom to Fly to their fellow Americans. They

take pride in doing well for themselves by doing good for others. They have built a unique and powerful culture that demonstrates that the only way to accomplish our mission to make air travel affordable for others, while ensuring ample profitability, job security, and plentiful Profitsharing for ourselves, is to keep our costs low and Customer Service quality high.

> At Southwest, our People are our greatest assets, which is why we devote so much time and energy to hiring great People with winning attitudes. Because we are well known as an excellent place to work with great career opportunities and a secure future, lots of People want to work for Southwest. . . . Once hired, we provide a nurturing and supportive work environment that gives our Employees the freedom to be creative, have fun, and make a positive difference. Although we offer competitive compensation packages, it's our Employees' sense of ownership, pride in team accomplishments, and enhanced job satisfaction that keep our Culture and Southwest Spirit alive and why we continue to produce winning seasons.

Gary Kelly, the company's current CEO, echoed the views of his predecessors: "Our People are our single greatest strength and our most enduring long term competitive advantage."[20]

The company changed the Personnel Department's name to the People Department in 1989. Later, it was renamed the People and Leadership Development Department.

Recruiting, Screening, and Hiring

Southwest hired employees for attitude and trained for skills. Herb Kelleher explained:

> We can train people to do things where skills are concerned. But there is one capability we do not have and that is to change a person's attitude. So we prefer an unskilled person with a good attitude . . . [to] a highly skilled person with a bad attitude.[21]

Southwest recruited employees by means of newspaper ads, career fairs, and Internet job listings; a number of candidates applied because of Southwest's reputation as one of the best companies to work for in America and because they were impressed by their experiences as a customer on Southwest flights. Recruitment ads were designed to capture the attention of people thought to possess Southwest's "personality profile." For instance, one ad showed Herb Kelleher impersonating Elvis Presley and had the following copy:

> Work In A Place Where Elvis Has Been Spotted. The qualifications? It helps to be outgoing. Maybe even a bit off center. And be prepared to stay for a while. After all, we have the lowest employee turnover rate in the industry. If this sounds good to you, just phone our jobline or send your resume. Attention Elvis.[22]

Colleen Barrett elaborated on what the company looked for in screening candidates for job openings:

> We hire People to live the Southwest Way. They must possess a Warrior Spirit, lead with a Servant's Heart, and have a Fun-LUVing attitude. We hire People who fight to win, work hard, are dedicated, and have a passion for Customer Service. We won't hire People if something about their behavior won't be a Cultural fit. We hire the best. When our new hires walk through the door, our message to them is you are starting the flight of your life.[23]

All job applications were processed through the People and Leadership Development Department. Exhibit 11 details what the company called the "Southwest Way."

In hiring for jobs that involved personal contact with passengers, the company looked for people-oriented applicants who were extroverted and had a good sense of humor. It tried to identify candidates with a knack for reading peoples' emotions and responding in a genuinely caring, empathetic manner. Southwest wanted employees to deliver the kind of service that showed they truly enjoyed meeting people, being around passengers, and doing their job, as opposed to delivering the kind of service that came across as being forced or taught. Kelleher elaborated: "We are interested in people who externalize, who focus on other people, who are

Exhibit 11 **Personal Traits, Attitudes, and Behaviors That Southwest Wanted Employees to Possess and Display**

Living the Southwest Way		
Warrior Spirit	**Servant's Heart**	**Fun-LUVing Attitude**
• Work hard	• Follow the Golden Rule	• Have FUN
• Desire to be the best	• Adhere to the Basic Principles	• Don't take yourself too seriously
• Be courageous	• Treat others with respect	• Maintain perspective (balance)
• Display a sense of urgency	• Put others first	• Celebrate successes
• Persevere	• Be egalitarian	• Enjoy your work
• Innovate	• Demonstrate proactive Customer Service	• Be a passionate team player
	• Embrace the SWA Family	

Source: Southwest Airlines, www.southwest.com, accessed August 18, 2010.

motivated to help other people. We are not interested in navel gazers."[24] In addition to a "whistle while you work" attitude, Southwest was drawn to candidates who it thought would be likely to exercise initiative, work harmoniously with fellow employees, and be community-spirited.

Southwest did not use personality tests to screen job applicants, nor did it ask them what they would or should do in certain hypothetical situations. Rather, the hiring staff at Southwest analyzed each job category to determine the specific behaviors, knowledge, and motivations that job holders needed and then tried to find candidates with the desired traits—a process called targeted selection. A trait common to all job categories was teamwork; a trait deemed critical for pilots and flight attendants was judgment. In exploring an applicant's aptitude for teamwork, interviewers often asked applicants to tell them about a time in a prior job when they went out of their way to help a coworker or to explain how they had handled conflict with a coworker. Another frequent question was "What was your most embarrassing moment?" The thesis here was that having applicants talk about their past behaviors provided good clues about their future behaviors.

To test for unselfishness, Southwest interviewing teams typically gave a group of potential employees ample time to prepare five-minute presentations about themselves; during the presentations in an informal conversational setting, interviewers watched the audience to see who was absorbed in polishing their presentations and who was listening attentively, enjoying the stories being told, and applauding the efforts of the presenters. Those who were emotionally engaged in hearing the presenters and giving encouragement were deemed more apt to be team players than those who were focused on looking good themselves. All applicants for flight attendant positions were put through such a presentation exercise before an interview panel consisting of customers, experienced flight attendants, and members of the People and Leadership Department. Flight attendant candidates that got through the group presentation interviews then had to complete a three-on-one interview conducted by a recruiter, a supervisor from the hiring section of the People and Leadership Department, and a Southwest flight attendant; following this interview, the three-person panel tried to reach a consensus on whether to recommend or drop the candidate.

Southwest received 90,043 résumés and hired 831 new employees in 2009. In 2007, prior to the onset of the recession, Southwest received 329,200 résumés and hired 4,200 new employees.

Training

Apart from the FAA-mandated training for certain employees, training activities at Southwest were designed and conducted by Southwest's University for People. The curriculum included courses for new recruits, employees, and managers. Learning was viewed as a never-ending process for all company personnel; the expectation was that each employee should be an "intentional learner," looking to grow and develop not just from occasional classes taken at Southwest's festive University for People learning center but also from their everyday on-the-job experiences.

Southwest's University for People conducted a variety of courses offered to maintenance personnel and other employees to meet the training and safety requirements of the Federal Aviation Administration, the U.S. Department of Transportation, the Occupational Safety and Health Administration, and other government agencies. And there were courses on written communications, public speaking, stress management, career development, performance appraisal, decision making, leadership, customer service, corporate culture, and employee relations to help employees advance their careers.

Employees wanting to explore whether a management career was for them could take Leadership 101 and 201. One of the keystone course offerings for new frontline managers was a four-session "Leadership Southwest Style" course, which made extensive use of the Myers-Briggs personality assessment to help managers understand the "why" behind coworkers' behaviors and to learn how to build trust, empathize, resolve conflicts, and do a better job of communicating. There was a special "manager-in-training" course for high-potential employees wanting to pursue a long-term career at Southwest. Leadership courses for people already in supervisory or managerial positions emphasized a management style based on coaching, empowering, and encouraging, rather than supervising or enforcing rules and regulations. From time to time, supervisors and executives attended courses on corporate culture, intended to help instill, ingrain, and nurture such cultural themes as teamwork, trust, harmony, and diversity.

All employees who came into contact with customers, including pilots, received customer care training. Southwest's latest customer-related training initiative involved a course called "Every Customer Matters"; by the end of 2009, 14,225 employees had completed the course. Altogether, Southwest employees spent more than 720,000 hours in training sessions of one kind or another in 2009:[25]

Job Category	Amount of Training
Maintenance and support personnel	81,633 hours
Customer support and services personnel	106,480 hours
Flight attendants	109,450 hours
Pilots	199,500 hours
Ground operations personnel	224,799 hours

The OnBoarding Program for Newly Hired Employees Southwest had a program called OnBoarding "to welcome New Hires into the Southwest Family" and provide information and assistance from the time they were selected until the end of their first year. Orientation for new employees included a one-day orientation session, videos on Southwest's history, an overview of the airline industry and the competitive challenges that Southwest faced, and an introduction to Southwest's culture and management practices. The culture introduction included a video called the *Southwest Shuffle,* which featured hundreds of Southwest employees rapping about the fun they had on their jobs (at many Southwest gatherings, it was common for a group of employees to do the Southwest Shuffle, with the remaining attendees cheering and clapping). There were also exercises that demonstrated the role of creativity and teamwork and a scavenger hunt in which new hires were given a timeline with specific dates in Southwest's history and were asked to fill in the missing details by viewing the memorabilia decorating the corridors of the Dallas headquarters and getting information from people working in various offices. During their first 30 days at Southwest,

new employees could access an interactive online tool—OnBoarding Online Orientation—to learn about the company.

An additional element of the Onboarding Program involved assigning each new employee to an existing Southwest employee who had volunteered to sponsor a new hire and be of assistance in acclimating the new employee to his or her job and the Southwest Way; each volunteer sponsor received training from Southwest's Onboarding Team in what was expected of a sponsor. Much of the indoctrination of new employees into the company's culture was done by the volunteer sponsor, coworkers, and the new employee's supervisor. Southwest made active use of a one-year probationary employment period to help ensure that new employees fit in with the company's culture and adequately embraced its cultural values.

Promotion

Approximately 80 to 90 percent of Southwest's supervisory positions were filled internally, reflecting management's belief that people who had "been there and done that" would be more likely to appreciate and understand the demands that people under them were experiencing and, also, more likely to enjoy the respect of their peers and higher-level managers. Employees could either apply for supervisory positions or be recommended by their present supervisor. New appointees for supervisor, team leader, and manager attended a three-day class called Leading with Integrity and aimed at developing leadership and communication skills. Employees being considered for managerial positions of large operations (Up and Coming Leaders) received training in every department of the company over a six-month period in which they continued to perform their current job. At the end of the six-month period, candidates were provided with 360-degree feedback from department heads, peers, and subordinates; representatives of the People and Leadership Department analyzed the feedback in deciding on the specific assignment of each candidate.[26]

Compensation

Southwest's pay scales compared quite favorably with other major U.S. airlines (see Exhibit 12).

Exhibit 12   **Estimated Employee Compensation and Benefits at Selected U.S. Airlines, 2008 and 2009**

	Southwest Airlines	American Airlines	Delta	Continental Airlines	JetBlue	United Airlines	US Airways
Average Pilot Wage/Salary							
2008	**$172,800**	$138,800	$125,600	$136,300	$112,000	$119,500	$113,900
2009	**176,200**	137,500	137,900	150,200	124,700	125,500	111,300
Average Flight Attendant Wage/Salary							
2008	**$ 53,000**	$ 49,800	$ 37,000	$ 49,100	$ 33,000	$ 40,100	$ 39,700
2009	**46,800**	50,900	39,200	51,200	33,800	40,600	40,600
All-Employee Average Wage/Salary							
2008	**$ 72,100**	$ 60,900	$ 56,100	$ 54,400	$ 54,400	$ 58,100	$ 53,800
2009	**75,600**	63,000	59,600	56,800	58,600	58,200	55,500
Average Benefits per Employee							
2008	**$ 24,200**	$ 24,300	$ 45,100	$ 15,800	$ 13,800	$ 25,600	$ 14,500
2009	**23,800**	30,500	30,100	19,900	14,800	22,700	13,500

Note: The compensation and benefits numbers are estimated from compensation cost and workforce size data reported by the airlines to the Bureau of Transportation Statistics. The number of employees at year-end were used to calculate the averages, which may cause distortions in the event of significant changes in a company's workforce size during the year. In addition, several companies were engaged in mergers and/or major cost restructuring initiatives during 2008–2009, which in some instances (notably Delta) resulted in significant within-company changes from 2008 to 2009.

Source: Derived from data in various airline industry reports published by the Bureau of Transportation Statistics and from information posted at www.airlinefinancials.com.

Southwest's average pay for pilots and its all-employee average compensation were the highest of all the major U.S. airlines—sometimes even at or near the top of the industry—and its benefit packages were quite competitive.

Southwest introduced a profit-sharing plan for senior employees in 1973, the first such plan in the airline industry. By the mid-1990s, the plan had been extended to cover most Southwest employees. As of 2010, Southwest had stock option programs for various employee groups (including those covered by collective bargaining agreements), a 401(k) employee savings plans that included company-matching contributions, an employee stock purchase plan, and a profit-sharing plan covering virtually all employees that consisted of a money purchase defined-contribution plan to which Southwest contributed 15 percent of eligible pretax profits. Company contributions to employee 410(k) and profit-sharing plans totaled

$1.3 billion during 2005–2009; in recent years, the annual contribution had represented 6 to 12 percent of base pay. Employees participating in stock purchases via payroll deduction bought 1.3 million shares in 2007, 1.3 million shares in 2008, and 2.2 million shares in 2009 at prices equal to 90 percent of the market value at the end of each monthly purchase period. Southwest employees owned about 10 percent of Southwest's outstanding shares and, as of December 31, 2009, held options to buy some 78.2 million additional shares.

Employee Relations

About 82 percent of Southwest's 34,700 employees belonged to a union, making Southwest one of the most highly unionized U.S. airlines. An in-house union—the Southwest Airline Pilots Association—represented the company's pilots. The Teamsters Union represented Southwest's stock clerks and flight simulator technicians; a local of the Transportation Workers of America represented flight attendants; another local of the Transportation Workers of America represented baggage handlers, ground crews, and provisioning employees; the International Association of Machinists and Aerospace Workers represented customer service and reservation employees; and the Aircraft Mechanics Fraternal Association represented the company's mechanics.

Management encouraged union members and negotiators to research their pressing issues and to conduct employee surveys before each contract negotiation. Southwest's contracts with the unions representing its employees were relatively free of restrictive work rules and narrow job classifications that might impede worker productivity. All of the contracts allowed any qualified employee to perform any function—thus pilots, ticket agents, and gate personnel could help load and unload baggage when needed and flight attendants could pick up trash and make flight cabins more presentable for passengers boarding the next flight.

Except for one brief strike by machinists in the early 1980s and some unusually difficult negotiations in 2000–2001, Southwest's relationships with the unions representing its employee groups were harmonious and nonadversarial for the most part—even though there were sometimes spirited disagreements over particular issues.

In 2000–2001, the company had contentious negotiations with Local 555 of the Transportation Workers of America (TWU) over a new wage and benefits package for Southwest's ramp, baggage operations, provisioning, and freight personnel; the previous contract had become open for renegotiation in December 1999, and a tentative agreement reached at the end of 2000 was rejected by 64 percent of the union members who voted. A memo from Kelleher to TWU representatives said, "The cost and structure of the TWU 555 negotiating committee's proposal would seriously undermine the competitive strength of Southwest Airlines; endanger our ability to grow; threaten the value of our employees' profit-sharing; require us to contract out work in order to remain competitive; and threaten our 29-year history of job security for our employees." In a union newsletter in early 2001, the president of the TWU local said, "We asked for a decent living wage and benefits to

support our families, and were told of how unworthy and how greedy we were." The ongoing dispute resulted in informational picket lines in March 2001 at several Southwest locations, the first picketing since 1980. Later in 2001, with the help of the National Mediation Board, Southwest and the TWU reached an agreement covering Southwest's ramp, operations, and provisioning employees.

Prior to 9/11, Southwest's pilots were somewhat restive about their base pay relative to pilots at other U.S. airlines. The maximum pay for Southwest's 3,700+ pilots (before profit-sharing bonuses) was $148,000, versus maximums of $290,000 for United's pilots, $262,000 for Delta's pilots, $206,000 for American's pilots, and $199,000 for Continental's pilots.[27] Moreover, some veteran Southwest employees were grumbling about staff shortages in certain locations (to hold down labor costs) and cracks in the company's close-knit family culture due to the influx of so many new employees over the past several years. A number of employees who had accepted lower pay because of Southwest's underdog status were said to feel entitled to "big airline" pay now that Southwest had emerged as a major U.S. carrier.[28] However, when airline traffic dropped precipitously following 9/11, Southwest's major airline rivals won big wage and salary concessions from unions representing pilots and other airline workers; moreover, about 1 in 5 airline jobs—some 120,000 in all—were eliminated. In 2006, a senior Boeing 737 pilot at Delta Air Lines working a normal 65-hour month made $116,200 annually, down 26 percent from pre-9/11 wages. A comparable pilot at United Airlines earned $102,200, down 34 percent from before 9/11, and at American Airlines such a pilot made $122,500, 18 percent less than in the days before 9/11.

In 2004, 2007, and 2009, in an attempt to contain rising labor costs and better match workforce size to its operating requirements, Southwest offered voluntary buyout or early retirement packages to selected groups of employees. The 2004 buyout package was offered to approximately 8,700 flight attendants, ramp workers, customer service employees, and those in reservations, operations, and freight who had reached a specific pay scale; the buyout consisted of a $25,000 payment and medical and dental benefits for a specified period. About

1,000 employees accepted the 2004 buyout offer. In 2009, Southwest announced Freedom '09, a one-time voluntary early retirement program offered to older employees, in which the company offered cash bonuses, medical/dental coverage for a specified period of time, and travel privileges based on work group and years of service; some 1,400 employees elected to participate in Freedom '09, resulting in payouts of $66 million.

The No-Layoff Policy

Southwest Airlines had never laid off or furloughed any of its employees since the company began operations in 1971. The company's no-layoff policy was seen as integral to how the company treated its employees and management efforts to sustain and nurture the culture. According to Kelleher:

> Nothing kills your company's culture like layoffs. Nobody has ever been furloughed here, and that is unprecedented in the airline industry. It's been a huge strength of ours. It's certainly helped negotiate our union contracts. . . . We could have furloughed at various times and been more profitable, but I always thought that was shortsighted. You want to show your people you value them and you're not going to hurt them just to get a little more money in the short term. Not furloughing people breeds loyalty. It breeds a sense of security. It breeds a sense of trust.[29]

Southwest had built up considerable goodwill with its employees and unions over the years by avoiding layoffs. Both senior management and Southwest employees regarded the three recent buyout offers as a better approach to workforce reduction than involuntary layoffs.

Operation Kick Tail

In 2007, Southwest management launched an internal initiative called Operation Kick Tail, a multiyear call to action for employees to focus even more attention on providing high-quality customer service, maintaining low costs, and nurturing the Southwest culture. One component of Operation Kick Tail involved singling out employees for special recognition when they did something to make a positive difference in a customer's travel experience or in the life of a coworker.

Gary Kelly saw this aspect of Operation Kick Tail as a way to foster the employee attitudes and commitment needed to provide "Positively Outrageous Customer Service." He explained:

> One of Southwest's rituals is finding and developing People who are "built to serve." That allows us to provide a personal, warm level of service that is unmatched in the airline industry.

Southwest management viewed Operation Kick Tail as a means to better engage and incentivize employees to strengthen their display of the traits included in the Southwest Way and achieve a competitive edge keyed to superior customer service.

Management Style

At Southwest, management strove to do things in a manner that would make Southwest employees proud of the company they worked for and its workforce practices. Managers were expected to spend at least one-third of their time walking around the facilities under their supervision, observing firsthand what was going on, listening to employees, and being responsive to their concerns. A former director of people development at Southwest told of a conversation he had with one of Southwest's terminal managers:

> While I was out in the field visiting one of our stations, one of our managers mentioned to me that he wanted to put up a suggestion box. I responded by saying, "Sure—why don't you put up a suggestion box right here on this wall and then admit you are a failure as a manager?" Our theory is, if you have to put up a box so people can write down their ideas and toss them in, it means you are not doing what you are supposed to be doing. You are supposed to be setting your people up to be winners. To do that, you should be there listening to them and available to them in person, not via a suggestion box. For the most part, I think we have a very good sense of this at Southwest. I think that most people employed here know that they can call any one of our vice presidents on the telephone and get heard, almost immediately.
>
> The suggestion box gives managers an out; it relinquishes their responsibility to be accessible to their people, and that's when we have gotten in trouble at Southwest—when we can no longer be responsive to our flight attendants or customer service agents, when they can't gain access to somebody who can give them resources and answers.[30]

Company executives were very approachable, insisting on being called by their first names. At new employee orientations, people were told, "We do not call the company chairman and CEO Mr. Kelly, we call him Gary." Managers and executives had an open-door policy, actively listening to employee concerns, opinions, and suggestions for reducing costs and improving efficiency.

Employee-led initiatives were common. Southwest's pilots had been instrumental in developing new protocols for takeoffs and landings that conserved fuel. Another frontline employee had suggested not putting the company logos on trash bags, saving an estimated $250,000 annually. Rather than buy 800 computers for a new reservations center in Albuquerque, company employees determined that they could buy the parts and assemble the PCs themselves for half the price of a new PC, saving the company $1 million. It was Southwest clerks who came up with the idea of doing away with paper tickets and shifting to e-tickets.

There were only four layers of management between a frontline supervisor and the CEO. Southwest's employees enjoyed substantial authority and decision-making power. According to Kelleher:

> We've tried to create an environment where people are able to, in effect, bypass even the fairly lean structures that we have so that they don't have to convene a meeting of the sages in order to get something done. In many cases, they can just go ahead and do it on their own. They can take individual responsibility for it and know they will not be crucified if it doesn't work out. Our leanness requires people to be comfortable in making their own decisions and undertaking their own efforts.[31]

From time to time, there were candid meetings of frontline employees and managers where operating problems and issues between/among workers and departments were acknowledged, openly discussed, and resolved.[32] Informal problem avoidance and rapid problem resolution were seen as managerial virtues.

Southwest's Two Big Core Values—LUV and Fun

Two core values—LUV and fun—permeated the work environment at Southwest. LUV was much more than the company's ticker symbol and a recurring theme in Southwest's advertising campaigns. Over the years, LUV grew into Southwest's code word for treating individuals—fellow employees and customers—with dignity and respect and demonstrating a caring, loving attitude. The code word *LUV* and red hearts commonly appeared on banners and posters at company facilities, as reminders of the compassion that was expected toward customers and other employees. Practicing the Golden Rule, internally and externally, was expected of all employees. Employees who struggled to live up to these expectations were subjected to considerable peer pressure and usually were asked to seek employment elsewhere if they did not soon leave on their own volition.

Fun at Southwest was exactly what the word implies—and it occurred throughout the company in the form of the generally entertaining behavior of employees in performing their jobs, the ongoing pranks and jokes, and frequent company-sponsored parties and celebrations (which typically included the Southwest Shuffle). On holidays, employees were encouraged to dress in costumes. There were charity benefit games, chili cook-offs, Halloween parties, new Ronald McDonald House dedications, and other special events of one kind or another at one location or another almost every week. According to one manager, "We're kind of a big family here, and family members have fun together."

Culture Building

Southwest executives believed that the company's growth was primarily a function of the rate at which it could hire and train people to fit into its culture and consistently display the desired traits and behaviors. CEO Gary Kelly said, "Some things at Southwest won't change. We will continue to expect our people to live what we describe as the 'Southwest Way,' which is to have a Warrior Spirit, Servant's Heart, and Fun-Loving Attitude. Those three things have defined our culture for 36 years."[33]

The Corporate Culture Committee

Southwest formed its Corporate Culture Committee in 1990 to promote "Positively Outrageous Service" and devise tributes, contests, and celebrations intended to nurture and perpetuate the Southwest Spirit and Living the Southwest Way. The committee, chaired by Colleen Barrett until mid-2008 and then by Ginger Hardage (who was given lead executive responsibility for cultural aspects at Southwest when Barrett retired), was composed of 100 employees who had demonstrated their commitment to Southwest's mission and values and zeal in exhibiting the Southwest Spirit and Living the Southwest Way. Members came from a cross-section of departments and locations and functioned as cultural ambassadors, missionaries, and storytellers during their two-year term.

The Corporate Culture Committee had four all-day meetings annually; ad hoc subcommittees formed throughout the year met more frequently. Over the years, the committee had sponsored and supported hundreds of ways to promote and ingrain the traits and behaviors embedded in Living the Southwest Way—examples included promoting the use of red hearts and LUV to embody the spirit of Southwest employees caring about each other and Southwest's customers, showing up at a facility to serve pizza or ice cream to employees or to remodel and decorate an employee break room. Kelleher indicated, "We're not big on Committees at Southwest, but of the committees we do have, the Culture Committee is the most important."[34]

Efforts to Nurture and Sustain the Southwest Culture

Apart from the efforts of the Corporate Culture Committee, Southwest management had sought to reinforce the company's core values and culture via its annual Heros of the Heart Award, its CoHearts mentoring program, its Day in the Field program in which employees spent time working in another area of the company's operations, its Helping Hands program in which volunteers from around the system traveled to work two weekend shifts at other Southwest facilities that were temporarily shorthanded or experiencing heavy work-

loads, and periodic Culture Exchange meetings to celebrate the Southwest Spirit and company milestones. Almost every event at Southwest was videotaped, which provided footage for creating multipurpose videos, such as *Keepin' the Spirit Alive,* that could be shown at company events all over the system and used in training courses. The concepts of LUV and fun were spotlighted in all of the company's training manuals and videos.

Southwest's monthly employee newsletter often spotlighted the experiences and deeds of particular employees, reprinted letters of praise from customers, and reported company celebrations of milestones. A quarterly news video, *As the Plane Turns,* was sent to all facilities to keep employees up to date on company happenings, provide clips of special events, and share messages from customers, employees, and executives. The company had published a book for employees describing "outrageous" acts of service.

Employee Productivity

Management was convinced the company's strategy, culture, esprit de corps, and people management practices fostered high labor productivity and contributed to Southwest's having low labor costs in comparison to the labor costs at its principal domestic rivals. When a Southwest flight pulled up to the gate, ground crews, gate personnel, and flight attendants hustled to perform all the tasks requisite to turn the plane quickly—employees took pride in doing their part to achieve good on-time performance. Southwest's turnaround times were in the range of 25 to 30 minutes, versus an industry average of around 45 minutes. In 2009, Southwest's labor productivity compared quite favorably with its chief domestic competitors (as shown below):

	Productivity Measure	
	Passengers Enplaned per Employee, 2009	Employees per Plane, 2009
Southwest Airlines	2,475	65
American Airlines	1,289	109
Continental	1,177	115
Delta	1,430	103
JetBlue	2,121	70
United	1,204	129
US Airways	1,628	90

Source: Calculated from data in Southwest Airlines' 10-K reports.

System Operations

Under Herb Kelleher, instituting practices, procedures, and support systems that promoted operating excellence had become a tradition and a source of company pride. Much time and effort over the years had gone into finding the most effective ways to do aircraft maintenance, to operate safely, to make baggage handling more efficient and baggage transfers more accurate, and to improve the percentage of on-time arrivals and departures. Believing that air travelers were more likely to fly Southwest if its flights were reliable and on time, Southwest's managers constantly monitored on-time arrivals and departures, making inquiries when many flights ran behind and searching for ways to improve on-time performance. One initiative to help minimize weather and operational delays involved the development of a state-of-the-art flight dispatch system.

Southwest's current CEO, Gary Kelly, had followed Kelleher's lead in pushing for operating excellence. One of Kelly's strategic objectives for Southwest was "to be the safest, most efficient, and most reliable airline in the world." Southwest managers and employees in all positions and ranks were proactive in offering suggestions for improving Southwest's practices and procedures; those with merit were quickly implemented. Southwest was considered to have one of the most competent and thorough aircraft maintenance programs in the commercial airline industry and, going into 2008, was widely regarded as the best operator among U.S. airlines. Its recent record vis-à-vis rival airlines on four important measures of operating performance was commendable—see Exhibit 13.

The First Significant Blemish on Southwest's Safety Record

While no Southwest plane had ever crashed and there had never been a passenger fatality, there was an incident in 2005 in which a Southwest plane landing in a snow storm with a strong tailwind at Chicago's Midway airport was unable to stop before overrunning a shorter-than-usual runway, rolling onto a highway, crashing into a car, killing one of the occupants, and injuring 22 of the passengers on the plane. A National Traffic Safety Board investigation concluded that "the pilot's failure to use available reverse thrust in a timely manner to safely slow or stop the airplane after landing" was the probable cause.

Belated Aircraft Inspections Further Tarnish Southwest's Reputation

In early 2008, various media reported that Southwest Airlines over a period of several months in 2006 and 2007 had knowingly failed to conduct required inspections for early detection of fuselage fatigue cracking on 46 of its older Boeing 737-300 jets. The company had voluntarily notified the Federal Aviation Administration about the lapse in checks for fuselage cracks but continued to fly the planes until the work was done—about eight days. The belated inspections revealed tiny cracks in the bodies of six planes, with the largest measuring four inches; none of the cracks impaired flight safety. According to CEO Gary Kelly, "Southwest Airlines discovered the missed inspection area, disclosed it to the FAA, and promptly re-inspected all potentially affected aircraft in March 2007. The FAA approved our actions and considered the matter closed as of April 2007." Nonetheless, on March 12, 2008, shortly after the reports in the media surfaced about Southwest's failure to meet inspection deadlines, Southwest canceled 4 percent of its flights and grounded 44 of its Boeing 737-300s until it verified that the aircraft had undergone required inspections. Gary Kelly then initiated an internal review of the company's maintenance practices; the investigation raised "concerns" about the company's aircraft maintenance procedures, prompting Southwest to put three employees on leave. The FAA subsequently fined Southwest $10.2 million for its transgressions. In an effort to help restore customer confidence, Kelly publicly apologized for the company's wrongdoing, promised that such a lapse would not occur again, and reasserted the company's commitment to safety. He said:

> From our inception, Southwest Airlines has maintained a rigorous Culture of Safety—and has maintained that same dedication for more than 37 years. It is and always has been our number one priority to ensure safety.
>
> We've got a 37-year history of very safe operations, one of the safest operations in the world, and we're safer today than we've ever been.

Exhibit 13   **Comparative Statistics on On-Time Flights, Mishandled Baggage, Boarding Denials Due to Oversold Flights, and Passenger Complaints for Eight Major U.S. Airlines, 2000 through Quarter 1 of 2010**

Percentage of Scheduled Flights Arriving within 15 Minutes of the Scheduled Time (during the previous 12 months ending in May of each year)							
Airline	2000	2005	2006	2007	2008	2009	Q1 2010
American Airlines	75.8%	78.0%	75.6%	72.4%	66.9%	75.2%	77.5%
Continental Air Lines	76.7	78.7	74.8	73.5	74.1	75.6	80.4
Delta Air Lines	78.3	76.4	76.2	76.6	75.7	76.3	79.3
JetBlue Airways	n.a.	76.3	73.1	69.4	73.3	74.0	77.3
Northwest Airlines*	80.7	79.3	75.1	71.4	71.1	80.5	—
Southwest Airlines	**78.7**	**79.9**	**80.3**	**80.7**	**78.5**	**83.3**	**81.5**
United Air Lines	71.6	79.8	75.7	73.0	69.1	76.2	82.5
US Airways	72.7	76.0	78.9	69.7	75.5	79.9	81.9

Mishandled Baggage Reports per 1,000 Passengers (in May of each year)							
Airline	2000	2005	2006	2007	2008	2009	Q1 2010
American Airlines	5.44	4.58	4.91	6.40	5.82	4.32	3.87
Continental Air Lines	4.11	3.30	3.85	5.02	3.78	2.32	2.27
Delta Air Lines	3.64	6.21	4.75	5.26	3.81	4.33	3.50
JetBlue Airways	n.a.	3.16	2.88	4.38	3.23	2.26	2.15
Northwest Airlines*	4.98	3.58	3.11	3.80	2.97	2.11	—
Southwest Airlines	**4.14**	**3.46**	**3.66**	**5.54**	**4.41**	**3.30**	**3.09**
United Air Lines	6.71	4.00	3.89	4.83	4.76	3.67	3.05
US Airways	4.57	9.73	5.69	7.17	3.86	2.91	2.27

Involuntary Denied Boardings per 10,000 Passengers Due to Oversold Flights (January through March of each year)							
Airline	2000	2005	2006	2007	2008	2009	Q1 2010
American Airlines	0.59	0.72	1.16	1.06	0.98	0.43	1.28
Continental Air Lines	0.50	3.01	2.60	1.93	1.57	1.42	2.73
Delta Air Lines	0.44	1.06	2.68	3.47	1.80	1.64	0.63
JetBlue Airways	n.a.	0.00	0.01	0.04	0.02	0.00	0.01
Northwest Airlines*	0.12	1.70	1.00	1.25	1.15	0.68	—
Southwest Airlines	**1.70**	**0.74**	**1.81**	**1.25**	**1.68**	**1.42**	**2.59**
United Air Lines	1.61	0.42	0.88	0.4	0.89	1.30	1.92
US Airways	0.80	1.01	1.07	1.68	2.01	1.50	2.96

Complaints per 100,000 Passengers Boarded (in May of each year)							
Airline	2000	2005	2006	2007	2008	2009	Q1 2010
American Airlines	2.77	1.01	1.22	1.44	1.30	1.18	1.61
Continental Air Lines	2.25	0.89	0.85	0.75	1.03	1.03	1.36
Delta Air Lines	1.60	0.91	0.93	1.50	2.10	1.85	1.57
JetBlue Airways	n.a.	0.00	0.22	0.40	0.56	0.93	1.72
Northwest Airlines*	2.17	0.83	0.69	1.13	0.94	0.88	—
Southwest Airlines	**0.41**	**0.17**	**0.18**	**0.19**	**0.32**	**0.13**	**0.26**
United Air Lines	5.07	0.87	1.19	2.00	1.61	1.16	1.67
US Airways	1.63	0.99	1.22	2.65	1.94	1.34	1.19

*Effective January 2010, data of the merged operations of Delta Air Lines and Northwest Airlines were combined and reported as Delta for Q1 2010.

Source: Office of Aviation Enforcement and Proceedings, Air Travel Consumer Report, various years.

In the days following the public revelation of Southwest's maintenance lapse and the tarnishing of its reputation, an industry-wide audit by the FAA revealed similar failures to conduct timely inspections for early signs of fuselage fatigue at five other airlines—American, Continental, Delta, United, and Northwest. An air travel snafu ensued, with more than a thousand flights subsequently being canceled due to FAA-mandated grounding of the affected aircraft while the overdue safety inspections were performed. Further public scrutiny, including a congressional investigation, turned up documents indicating that, in some cases, planes flew for 30 months after the inspection deadlines had passed. Moreover, high-level FAA officials were apparently aware of the failure of Southwest and other airlines to perform the inspections for fuselage cracks at the scheduled times and chose not to strictly enforce the inspection deadlines—according to some commentators, because of allegedly cozy relationships with personnel at Southwest and the other affected airlines. Disgruntled FAA safety supervisors in charge of monitoring the inspections conducted by airline carriers testified before Congress that senior FAA officials frequently ignored their reports that certain routine safety inspections were not being conducted in accordance with prescribed FAA procedures. Shortly thereafter, the FAA issued more stringent procedures to ensure that aircraft safety inspections were properly conducted.

A SUDDEN SHIFT IN STRATEGY

In September 2010, Southwest announced that it had entered into a definitive agreement to acquire all of the outstanding common stock of AirTran Holdings, Inc. (NYSE: AAI), the parent company of AirTran Airways (AirTran), for a combination of cash and Southwest Airlines' common stock. The transaction was valued at about $1.4 billion; Southwest planned to fund approximately $670 million of the acquisition cost out of cash on hand.[35] For the twelve months ending June 30, 2010, AirTran had revenues of $2.5 billion and operating income (excluding special items) of $128 million. Like Southwest, AirTran was also a low-fare, low-cost airline. AirTran served 70 airports in the United States, Mexico, and the Caribbean; nineteen of these coincided with airports already served by Southwest. AirTran's hub was Atlanta's Hartsfield-Jackson International Airport, the busiest airport in the United States and the largest domestic airport not served by Southwest; AirTran had 202 daily departures out of Atlanta.[36] Some analysts believed that Southwest's entry into the Atlanta market alone could translate into 2 million additional passengers for Southwest annually. AirTran had 8,033 employees, 138 aircraft, and 177 nonstop routes; in 2009 AirTran transported 24.0 million passengers, the seventh largest number of all U.S. airlines. Based on current operations, the combined organization would have nearly 43,000 employees and serve more than 100 million passengers annually. In addition, the combined carriers' all-Boeing fleet consisting of 685 active aircraft would include 401 Boeing 737-700s, 173 Boeing 737-300s, 25 Boeing 737-500s, and 86 Boeing 717s, with an average age of approximately 10 years, one of the youngest fleets in the industry. The companies hoped to close the merger deal in early 2011 and then begin integration of AirTran into the Southwest Airlines brand—a process which Southwest management said might take as long as two years in order to maintain Southwest's standards for customer service.

ENDNOTES

1 Kevin Freiberg and Jackie Freiberg, *NUTS! Southwest Airlines' Crazy Recipe for Business and Personal Success* (New York: Broadway Books, 1998), p.15.
2 Ibid., pp. 16–18.
3 Katrina Brooker, "The Chairman of the Board Looks Back," *Fortune*, May 28, 2001, p. 66.
4 Freiberg and Freiberg, *NUTS*, p. 31.
5 Ibid., pp. 26–27.
6 Ibid., pp. 246–47.
7 Quoted in the *Dallas Morning News*, March 20, 2001.
8 Quoted in Brooker, "The Chairman of the Board Looks Back," p. 64.
9 Ibid., p. 72.
10 Quoted in *Seattle Times*, March 20, 2001, p. C3.
11 Speech at Texas Christian University, September 13, 2007; accessed at www. southwest.com on September 8, 2008.
12 Freiberg and Freiberg, *NUTS!*, p. 163.
13 Company press release, July 15, 2004.

Case 20   Southwest Airlines in 2010: Culture, Values, and Operating Practices   C-309

14 Speech to Greater Boston Chamber of Commerce, April 23, 2008, www.southwest.com, accessed September 5, 2008.
15 Speech to Business Today International Conference, November 20, 2007, www.southwest.com, accessed September 8, 2008.
16 As cited in Freiberg and Freiberg, *NUTS!*, p. 288.
17 Speech by Colleen Barrett on January 22, 2007 and posted at www.southwest.com; accessed on September 5, 2008.
18 Brenda Paik Sunoo, "How Fun Flies at Southwest Airlines," *Personnel Journal* 74, no. 6 (June 1995), p. 70.
19 Statement made in a 1993 Harvard Business School video and quoted in Roger Hallowell, "Southwest Airlines: A Case Study Linking Employee Needs Satisfaction and Organizational Capabilities to Competitive Advantage," *Human Resource Management* 35, no. 4 (Winter 1996), p. 517.

20 Statement posted in the Careers section at www.southwest.com, accessed August 18, 2010.
21 Quoted in James Campbell Quick, "Crafting an Organizational Structure: Herb's Hand at Southwest Airlines," *Organizational Dynamics* 21, no. 2 (Autumn 1992), p. 51.
22 Southwest's ad entitled "Work in a Place Where Elvis Has Been Spotted," and Sunoo, "How Fun Flies at Southwest Airlines," pp. 64–65.
23 Speech to the Paso Del Norte Group in El Paso Texas, January 22, 2007, www.southwest.com, accessed September 5, 2008.
24 Quick, "Crafting an Organizational Structure," p. 52.
25 Southwest's "2009 One Report," p. 20, www.southwest.com, accessed August 19, 2010.
26 Sunoo, "How Fun Flies at Southwest Airlines," p. 72.

27 Shawn Tully, "From Bad to Worse," *Fortune*, October 15, 2001, p. 124.
28 Melanie Trottman, "Amid Crippled Rivals, Southwest Tries to Spread Its Wings," *Wall Street Journal*, October 11, 2001, p. A10.
29 Brooker, "The Chairman of the Board Looks Back," p. 72.
30 Freiberg and Freiberg, *NUTS!*, p. 273.
31 Ibid., p. 76.
32 Hallowell, "Southwest Airlines," p. 524.
33 Speech to Business Today International Conference, November 20, 2007; accessed at www.southwest.com on September 8, 2008.
34 Freiberg and Freiberg, *NUTS!*, p. 165.
35 Southwest Airlines press release, September 27, 2010.
36 Rhonda Cook and Kelly Yamanouchi, "Southwest Buying AirTran for $1.4 Billion," *Atlanta Journal-Constitution*, September 27, 2010, accessed at www.ajc.com on October 26, 2010.